Recent studies of the concepts and ideologies of Romanticism have neglected to explore the way in which Romanticism defined itself by reconfiguring its literary past. In *Wordsworth's Pope* Robert J. Griffin shows that many of the basic tenets of Romanticism derive from mid-eighteenth-century writers' attempts to free themselves from the literary dominance of Alexander Pope. As a result, a narrative of literary history in which Pope figured as an alien poet of reason and imitation became the basis for nineteenth-century literary history, and still affects our thinking on Pope and Romanticism. Griffin traces the genesis and transmission of "romantic literary history," from the Wartons to M. H. Abrams; in so doing, he calls into question some of our most basic assumptions about the chronological and conceptual boundaries of Romanticism.

CAMBRIDGE STUDIES IN ROMANTICISM 17

WORDSWORTH'S POPE

CAMBRIDGE STUDIES IN ROMANTICISM

General editors
Professor Marilyn Butler   Professor James Chandler
University of Oxford   *University of Chicago*

Editorial board
John Barrell, *University of York*   Paul Hamilton, *University of Southampton*
Mary Jacobus, *Cornell University*   Kenneth Johnston, *Indiana University*
Alan Liu, *University of California, Santa Barbara*
Jerome McGann, *University of Virginia*   David Simpson, *University of Colorado*

This series aims to foster the best new work in one of the most challenging fields within English literary studies. From the early 1780s to the early 1830s a formidable array of talented men and women took to literary composition, not just in poetry, which some of them famously transformed, but in many modes of writing. The expansion of publishing created new opportunities for writers, and the political stakes of what they wrote were raised again and again by what Wordsworth called those "great national events" that were "almost daily taking place": the French Revolution, the Napoleonic and American wars, urbanization, industrialization, religious revival, an expanded empire abroad, and the reform movement at home. This was an enormous ambition, even when it pretended otherwise. The relations between science, philosophy, religion, and literature were reworked in texts such as *Frankenstein* and *Biographia Literaria*; gender relations in *A Vindication of the Rights of Woman* and *Don Juan*; journalism by Cobbett and Hazlitt; poetic form, content, and style by the Lake School and the Cockney School. Outside Shakespeare studies, probably no body of writing has produced such a wealth of response or done so much to shape the responses of modern criticism. This indeed is the period that saw the emergence of those notions of "literature" and of literary history, especially national literary history, on which modern scholarship in English has been founded.

The categories produced by Romanticism have also been challenged by recent historicist arguments. The task of the series is to engage both with a challenging corpus of Romantic writings and with the changing field of criticism they have helped to shape. As with other literary series published by Cambridge, this one will represent the work of both younger and more established scholars, on either side of the Atlantic and elsewhere.

For a complete list of titles published see back of book.

WORDSWORTH'S POPE

A study in literary historiography

ROBERT J. GRIFFIN

Tel Aviv University

Published by the Press Syndicate of the University of Cambridge
The Pitt Building, Trumpington Street, Cambridge CB2 1RP
40 West 20th Street, New York, NY 10011-4211, USA
10 Stamford Road, Oakleigh, Melbourne 3166, Australia

© Cambridge University Press 1995

First published 1995

Printed in Great Britain at the University Press, Cambridge

A catalogue record for this book is available from the British Library

Library of Congress cataloguing in publication data

Griffin, Robert J.
Wordsworth's Pope : a study in literary historiography / Robert J. Griffin.
p. cm. – (Cambridge studies in Romanticism)
Includes bibliographical references and index.
ISBN 0 521 48171 6 (hardback)
1. Wordsworth, William, 1770–1850 – Knowledge – Literature.
2. English poetry – History and criticism – Theory, etc. 3. Pope, Alexander, 1688–1744 – Influence. 4. Influence (Literary, artistic, etc.) 5. Romanticism – England. 6. Classicism – England. I. Title. II. Series.
PR5892.L5G75 1996
821'.7 – dc20   95-7147 CIP

ISBN 0 521 48171 6 hardback

SE

for Ariela

Though the Romantics and the Victorians steadily depreciated Pope and even went so far as to call him no poet at all, they continued to accord him practically the status of a major poet by showing that they were unable to ignore and forget him.

                                      Frederick A. Pottle, "The Case of Shelley"

Contents

List of illustrations	*page* x
Acknowledgments	xi
Introduction	1
1. The eighteenth-century construction of Romanticism	24
2. Refinement, Romanticism, Francis Jeffrey	64
3. Wordsworth's Pope	88
4. Mirror and lamp	111
Conclusion, with thoughts on method in literary historiography	133
Notes	146
Bibliography	170
Index	184

Illustrations

1. *Alexander Pope* by William Blake. Manchester City Art Gallery. *page* 30

2. "The Death of Dido" by Franz Cleyn, from *The Works of Virgil*, translated by John Dryden (London, 1697), p. 327. Beinecke Rare Book and Manuscript Library, Yale University. 105

Acknowledgments

The germ of the idea for this study came to me in a specific time and place, when I happened to take a graduate seminar on "Dryden, Swift, and Pope" simultaneously with a seminar on "Wordsworth and Coleridge." I wish to thank James Winn and Leslie Brisman for initiations that were comprehensive yet detailed, rigorous yet humane. Further investigations in these areas were stimulated by seminars with Ronald Paulson, Geoffrey Hartman, Harold Bloom, and one conducted jointly by Hartman and Paul de Man. I count myself very fortunate, since that time, to have engaged in ongoing conversations with Ronald Paulson and Geoffrey Hartman.

After completing a dissertation on another subject, I began to investigate this topic in earnest while teaching at Bowdoin College in Brunswick, Maine. Joe Litvak, Marilyn Reizbaum, and Frank Burroughs helped orient me on the way. Bill Watterson's unexpected gift of a meaningful book will always be cherished. President Roy Greason's generosity permitted me to attend the Wordsworth Summer Conference at Grasmere, and thus to test my first ideas against the experts. I remain grateful to Jonathan Wordsworth for his invitation.

At Tel Aviv, I have received timely support from Hana Wirth-Nesher and Zephyra Porat. Colleagues' questions in staff seminars have forced me to clarify specific issues. I have gained also by contact with a distinguished series of visitors. Thus I have received, at various times, direction and encouragement from Jerome McGann, Wendy Steiner, Don Kartiganer, and Ted Tayler. In Jerusalem, Larry Besserman and Sandy Budick have been especially helpful.

I am thankful to two friends, Brian McHale and Jim Shapiro, who had patience enough to read an inchoate version of the first chapters, and whose criticisms helped pull them in the direction of greater coherence and polish. Jim Shapiro, moreover, read drafts of the final chapters, and aside from his valuable observations, would not let me not finish the book. His support throughout the entire process has been priceless. Annette Cafarelli offered incisive criticisms of the first two chapters at a later stage. Meir Sternberg read and improved the Introduction and challenged me to make the reflections that became the Conclusion. Of those with whom I have discussed this project at various times, I want to thank in particular William Keach, Anca Vlasopolos, Marshall Brown, Jonathan Arac, David Fairer, Lee Erickson, Menachem Fisch, John Richetti, Bruce Graver, and Douglas Lane Patey.

The anonymous readers for Cambridge University Press improved the manuscript considerably by their suggestions. I am grateful for their time and effort. I am likewise sensible of a debt to the Series Editors, Marilyn Butler and James Chandler, especially the latter with whom I was directly in contact. Josie Dixon's intelligence and tact have made my dealings with the Press a pleasure.

While most of the book was written in Tel Aviv, most of the research needed to be done in London, New York, and New Haven. I thank the staffs of the British Library, the Senate House Library of the University of London, the Butler Library of Columbia University, and the Sterling and Cross-Campus Libraries as well as the Beinecke Rare Book and Manuscript Library of Yale University.

This book could not have been written without research and sabbatical funds granted by Tel Aviv University and by the Cohen-Porter Fund of the Department of English. Dr. Michael Murphy of the British Council, a well-travelled observer of the human condition and a valued friend, approved a travel grant to London at a crucial stage of investigation.

Parts of Chapter 3 and a section of Chapter 1 have appeared previously in print: "Wordsworth's Pope: The Language of His Former Heart," *ELH* 54 (1987): 695–715; and "The Eighteenth-Century Construction of Romanticism: Thomas Warton and the Pleasures of Melancholy," *ELH* 59 (1992): 799–815. This material is reprinted here by permission of the Johns Hopkins University Press. I thank also the Beinecke Rare Book and Manuscript Library and the Manchester City Art Gallery for allowing me to reproduce images from their collections.

I take this opportunity to acknowledge a longstanding intellectual debt to Blaine Bocarde.

As I look back on the aid I have received from so many sources, I feel both humbled and privileged. The book might have been written sooner, or might have been written better, were it not for my own unavoidable limitations. But such as it is, it is dedicated to the person with whom I share this life.

Introduction

THESIS

Let me sketch out my thesis by explaining its title, for the title, like most parts that attempt to represent a whole, is inevitably inadequate to its task, and thus requires some kind of supplementary explanation. "Wordsworth's Pope" is another way of saying "Romanticism's Pope," but I have subsumed Romanticism under Wordsworth for several reasons. There is a tradition of doing so, one associated with René Wellek and Meyer H. Abrams, and one that has come under attack in the last decade or so. My own critique is equally skeptical of that tradition, but it simultaneously acknowledges how much our notions of Romanticism have been influenced by Wordsworth's writings either directly, or indirectly through the critical tradition established in the nineteenth century and renewed in the academy forty years ago. I put forward here the argument that, however much the term "Romanticism" is under dispute, what we recognize today as "Romantic" is directly related to its view of Pope and the eighteenth century, and that it is primarily Wordsworth's polemical attacks on Pope that establish for us our notions of both "Pope" and the Romantic difference. "Wordworth's Pope," then, is the name of a recognizable relation, one crucial to literary history, for the debate over Pope in the early nineteenth century is accurately characterized by James Chandler as "arguably the canonical canon controversy in English literary history, the one associated with that nation's major revolution in poetry and taste."[1] But "Wordsworth's Pope" is also precisely what this study seeks to reveal as an interested construction, and thus to displace. It will become clear that Wordsworth's Pope is not really Wordsworth's, in that he inherited the terms of the debate, just as "Pope" is not really Pope, in that the Romantic view of Pope is a very narrow and ambivalent construction of the texts associated with that name.

As for the subtitle, this is a study in "literary historiography" because it is my argument that the Romantic view of Pope, the one that confirms by contrast the identity of "Romanticism," originates and is transmitted through a particular version of English literary history, one that is second nature to us and thus never questioned. What this book does, in particular, is trace the genesis, structure, and fate of that narrative of literary history. It should not be news to literary and cultural critics that ideology is naturalized in the stories we tell each other.

This study is not a comprehensive survey of Pope's influence on the early nineteenth-century poets, nor is it a full-scale history of Romanticism, nor a tracing of all the complicated turns in the reception of Romantic ideology in the nineteenth and twentieth centuries. I simply try to identify a particular discursive formation that comes into being in the 1740s in England and whose outlines are still visible in Romantic criticism today. My claim, which the reader can test in viewing the evidence, is that it is this discursive formation, this narrative structure, that holds together the diversity we call "Romanticism." Therefore, Chapter 1 describes how the central narrative of Romantic literary history was formulated in an ambivalent reaction to Pope in the writings of Thomas and Joseph Warton, and Edward Young; Chapter 2 shows how this narrative became established in the early nineteenth century, particularly, if unexpectedly, through the influence of Francis Jeffrey; Chapter 3 focuses on Wordsworth's relation to Pope; and Chapter 4 shows how the same narrative structure used by the writers of the 1740s and 1750s, inherited by Wordsworth and the early nineteenth century, is applied very successfully by M. H. Abrams in *The Mirror and the Lamp* (1953) to become the basis of modern critical studies of Romanticism. To compare small things with great, this is a "tunnel history," which is the way J. G. A. Pocock describes his own and related projects: "The works just mentioned form a 'tunnel history,' selecting a single theme and pushing it through until it emerges in the daylight of a new country; they do not and cannot claim to have told all there is to tell."[2]

My research supports the central conclusion that our received picture of Romantic literary history is a significantly distorted one because it derives from Romanticism's view of itself. This project, therefore, should be seen in the context of recent work that looks critically at Romantic self-definitions, and attempts to assess the influence of Romantic values on our current thinking. Marilyn Butler in *Romantics, Rebels and Reactionaries* (1981), Jerome McGann in *The Romantic Ideology* (1983), and Clifford Siskin in *The Historicity of Romantic Discourse* (1988), have begun to criticize the way scholars of Romanticism have themselves been shaped by Romantic values. As Siskin observes: "No issue is more central to today's Romanticists than clarifying their historical relationship to their subject matter."[3] As opposed to uncritical identification, what is developing in recent innovative criticism is a form of historical consciousness sensitive to differences between then and now. My project differs from these efforts of critical self-consciousness only in arguing that, however radical the effort, the analysis of Romanticism and its subsequent effects remains "Romantic" unless we scrutinize thoroughly the fact that a crucially defining feature of Romanticism is its rejection of the eighteenth century.

Alan Liu, in an elaborate and very shrewd essay on the New Historicism, simply takes as an unquestioned given "the transition between mimesis and symbolism initiated in Romanticism and its sequalia."[4] In my chapter on Abrams I will subject such an assumption to an unrelenting critique. Liu's re-telling of this story, however, suffices of itself to indicate that the transition from Classic to Romantic, Mirror to Lamp, taken as a straight developmental sequence, at a very fundamental level continues to shape attitudes towards the periods in question, and effectively prevents inquiries into the grounds upon which it was constructed. Even in sophisticated critics with a command of the tradition, the need to define Wordsworth and Romanticism honorifically in explicit opposition to Pope and the eighteenth century remains constant, suggesting that the opposition is in some way constitutive of Romantic identity.

Another example is Jonathan Bate: "Wordsworth and Coleridge were walking poets every bit as much as they were poets of the imagination. Imagine Alexander Pope composing poetry: we see him sitting in a patron's house or a coffee-house. Imagine Wordsworth or Coleridge composing; we see them in the open air."[5] There appears to be something gratuitous about such a comparison. Why put them together at all? And if one does, why not just as easily imagine Pope in Windsor Forest? And if "in a patron's house," why not correlate the facts that Wordsworth owed much more to patrons like Raisley Calvert and George Beaumont (including a winter of housing, 1806–07) than Pope, who remained fiercely independent, even translating Homer to remain so? "But (thanks to Homer) since I live and thrive, / Indebted to no Prince or Peer alive."[6] We cannot, or routinely do not, question such a juxtaposition because, however gratuitous the comparison appears, it is actually a deeply obligatory gesture, one that structures for us what we traditionally call "Romanticism." It does not account for every positive manifestation of "Romanticism," but it exists as an enabling condition of romantic discourse.

This is palpably the case even in a type of criticism, cultural materialism, that would seem furthest from the assumptions of a critic like Meyer Abrams, and which has been useful in breaking down certain aspects of the Romantic paradigm. Here is the opening sentence of the introduction to Stephen Copley and John Whale's collection of essays:

> A "new" eighteenth century has recently been announced. In justification it has been claimed that literary criticism of the period on both sides of the Atlantic has resisted theory. To make such a claim for the romantic period would be thought absurd. Romantic criticism has long been theoretically sophisticated.[7]

"Romanticism" needs to define itself as superior to the eighteenth century, and here the condescension is reproduced in the arena of criticism and theory. This opening gesture of the volume establishes for its readers a common ground of self-congratulation. A very different response to the collection of essays titled *The New Eighteenth Century* (1987) is registered by Lawrence Lipking, whom I imagine no one would call theoretically naive:

> The old eighteenth century, according to the editors, was characterized by its resistance to theory. Yet their own choice of four major critics from whom "contemporary eighteenth-century studies received its definition" – R. S. Crane, W. K. Wimsatt, Earl Wasserman, and Reuben Brower – sufficiently refutes the generalization, since each of the four spelled out explicit theoretical assumptions.[8]

I have chosen these quotations from Liu, Bate, and Copley and Whale, because they are very recent, and because they represent no single position on the critical spectrum. Their agreement reinforces my claim that the deep structure of "Romanticism," its *episteme* so to speak, is a narrative of periodization that posits an epochal break at some indeterminate point in the eighteenth century. Wordsworth's rejection of Pope, a foundational gesture for modern Romantic studies, has never really been scrutinized. De Man, though, writing on the *Essays on Epitaphs*, noted in passing that there was something excessive about Wordsworth's rhetoric:

> The *Essays* speak out forcefully against the antithetical language of satire and invective and plead eloquently for a lucid language of repose, tranquillity, and serenity. Yet, if we ask the legitimate question which of the two prevails in this text, the mode of aggression or of repose, it is clear that the essays contain large

portions that are most openly antithetical and aggressive. "I cannot suffer any Individual, however highly and deservedly honoured by my Countryman, to stand in my way"; this reference to Pope, together with many others addressed to the same, are anything but gentle. Wordsworth is sufficiently bothered by the discrepancy – it *is* a discrepancy, for there is no reason in the world why Pope could not have been handled with the same dialectical generosity accorded to death – to generate an abundant discourse of self-justification that spills over into a redundantly insistent Appendix. The most violent language is saved however, not for Alexander Pope, but for language itself.[9]

Harold Bloom's oedipal interpretation of literary influence seems pertinent here, but a romantically constructed history like his simply does not take seriously Pope's impact on his successors. Bloom's application of his theory to Wordsworth, for instance, takes it for granted that Milton is the oedipal precursor. In fact, I will argue, the structure of ambivalence set out in Bloom's theory describes precisely Wordsworth's relation to Pope, not Milton. Instead of taking Wordsworth's denial of Pope as a watershed, we should see that, defining himself from the moment he emerges as a distinct poetic voice as *not* Pope, Wordsworth's negation is itself a form of relationship. Pope, even when denied, is constitutive of Wordsworth's self-definition.

The larger implications of this structure are far-reaching. Consider that in terms of the narrative by which a superior, modern poetry ousts an inferior one identified with an *ancien régime*, the signifiers "Pope," "Wordsworth," and "Romanticism" shift their meanings according to varying historical moments and their pressures. Before the second slot even was named "Wordsworth" or "Romanticism," it was simply a vacant space identified with a savior and then given the name "Cowper." By the 1960s, though, these counters will have taken on multiple and complicated meanings, and I would suggest that what is denied as an alien Other is actually an inseparable part of the internal structure of the Romantic subject.

The problem then with Romantic literary history is, first, that it has accepted Wordsworth's aesthetic quarrel with Pope without questioning its provenance, its motives, or what it implied about Pope's influence, and, second, that it has allowed a positive view of Wordsworth and a negative view of Pope to shape its conception of history. When such evaluations drive historiography, anomalies do not register as anomalies but are simply subordinated to the dominant paradigm. For example, a standard narrative tells us that Wordsworth is the central figure in the revolt against the eighteenth century, that the key year is 1798, and that *The Prelude* is the major Romantic poem in English. On the basis of such evaluation, the title of a new anthology of critical essays, *The Age of William Wordsworth* (1987), quite openly suggests that Wordsworth is the major literary figure of his age. Personally, I do not dispute Wordsworth's continuing importance. The problem, rather, is that this view has very little to do with an attempt at reconstructing the historical moment of the early nineteenth century and its climate of reception. The most popular poets of the "Age of Wordsworth" were Scott and Byron, with Campbell, Rogers, and Moore in the second rank. Wordsworth did not become popular in any general sense until the 1830s when Scott and Byron, Coleridge, Keats, Shelley, and the rest were already dead. *The Prelude* was not published until after Wordsworth's death, and the 1805 *Prelude*, so central to a normative reconstruction of the age, was not published until the 1920s. Although these facts are widely known, they rarely collide with the evaluative point of view. For to speak of an "Age of Wordsworth" – on analogy with an Age of Pope, of Johnson, or of Rousseau – clearly falsifies the cultural milieu of the late eighteenth and early nineteenth century in England. Some other pressure than historical accuracy is at work.

Similarly, Wordsworth's supersession of Pope is very much a posthumous critical phenomenon, as my extensive documentation in Chapters 1 and 2 demonstrates. The terms of Wordsworth's attack on Pope were not original with him, but ones that he inherited from the eighteenth century. The debate over Pope's position as the latest and best thing in English began shortly after his death with the Wartons in the 1740s and 1750s, but they convinced very few. The debate heated up in the 1790s with, among other things, a two-year-long exchange of letters in *The Gentleman's Magazine* disputing who was superior, Pope or Dryden. When the dust settled in the 1820s it was generally accepted that Pope was indeed very accomplished, but that the Elizabethans were of a higher rank. The Wartons' position, in a more moderate form, had become orthodoxy. Wordsworth's role in bringing about this revolutionary state of affairs was not particularly conspicuous to his contemporaries. His archenemy, Francis Jeffrey, played a much more influential role in canon-formation from his position as arbiter of taste for the powerful and widely circulated *Edinburgh Review*. As early as 1803 Jeffrey observed that the first poet to break Pope's hold on posterity was Cowper, and later would add Burns and Scott; by 1808 he was already proclaiming the superiority of the

Elizabethans to the Queen Anne's men. We gain a much clearer picture of Wordsworth's position if we take into account here his statement that it was Burns and Cowper who liberated him in the early 1790s from the gaudy phraseology he had admired in Erasmus Darwin.[10] Jeffrey, for his part, considered Wordsworth a part of this dominant trend in modern poetry, but thought him both original and misguided, someone who did not even lead the Lake school, a position reserved for Southey. It is clear to us that Jeffrey could not appreciate Wordsworth's special achievement, but it should also be clear that very few in his time did. But Jeffrey was by no means an anti-romantic chained to outdated values, as his celebration of Keats upon his first appearance makes clear.

Because Romantic ideology was available since the 1740s, and because it was disseminated publicly by many, including Jeffrey, well before 1815, it is simply not possible to agree with Stephen Parrish when he states of the "Essay, Supplementary 1815":

The Romantic revolution of taste was nowhere more firmly established than in this important undervalued essay, which appeared before Coleridge's *Biographia Literaria*, before Keats had left medical school, before Shelley had published any verse except *Queen Mab* and a few scattered lyrics, before Blake was known to anyone beyond his circle, before Hazlitt had begun to collect his influential essays, before De Quincey had come into view outside of Westmorland. Wordsworth's essay (which, with the 1815 Preface, stimulated Coleridge to put the *Biographia* together) ranks with the prefaces to *Lyrical Ballads* as central documents of the most important critical revolution of the century.[11]

There are several revisionist historical projects ongoing in contemporary Romantic studies. But none that I know takes Thomas and Joseph Warton and Francis Jeffrey as central to their thesis. My argument may strike some as strange, if not perverse. It is counter-intuitive, but that is only because our "intuitions" have been trained to the point of automatic response by the Romantic point of view. What I have written is a defamiliarized history, and for that reason alone I expect it will rub many readers the wrong way. Everything depends on convincing the reader that we must take seriously "minor" mid-eighteenth-century figures, and see that these least familiar writers were most crucial in establishing the Romantic paradigm as we know it. We must put aside the condescension coded in the term "pre-Romantic" and recognize in them the first, earliest Romantics. In the section that follows I hope to convince the reader that what may look at first like an odd claim is actually a next logical step.

THE CONTEXT OF RECENT SCHOLARSHIP

I have deliberately stressed the novelty of my thesis because I believe it is true that, for many critics of Romanticism, to accept its findings requires a fundamental kind of conceptual reorientation. Yet what looks from one angle to be an eccentric fringe phenomenon, from another is no more than an extension of what several Romantic critics are already practicing, that is, working with the eighteenth century in a non-condescending, non-hierarchical way. In this section, though, rather than locate and cite all works that hint toward, or run parallel to, my point of view, I prefer to trace out a conceptual development that, I hope, establishes the plausibility of my undertaking.

Several critics and literary historians claim Romanticism for modernity and look forward from the 1790s. That approach certainly has its uses. But first, "modernity" is a problematic term; and second, the cultural semiotics of early nineteenth-century Britain require the observer to be competent in events going back to the mid-seventeenth century. What I want to urge explicitly is that the Romantic period – so often confined to a thirty- or forty-year stretch from the end of the eighteenth century to, roughly, the Reform Bill of 1832 – be absorbed into, and be seen as playing a natural role in, the period 1660 to 1832 that is coming to be recognized as the "long" eighteenth century. I make this suggestion not because I put faith in period constructions (as my next section will make clear), although the historians do in fact often treat these years as a kind of unit; the boundaries vary at times to 1688–1815, but the general sense is that it is profitable to view post-Civil War developments as reaching some sort of culmination in the early nineteenth century. Rather this viewpoint seems compelling because it is time for a fresh look, not at Romanticism as an origin of modernity, but in terms of its own origins, and precisely not in terms of its own narrative of its origins. Moreover, it is increasingly clear that one cannot study early nineteenth-century literature in isolation from broader social, cultural, economic, and political forces, and, to understand these, one needs a wider focus than a few decades can provide. The visible shift in literary criticism of the past decade precisely toward taking into account these forces, often only synchronically, nevertheless opens the way toward a reconsideration of Romanticism's attitude toward the eighteenth century. Two writers in particular, J. G. A. Pocock and Raymond Williams, seem to me highly influential in establishing the conditions for further inquiry.

Pocock, particularly in *The Machiavellian Moment* (1975), is associated with the study of the set of values called classical republicanism, which refers back to the landowner, like Cincinnatus in Livy, whose sense of civic virtue is grounded in a confederation of equals whose interests in maintaining the general good, the "good of the country," is identical with the interests of the enfranchised landowning class. Pocock shows how this republican ideal, opposed to monarchy in the 1640s, later became a leading theme of the country party opposed to commercial interests at the end of the seventeenth century with the establishment of the Bank of England in 1694 and, concomitantly, the national debt. Land, in short, as opposed to paper, although this simple dichotomy, as we learn, proves impossible to maintain. Nonetheless, the rhetoric of civic virtue became the paradigm of opposition to the Whig aristocratic-commercial oligarchy of the eighteenth century, and its force continued well into the nineteenth century.

Pocock's account of these developments, elaborated in several essays following upon the book, is so detailed, dialectical, and nuanced, that easy generalizations and stereotyped narratives are discouraged. For example, we are warned not to attribute "commerce" to a bourgeois middle class opposed to an aristocratic landed feudalism since the Whig oligarchy represented an aristocratic capitalism. Similarly, opposition rhetoric is shared by commonwealth Whigs and Tories, groups who would seem to have little in common. Pocock is particularly hard on Marxist historians:

Historians of this persuasion have been offended by the suggestion that radicalism in the eighteenth century consisted largely of a polemic against a system of public credit dominated by a landed aristocracy, that it was conducted largely in the name of classical-republican and agrarian-military values, and that it was in defense of the Whig aristocracy that an ethos of commercial individualism was first elaborated.[12]

The implications of Pocock's narrative for literary study are many, the potential for irony great, and I will develop some of these as we go along. For the moment it is enough to point out that his description of civic virtue has broadly influenced studies such as James Chandler's *Wordsworth's Second Nature* (1984) and David Simpson's *Wordsworth's Historical Imagination* (1987), as well as the series of studies that John Barrell has undertaken in the last decade.

Barrell provides us with an easy transition to Raymond Williams, for his Preface to *English Literature in History, 1730–1780: An Equal, Wide Survey* (1983) explicitly acknowledges Pocock in a book whose Series Editor is

Raymond Williams, and whose periodization draws upon the eras defined by Williams in *The Long Revolution* (1961). Moreover, when Simpson discusses Wordsworth's "Gypsies" in terms of Goldsmith's "Deserted Village" (and apologizes for doing so) he draws on Raymond Williams' discussion of Goldsmith in *The Country and the City* (1973) and of the romantic artist in *Culture and Society* (1958). Williams' work dovetails with Pocock's in many ways, particularly his focus on the role of "agrarian capitalism" in *The Country and the City*, and perhaps also for its long view of things. As a critic, moreover, Williams' work is a milestone in an attitudinal change, one that, whatever their differences of style and tradition, is similar to what one finds in post-structuralist criticism.[13] Stephen Greenblatt, who studied briefly at Cambridge, describes Williams' teaching in this way: "In Williams' lectures all that had been carefully excluded from the literary criticism in which I had been trained – who controlled access to the printing press, who owned the land and the factories, whose voices were being repressed as well as represented in literary texts, what social strategies were being served by the aesthetic values we constructed – came pressing back in upon the act of interpretation."[14]

The conjunction of Williams, Barrell, Simpson, and others, at Cambridge in the late 1970s and early 1980s allows us, perhaps, to speak loosely of a Cambridge School. Within the general goal of historicizing literary study, a central concern of this work is the ambivalent role of the poet and artist in a commercial society. Not that these critics are the only ones to take up these issues, for, as we know, the trend toward historicization is general across the 1980s. My point is that critics of Romanticism who take seriously the concern with material and historical points of view are more likely than others to place Romanticism in a wider perspective, and the Cambridge-affiliated critics are a good example. Jonathan Arac, a critic influenced by Williams and the Marxist tradition as well as by post-structuralist theory, similarly identifies what is at stake across the board in the eighteenth century in the artist's anxiety over the marketplace when he notes that the Preface to *Lyrical Ballads* "proclaimed the need for sober and serious opposition to what Pope and Swift had dismissed with satiric scorn."[15] That is, Swift, Pope, and Wordsworth are opposed to the same phenomenon but by Wordsworth's time the problem had become more acute. In Pocock's terms, all of these writers draw upon civic humanism as a weapon against the spread of commercial values. An irony Pocock registers is that commercial society in this period helped promote the growth of the arts, a fact which places our poets in a tricky relation to the market given the gradual decline in patronage.[16]

Certain opportunities, then, present themselves. Although I do not discuss him, Burke is a key figure because it is he who sums up and codifies a national consensus that had been forming since the Restoration. His debate with Price, we recall, is conducted in terms of whether what happens in France can be read in terms of the England of 1649, or of 1688. As Peter Manning puts it: "Because the French had taken inspiration from seventeenth-century English republican thought, the pressing contemporary situation made interpretation of England's own revolution a subject of renewed debate."[17] Chandler's carefully detailed study of Wordsworth as already Burkean in the 1790s is particularly suggestive, for it enables us to establish a link between a certain strain of Augustan reaction to the Civil War and a similar kind of Romantic reaction to the French Revolution. Both eschew political enthusiasm, something which reminds us that Coleridge, in *Aids to Reflection*, recommended Swift's *A Tale of a Tub* as a caution against self-inflation. Enthusiasm in the intervening years had become aesthetic, as my discussion of Edward Young's *Conjectures on Original Composition* (1759) in Chapter 1 will propose.

There are at least two kinds of continuity between the position of Pope and the position of Wordsworth that I wish to make clear. First, both subscribe to the values of classical republicanism and oppose themselves to what they perceive as the threat posed to their cultural values by what we call capitalism. This has not always been clear because, together with embarrassment over his later conservatism, critics often portray Wordsworth, in a confusion of aesthetic with political debate, as a revolutionary opposed to the reactionary conservatism of Swift and Pope. Which is to say that Wordsworth's republicanism has been interpreted as *exclusively* progressive. This is not wrong, so much as it is partial. Pocock, once again, is useful because he reminds us that "romantic radicalism, like other radicalisms before it, flowed from both a republican and a Tory source; this may help us understand the movement of Coleridge, Southey, and Wordsworth from republican youth to Tory old age."[18] It may also help us to understand, without minimizing differences, how much the Lake poets have in common with the Queen Anne Tory satirists.

Second, I wish to stress another kind of continuity that only seems to be contradictory to the first, that of "refinement" and "politeness," which was historically the ideology that merged the interests of the aristocratic and the commercial classes, often if not always the same people.

Pocock points out the contrast between the patriot and the man of commerce, between "virtue" and "politeness," with politeness and refinement as crucial elements of the ideology of commercial culture. But politeness had also a wider appeal:

> The ideal of politeness had first appeared in the Restoration, where it formed part of the latitudinarian campaign to replace prophetic by sociable religiosity. This campaign is carried on by Addison, a sound churchman by the new Whig standards, whose supreme achievement we see as the advancement of a polite style, and so of a politics of style accompanied by a morality of politeness. The polemic against enthusiasm was to continue for another hundred years – so deep were the scars of the Puritan interregnum on the governing-class mind – and the concepts of politeness, manners, and taste were to remain integral parts of its strategy.[19]

In commercial culture, polite manners, the ability to mix smoothly with a wide range of people, replaced a sterner notion of civic virtue. But, as this quotation makes clear, politeness appealed across the culture to court, church, country, and merchant, and for at least a hundred years, if not beyond up to our own time, opposed itself to political and religious enthusiasm. It is fair to describe one characteristic of "Romanticism," already in the 1740s, as a displacement of enthusiasm into poetry, but this necessarily occurs *within* the discourse of politeness and is opposed to it only in its excessive form as "false refinement," a term first used by Swift as far as I can tell. In the opposition that develops between the "polite" and the "vulgar," Romantic poets are definitely polite, even when their subjects are not. Percy's *Reliques*, we recall, were touched up to suit the taste of the age, and *Lyrical Ballads* necessarily participated in the same aesthetic. An early reviewer, Charles Burney, wrote: "Each ballad is a tale of woe. The style and versification are those of our ancient ditties; but much polished, and more consistently excellent."[20]

The debate between civic virtue and commerce is a real one. But the debate should not obscure how much both sides have in common. What is at stake is not a division of property between the haves and the have-nots. The dispute is between two kinds of property: "We are contrasting a conception of property which stresses possession and civic virtue with one that stresses exchange and the civilization of the passions, and thereby disclosing that the debate between the two is a major key to eighteenth-century social thought."[21] The poet is caught between. Writing implies exchange, but the writer defends the order that exchange will eventually undermine.

This second continuity, then, reminds us that although our poets disdained commerce, they had little choice but to sell their wares to the public. If Pope and Wordsworth, identifying as they do with the landed interest, react instinctively against the de-stabilizing forces of a growing commercial economy, yet neither owns independent estates himself and so both are dependent on the very market they fear and attack for its production of hacks, dunces, and sickly German tragedies. Now that critics are beginning to explore these issues in Wordsworth, Byron, and others, it is time to notice that Wordsworth's attacks on Pope suppress the very real investment in civic virtue that they hold in common, while they maximize Pope's involvement with the market. As I discuss in Chapter 3, Wordsworth accuses Pope of debasing himself by pandering to the public. As Simpson observes: "Writers such as Pope and Gray themselves opposed the same commercial culture that Wordsworth criticizes; but, in terms of his account, their writings none the less reproduce the stylistic symptoms of the very forces that they deplore."[22] In this passage, Simpson distances himself from Wordsworth's "account," but it is not in his way to offer an extended critique of it, which is what I set out to do. For the irony is that Wordsworth has simply usurped Pope's rhetoric of self-righteous disdain and turned it against him. Pope and Wordsworth had ambivalent relations to commerce, but both their criticisms come from the conservative side.

This is important to note, for the very critics whose profession of cultural materialism, when thought through diachronically, has granted them a valuable perspective on the eighteenth and early nineteenth century, do not always sufficiently distance themselves from Wordsworth's perspective on Pope. If we compare Pocock's treatment of this period, for example, with Raymond Williams', the historian's with the critic's, what stands out is the residual Romanticism of the materialist critic. This is especially clear in *The Country and the City*. What is pointed out in Pope is his affiliation with the commercial development of his friends' estates, the "morality of improvement," while what is pointed out in Wordsworth is his resistance to modern industrialization.[23] The selection is tilted in such a way as to valorize Romanticism, even when reactionary.

A different principle of selection could make Pope look noble and Wordsworth somewhat less so, for the material is there.[24] Not that the situation would be any better if we simply turned the tables. For quite aside from the fact that art cannot be reduced to biography, and that our continuing interest in these poets derives from the power of their writings, my point is that we must get beyond the insistent antithesis of

Wordsworth to Pope, but the very structure of Romantic literary history works against it. Here is Williams on Goldsmith's *The Deserted Village*:

> Here, with unusual precision, what we can later call a Romantic structure of feeling – the assertion of nature against industry and of poetry against trade; the isolation of humanity and community into the idea of culture, against the real social pressures of the time – is projected. We can catch its echoes, exactly, in Blake, in Wordsworth, and in Shelley.[25]

I find this passage of enormous significance. "[P]oetry against trade," and with it "the idea of culture," is defined as exclusively a "Romantic structure of feeling." Notice, too, how it embraces radicals (Blake, Shelley) and conservatives (Wordsworth). But, actually, such criteria can take in almost all of the major writers and critics from the Elizabethan period (if not before) right up to Williams' time (including Dryden, Pope, and Swift), and is thus useless as a way of making distinctions. As it stands, this definition romanticizes the entire tradition, but implicitly excludes the Augustans who, as everyone knows, are by definition not "Romantic."

In this way, a perspective that has contributed to the critique of "Romanticism" by subjecting aesthetics to materialist questionings, can if not careful end up simply reproducing Romantic ideology in another guise: Pope as capitalist, the Romantic as prophet in the wilderness. The irony, of course, is that the persona of cultural prophet condemning commercial values was invented most powerfully by Pope in *The Dunciad*. As Leopold Damrosch argues, Pope's attack on the dunces masks his own ambivalent relationship to the market, and "permits him further to distinguish between acceptable and unacceptable aspects of himself."[26] So, too, I will argue, the Romantic attack on Pope masks how much they have in common, how much "Pope" is an aspect of themselves. In the meantime, Williams' treatment of these poets provides another illustration to my general thesis that the core of "Romanticism" is the Pope/Wordsworth antithesis, and that we need to reflect deeply on how it came into being and what its transformations have been. That also means undertaking what is not simply heretical but nearly unthinkable for most Romanticists, a sustained study of texts they have been trained to disregard.

A CRITIQUE OF ROMANTIC PERIODIZATION

The recent conversation about Romantic periodization, or rather, over ways of constructing the late eighteenth and early nineteenth centuries in England, returns inevitably to what is styled the "Lovejoy–Wellek debate" of forty years ago.[27] Lovejoy, in 1924, responding to confusion in the way the term "Romanticism" was being used by his contemporaries, set out to make, to my mind, very useful philosophical and historical distinctions. He argued that the differences between what began in England in the 1740s, in Germany in the 1790s, in France in 1801, etc., should not be obscured by grouping them under one hypostatized term, for they differ from each other on such apparent essentials as primitivism, naturalism, and the relation to Christianity and the classics of Greece and Rome. Moreover, he claimed that within themselves they are not totally consistent: "each of these so-called Romanticisms was a highly complex and usually an exceedingly unstable intellectual compound." His chief recommendation, therefore, was "that we should learn to use the word 'Romanticism' in the plural." Lovejoy was analytical, not dogmatic. He allowed that there may be "some common denominator of them all; but if so, it has never yet been clearly exhibited, and its presence is not to be assumed *a priori*."[28]

René Wellek, in 1949, admitting ruefully that Lovejoy's thesis was "established securely," took up the challenge with a vengeance. Basing his view on a display of vast erudition, Wellek argued for an essential unity of European Romanticism consisting of common concerns for imagination, nature, myth, and symbol.[29] Wellek "won," so to speak. As Jerome McGann recently noted, Wellek's formulation represents "on the one hand, a synthesis of an originary romantic tradition of thought, and, on the other, the bounding horizon for much of the work on romanticism done between World War II and the early 1980s." But McGann goes on to observe: "today that synthesis has collapsed and the debate about theory of romanticism is vigorous."[30]

Although Lovejoy was a philosopher and not a literary critic, it is not difficult to see this sequence in twentieth-century conceptualizations of the Romantic period – Lovejoy, Wellek, followed by revisionists like McGann and Marilyn Butler – as playing its role within a recognizable succession of dominant literary critical paradigms. Wellek's argument with Lovejoy, for instance, which is only part of his larger argument against "history" and for "evaluation," is emblematic of the emergence of criticism and the displacement of historical scholarship, just as the re-emergence of the historical emphasis in Romantic studies in the last ten years is part of the general dissatisfaction with an exclusively text-centered notion of criticism as explication.

I make what seems to be an obvious point in order to foreground the question of evaluation. The historical perspective tends to relativize value judgments. Lovejoy's sense of the need to discriminate began with the historical gap that had opened up between the early nineteenth century and a later century's perspectives on it. This gap, however, presented no obstacle for Wellek. Our interest, he says unequivocally, is with the "writers of greatest artistic importance." Thus, because of the imperative of evaluation, the "literary theories, terms, and slogans of a time need not have prescriptive force for the modern literary historian."[31] For all his considerable historical knowledge, Wellek set out to define a canon of values.

The undoing of Wellek's synthesis is part of the very stimulating, but also at times confusing situation that "theory" places us in. Mark Parker reads this new situation, quite accurately I think, as rehearsing, in its own way, the terms of the original debate: "Although McGann and Butler have been reliable guides to the route taken by subsequent researchers into the era traditionally called Romantic, it would be a mistake to see the Lovejoy/Wellek confrontation as solved or rendered irrelevant. The caution with which they invoke Lovejoy's position indicates the lingering force of Wellek's concept of a period."[32] In McGann's case the dialectic is very clear. As a Byron scholar, McGann dissented against Wellek's authority because the insistence on imagination, nature, and symbol, had the effect of putting Wordsworth and Coleridge in the center, and relegating Byron to an aberration. Hence, in *The Romantic Ideology* (1983), McGann used Lovejoy's notion of a plurality of Romanticisms in order to attack Wellek's reification and its implied standard of judgment. But in a recent essay he warns against "a neo-Lovejoyan skepticism": "To the extent that *The Romantic Ideology* was written as a critical polemic against what I took to be a false consciousness of romanticism, its arguments might be used to bolster such a pyrrhonist approach." But his own view, he tells us, is very different. Wellek's definition of Romanticism "is not so much wrong as it is abstract and preliminary." We cannot dispense with terms like "nature" and "imagination," McGann argues, because these terms "are primary philological data" of historical Romanticism. Rather we must see that a term like "imagination" is radically dialogical, and that poets like Coleridge and Shelley, for instance, set out to control its dynamism and limit it within "prescriptive and ideological frameworks."[33]

As a guide to a more accurate re-description of the early nineteenth century, McGann's scholarship cannot be ignored. McGann's example also shows, however, that recent historical criticism does not simply pick up where Lovejoy left off. Rather, very much like Wellek, the appeal to history functions as an argument for a new configuration of evaluations. Now revealed as a historical construction having a partial validity rather than constituting the "essence" of the period, the postwar generation's hierarchy of literary values has given way to an expanded canon in which Byron, Southey, Scott, Mary Shelley, Dorothy Wordsworth, and Charlotte Smith, for example, receive more critical attention.[34] This work is innovative and exciting. But I will argue that the opening up of the Romantic canon, the vigorous re-examination of the early nineteenth century, has had the paradoxical effect of reinforcing Romantic periodization.

By changing the canon, the thinking seems to go, one changes the conception of the period. To a certain extent the assumption is justified, for canon and period notions do overlap. The period does indeed look different when the traditional grouping (since the late nineteenth century) of five or six male poets loses its sacred aura, and when key terms are subjected to historical and ideological readings. But, in this criticism, canon and period are construed exclusively on a synchronic axis. What has not been investigated thoroughly, and what seems to me to be required, is the way Romantic canon and period constructions operate on a diachronic axis. Discussing historical construction in general, Fredric Jameson has made this point with clarity, observing "that individual period formulations always secretly imply or project narratives or 'stories' – narrative representations – of the historical sequence in which such individual periods take their place and from which they derive their significance."[35] For Jameson the diachronic problem is the prior one, because individual periods come into being diachronically as part of a more encompassing "master narrative" of history, whether Hegelian, Marxist, Viconian, or what have you. What happens if we transfer this insight to the master narratives of *literary* history?

A handful of critics, addressing themselves to the question of Romantic periodization, have raised the diachronic problem. By pointing out the shifting versions of the Romantic period they provide valuable perspectives from which to recognize the constructed nature of any given version.[36] But Jameson's insight supplies a perspective that has been missing, for these discussions do not locate a master narrative of literary history operating as a given in any particular construction of the early nineteenth century. They analyze various manifestations but do not address the underlying system. The focus of interest remains insistently the early nineteenth century, and then by a natural logic, its subsequent history as patterns of emphasis appear in various receptions in the later nineteenth century and up to our time.[37] I do not disparage this work; far from it. From my point of view, however, the assumption that Romanticism is essentially an affair of the 1790s and the first decades of the nineteenth century means that, whatever their disagreements and points of friction over canon and the theory of Romanticism, critics continue to participate uncritically in the master narrative within which the period "Romanticism" comes into being in the first place. Therefore, even in the attempt to measure our historical distance from "Romanticism," a Romantic narrative of English literary history continues to determine the possible limits of our discourse.

It is not that this narrative is unknown. It is rather that it has been relegated to the pre-history of Romanticism and its inventors labelled as pre-Romantics, and thus, as "background," does not enter the debate on the "Romantic period" in anything like its true dimensions. Nonetheless, as Chapter 1 shows in detail, the first appearance of a recognizably "Romantic" master narrative of literary history, the one which provides the necessary framework for the declaration of an epochal and irretrievable break from a recent past now to be understood as obsolete, occurs in the mid-eighteenth century with the poetry and criticism of Joseph and Thomas Warton. Wellek gives us the narrative of literary history that the Wartons themselves were influential in spreading:

> Without the term "romanticism" we can trace, within a short period, the shift from the earlier conception of the history of English poetry as one of uniform progress from Waller and Denham to Dryden and Pope, still accepted in Johnson's *Lives of the Poets*, to Southey's opposite view in 1807, that the "time which elapsed from the days of Dryden to those of Pope is the dark age of English poetry." The reformation began with Thomson and the Wartons.[38]

This is the story of a simple reversal of values. Within the space of a few decades a very high estimation of Dryden and Pope is replaced by a very low one. Wellek places Thomson and the Wartons at the beginning. It is really the Wartons, though, who set out to overturn Pope's reputation by argument, and by "reviving" the poetry of what we call the English Renaissance, which, however much respected in the early eighteenth century, was no longer considered a proper model for contemporary poetry. But by invoking Spenser, Shakespeare, and Milton, Joseph Warton, in his *Essay on the Writings and Genius of Pope* (1756), raises the question whether Pope was really a poet at all. Whereas post-Civil War poetry saw itself as refining upon a rich, but disorderly tradition, Warton's revised narrative claims that the aesthetic of polish and correctness is in effect a degeneration from "true" poetry, and that Pope is essentially outside of the tradition.

Wellek's *The Rise of English Literary History* (1941) gives us some perspective on the notion of "refinement." Apparently, Chaucer had been seen as a refiner, as had Wyatt and Surrey. There is evidence that the aesthetic of refinement is part of the vernacular's anxiety in relation to Greek and Latin. Nonetheless, the discourse of refinement in the eighteenth century is present in specific ways, and the standard version of Romanticism tells us that it rejects Popean refinement. I will argue, on the contrary, and taking my cue from Pocock's socio-political history, that the poetry of the late eighteenth and early nineteenth century maintains the aesthetic of refinement for both social and aesthetic reasons, but that this continuity presents no barrier whatsoever to writers condemning Pope for what they themselves practice.

The Wartonian version of English literary history is not only still with us, it is the one that everyone knows best. Here is Harold Bloom's concise and rhetorically powerful rendering of the Wartonian master narrative, updated to 1975:

The French in the seventeenth century . . . establish[ed] their permanent version of classicism, a version that the English Augustans bravely but vainly tried to emulate before they were flooded out by that great English renaissance of the English Renaissance we now call the Age of Sensibility or the Sublime, and date fairly confidently from the mid-1740s. This renaissance of the Renaissance was and is Romanticism, which is of course *the* tradition of the last two centuries.[39]

Lawrence Lipking, commenting on the Wartons, observes that a poet's history is "used to affirm a theory of poetic value, and to generate new poems"; hence it needs to be "generative, not rational and complete."[40] Accepting the poet's history, in this case most centrally and powerfully the re-statement of the Wartonian narrative by Wordsworth and Coleridge, we inherit the paradoxical situation in which Romanticism both begins and does not begin in the 1740s. Conventionally, we understand the Romantic period to begin with *Lyrical Ballads* in 1798, or perhaps earlier with Blake, or the French Revolution. Yet Lovejoy, Wellek, and Bloom all refer to 1740. The gap between these dates, 1740 and 1798, is opened up by means of the value judgment that the poetry of the later eighteenth century is not as interesting as one would desire. This is made clear in another of Bloom's declarations:

What allies Blake and Wordsworth, Shelley and Keats, is their strong mutual conviction that they are reviving the true English tradition of poetry, which they thought had vanished with the death of Milton, and had reappeared in diminished form, mostly after the death of Pope, in admirable but doomed poets like Chatterton, Cowper, and Collins, victims of circumstance and of their own false dawn of Sensibility.[41]

Now I am not going to argue that Collins, for example, is a better poet than Keats. Rather I want to reassert the claims of history in order to provide a genealogy of literary value judgments in the belief that such self-knowledge will be useful. By following Jameson's methodological lead, I identify "Romanticism" with the narrative of literary history that finds its first articulation in the 1740s. From there one can see that "Romanticism" assumes a protean number of literary forms, some now valued more highly than others. From there one sees also that the question of a Romantic canon must shift backward, for it is only much later that the center of gravity of Romanticism comes to be identified with the early nineteenth century. Joseph and Thomas Warton, and Joseph's friend and schoolmate at both Winchester and Oxford, William Collins, are, in my view, the first Romantics, and their poetry, whatever value we assign to it, can tell us much about the nature of romanticism.

The Wartonian narrative, it is crucial to note, is the foundation for literary history in the nineteenth century. As Wellek has pointed out, implied in Thomas Warton's *History of English Poetry* (1774–81), the starting point for nineteenth-century literary histories, is a "psychological concept of evolution" in which imagination is gradually overtaken by reason. Thus faculty psychology is projected as historical narrative: in the medieval period imagination predominated, in the Renaissance there was a balance between imagination and reason, whereas in the modern period, that is, since 1660, reason has predominated.[42] Nostalgia for imagination defines the emotional tone. Such a view of history would seem to be a fairly naive and transparent fiction. Yet its power should not be underestimated. As late as 1980, Howard Felperin protested that this Romantic perspective continued to dominate interpretations of Renaissance literature. Mentioning Thomas Warton and Schiller, among others, Felperin shows how Northrop Frye's theory of successive modes – from myth to romance down to irony – is based on the same structure. Against the view that presents literary history as a continual displacement and demystification of myth and romance in the movement toward "modern" irony, Felperin argues that a work like *The*

Tempest takes the demystification of romance as a central theme. Felperin ends his essay with harsh words:

> It is naive to place these great romances within an historical sequence of progressive demystification moving from myth to irony since each is demystified from the start. To do so is to patronize the past by oversimplifying it and to idealize the present by making it the source of complexity. The consequences of this procedure are not only bad literary history but bad literary interpretation.[43]

Felperin's protest highlights what I take to be the central issue. Modern criticism is deeply informed by Romantic literary history. More precisely, because it is a "master" narrative configuring not just Romanticism but other periods as well, the basic assumptions of Romantic literary history continue to shape modern critical attitudes about literature generally. For, when critics define the poetry of the early nineteenth century as a revival of medieval-Renaissance romance, then not just the early nineteenth century, but all English literary history has been thoroughly Romanticized. By means of this self-definition, all earlier periods are constructed from a Romantic perspective. In this reading, all of English literature, with the crucial exception of Dryden and Pope, is essentially Romantic in character. What is true of the tradition, moreover, has implications for the national character. Thus we find the editor of an anthology of English literature writing in 1941 that the Romantic movement "is in reality but a return to normal English currents of thought and expression." This is so because, note the use of the singular, "the mind of the Englishman, from the time of the Anglo-Saxon invasions of Britain to the present, has always been given more to emotion and imagination." In the early eighteenth century, of course, certain literary fashions had been "imposed upon the Englishman," but he followed them "reluctantly."[44]

What I have tried to sketch out very briefly is the narrative framework that has given shape not just to our notions of the Romantic period, but also, because of the values embedded in that narrative, to our view of literary history and, it follows, literature generally. I have stressed the role of evaluation in Romantic literary history, not because I wish to oppose it with my own evaluations and urge Romanticists to attempt an unprejudiced reading of the eighteenth century, although, in my estimation, such a project would have salutary effects. Rather, by exposing the foundations of Romantic literary history, I hope to reinforce the kind of work that sees the application of period terminology, not as a neutral tool in marking out chronological sequences, but rather as a form of discourse that imposes an implicit set of values upon its objects. The question of Pope then becomes, what is the romantic construction "Pope" a symptom of? There is no simple answer, and I will have to postpone speculation to a later moment.

Let me conclude this section with some general thoughts about periodization. One line of thinking suggests that, however partial or constricting, period constructions possess at least the heuristic value of introducing students to an era. The hope seems to be that more sophisticated study will qualify, refine, and even call into question the original generalizations. David Perkins, who has written literary history and devoted much thinking to the subject, summarizes this view as follows:

> At present, we tend to regard periods as necessary fictions. They are necessary because . . . one cannot write history or literary history without periodizing. Moreover, we require the concept of a unified period in order to deny it, and thus make apparent the particularity, local difference, heterogeneity, fluctuation, discontinuity, and strife that are now our preferred categories for understanding any moment of the past.[45]

The dilemma, for Perkins, is that the mind must necessarily seek to order and classify, and that this activity will necessarily distort the multiplicative and heterogeneous nature of the material under study. One can agree with the general point without accepting all of its applications. When Perkins himself concludes that "English romantic poetry seems to me a classification that is not well grounded," or when Annabel Patterson says that her study of the reception of Virgil's eclogues calls into question "already fragile" period demarcations, and sometimes, as with medievalism and romanticism, "subjected to skepticism even the semantic content of those terms" – when careful scholars come to these sorts of conclusions, the notion that we "require the concept of a unified period in order to deny it," as Perkins says, surely needs to be re-examined.[46] It may be true that we can never recover the past because of our own intellectual limitations, or even that our studies of the past will be inevitably determined by present concerns. But this is no reason to continue to accept and to teach period constructs when we know them to be fundamentally flawed.

The term "Romanticism," I have tried to argue, is anything but a neutral chronological indicator; it comes to us laden with whole strata of unconscious assumptions. I find it worthwhile to work against the grain of those assumptions, and to hope that, by identifying them, one can, by the abreactive process of dredging them up from the unconscious, loosen their hold on our thinking; there are several lines of inquiry in such a project that I have yet to pursue. Yet the very mention of the term "Romanticism" evokes such powerful associations, and so familiar a set of stock responses, that I have to wonder whether historical momentum simply overpowers the attempt to get free. For these assumptions are embedded not only in the texts we study, but are also institutionalized in course offerings, hiring decisions, dissertation topics, even in the Divisions of the Modern Language Association. Even if our thinking is inevitably shaped by a history that we haven't made, thought itself, I have to believe, is flexible enough and open-ended enough to allow for new ways of thinking to come into being. I take heart from Jerome McGann's observation on periodization: "We do not, after all, *have* to think in such terms."[47]

CHAPTER ONE

The eighteenth-century construction of Romanticism

The great merit of this writer appears to us to consist in the boldness and originality of his composition, and in the fortunate audacity with which he has carried the dominion of poetry into regions that had been considered as inaccessible to her ambition. The gradual refinement of taste had, for nearly a century, been weakening the force of original genius. Our poets had become timid and fastidious, and circumscribed themselves both in the choice and management of their subjects, by the observance of a limited number of models, who were thought to have exhausted all the legitimate resources of the art.
_____ was one of the first who crossed this enchanted circle; who reclaimed the natural liberty, and walked abroad in the open field of observation as freely as those by whom it was originally trodden. He passed from the imitation of poets to the imitation of nature.

This quotation expresses many of the essentials of the "Romantic" version of literary history. The chain of associations – boldness, original genius, break from a refined taste, natural liberty, direct observation, and imitation of nature – would lead most readers, I suggest, to complete the sequence and fill in the space I have left blank with the name "Wordsworth." Pressed to identify the author of the passage, one might reasonably guess it was Arnold, or some other Victorian influenced by Wordsworth, surveying the revolution in taste that occurred at the beginning of his/her century. In actual fact, this is an appreciation of William Cowper written in 1803 by the critic generally recognized to be Wordsworth's mortal enemy, Francis Jeffrey.[1] The feeling of disorientation that comes over one upon realizing this is caused by certainties rapidly dissolving. How is it that in 1803 Jeffrey writes in these terms? And if his subject is Cowper, why do we expect it to be Wordsworth?

It is certainly possible to argue that Jeffrey owes his critical perspective to Wordsworth's Preface to *Lyrical Ballads* published a few years earlier. But this response misses the broader cultural context: both Wordsworth and Jeffrey participate in a discourse that was formulated in the 1740s and 1750s, twenty years before they were born in the early 1770s. Jeffrey's placing of Cowper, for instance, which one easily mistakes for a much later critic's placing of Wordsworth using Wordsworthian terms, reads like a summary of the main points of Joseph Warton's *Essay on Pope* (1756) and Young's *Conjectures on Original Composition* (1759). To the extent, therefore, that we give assent to the "Romantic," or the "Wordsworthian" version of the eighteenth century, or agree with Arnold that that century was an age of reason and prose, we continue to participate uncritically in a narrative established by Pope's rivals in the decade after his death. Students of the eighteenth century have long abandoned such terminology but they have been talking mostly to themselves.

Marlon Ross has written that "romantic ideology began to dominate the literary establishment *before* the romantic canon, as we know it, was established."[2] I agree with the general statement, but, without altering the value of Ross's research, I would revise its application. First, I would substitute "romantic literary history" for "romantic ideology," because I assume throughout that ideological values require a narrative framework for their expression. Hence, what we call romantic ideology is inseparable from the narrative of diachronic periodization that organizes the field of literary history. Second, I would alter the chronology, for this statement occurs in a discussion of Wordsworth's reputation around 1820, whereas the burden of my argument is that we find essentially the same "Romantic" paradigm of literary history operative before Wordsworth was born. If the critical paradigm that prepared poets like Cowper, and Bowles, and Wordsworth to challenge Pope was already in place by 1760, though not widely accepted, this means that Romantic literary history existed *before* there was such a thing as romantic poetry, or rather, before a great romantic poet appeared. I agree completely with Ross's point that the Romantic paradigm is shared by those who divide sharply over the value of Wordsworth, as my opening citation of Jeffrey should make clear.

"Romantic" literary history, as I document in this chapter, originates with, and continues to function in relation to, an anxiety about Pope. It begins in the mid-eighteenth century and develops through the early nineteenth century as a polemical construction of Pope's place in English literary history. Pope's considerable influence throughout this period, even when construed as purely negative, is brought home by Byron's sardonic remark about his contemporaries in 1821: "The attempt of the poetical populace of the present day to obtain an ostracism against Pope is as easily accounted for as the Athenian's shell against Aristides; they are tired of hearing him always called 'the Just'.

They are also fighting for life; for, if he maintains his station, they will reach their own – by falling."[3]

The Wartons, William Collins, Gray, and Young are usually defined as minor, pre-Romantic poets, stock figures in a "Whig" history of ideas in which progress leads to the magic year, 1798. The teleological fallacy inherent in the notion "pre-Romanticism" has often been noticed.[4] The crudest, but also most telling, example of the logic of pre-Romanticism is Ernest Bernbaum's "Chronological Table of the Chief Pre-Romantic Works." The list begins with 1696 and includes *all* of the major and minor writers of the eighteenth century of every possible genre, with the exception of Dryden, Pope, Swift, Fielding, and Johnson.[5] My perspective, however, defines Romanticism not positively according to the very varied forms it takes, but negatively as a phenomenon that is intimately bound up in what it dislikes. The unity of Romanticism as an ideology, that is to say, is discovered in the agreement over what it rejects. From this perspective, the Wartons and Young, on whom I focus most of the attention here, are key figures, for they, in conscious but ambivalent rebellion against Pope, helped create the new paradigm out of old materials such as the hierarchy of genres, and the distinction between art and nature. For me, then, "pre-Romanticism" disappears entirely as a category, for these writers together with their followers in the nineteenth century, whatever their differences on the surface, participate in the same discursive formation. Critics from at least the 1930s to the present have argued that "Romanticism" is something that happened to Wordsworth or to Blake at a certain stage of their career, which is to say that before that they were pre-Romantic. This makes no sense to me because I see what is generally called Romanticism as neither a particular style (attention to details of nature, symbol, lyric expression, etc.), nor a particular content, but rather as a discourse that arises in response to a psychological dilemma in relation to modernity in general, and modern poetry, which is to say "Pope," in particular.

Though discredited as a concept by many, the point of view implied by the notion of "pre-Romanticism" continues to function as a mode of understanding literary history from Wordsworth's and Coleridge's point of view. This is only one example of the way that criticism, and with it literary history, tend to become simply satellites orbiting around the attractive power of "great writers." Since Wordsworth writes the poetry that is taken, retrospectively, to be the true alternative to Pope, criticism simply subsumes under his name a movement that had been gathering force for a half a century, labelling it "pre-". This leads to strange formulations which seem to corroborate Harold Bloom's notion of the way that strong poets are able to reverse chronological priority. Edith Morley, for example, cites Joseph Warton on the need to see the object steady and whole, and on the need for a simpler poetic diction. Rather than suggest that Wordsworth was influenced, or indeed shaped by Warton's discourse, Morley actually compliments Warton on agreeing with Wordsworth: "Wordsworth himself could say no more."[6]

The same dynamic is at work in the fate of Cowper, for Wordsworth would eventually assume the place in the Romantic paradigm that had once been held by the earlier poet. Chalmers, in 1810, wrote that Cowper, "above all poets of recent times, has become the universal favourite of his nation." Jeffrey, in 1811, repeated his estimate of 1803: "Cowper is, and is likely to continue, the most popular of all who have written for the present or the last generation." Coleridge in 1817 named the most recent era of English poetry, "from Cowper to the present day." In 1832, Christopher North reflects that "the era has been glorious," and that era includes "Cowper and Wordsworth, Burns and Byron."[7] But within the space of twenty years, by 1852, Wordsworth's reputation appears to have eclipsed Cowper's with the consequence that Cowper's priority was eclipsed as well. A reviewer thus protests against distortions of literary history:

It is constantly asserted that he [Wordsworth] effected a reform in the language of poetry, that he found the public bigoted to a vicious and flowery diction which seemed to mean a great deal and really meant nothing, and that he led them back to sense and simplicity. The claim appears to us to be a fanciful assumption, refuted by the facts of literary history. Feebler poetasters were no doubt read when Wordsworth began to write than would now command an audience, however small, but they had no real hold on the public, and Cowper was the only *popular* bard of the day. His masculine and unadorned English was relished in every cultivated circle in the land, and Wordsworth was the child, and not the father of the reaction, which after all, has been greatly exaggerated.[8]

My interest in the genealogy of literary values, in telling the story of "the story" – telling, that is, not how Mirror became Lamp, but how this particular episode of literary history came to be constructed in that way – focuses on the disjunction between today's dominant understanding of the relation between the Romantics and the eighteenth century, and the very different perspective that the following historical reconstruction opens up. The relegation of certain mid-eighteenth-century writers by literary history to the category of "pre-" is suggestive. From a more oblique angle, the prefix conjures up an archaeological level of romantic consciousness that has been labelled in order to be forgotten because it is meant to serve as a foundation we can confidently build upon in our discussions of what really matters. The uncanny, as defined by Freud, involves a confrontation with something strange, yet familiar, something that awakens in us something we thought was long put to rest. The notable obscurity of the figures I analyze in this chapter holds forth the possibility of moments of uncanny recognition on the margin – uncanny not simply because they appear so often as repressed doubles of our own discourse, but also because of the way they repeat Pope in the very act of displacing him.

THE WARTONS

Thomas Warton's "The Pleasures of Melancholy," written in 1745, a year after Pope's death, is a poem referred to more often than read. In the last forty years it has been addressed infrequently, but twice as a rough draft for Keats's "Ode on Melancholy."[9] Dismissing pre-Romanticism as the logic of the contradictions inherent in Romanticism proper, I find that nowhere is the genesis of Romanticism better studied than in Warton's poem.

Drawing upon "Il Penseroso" (and implicitly "L'Allegro") for its structure, "The Pleasures of Melancholy" constructs itself around the allegorical opposition between Day and Night, Mirth and Melancholy. The noise of the City is opposed to the quiet of Nature, Vice to Virtue, Summer to Winter, bright Sunshine to Fogs, Gloom, and Rain. The speaker's preference for solitude and night, emblems for "Virtue," expresses itself further in his choice between fictional women who are emblems of their authors. In this erotics of reading, Warton prefers Spenser's Una, alone in the wilderness, to Pope's Belinda, launched at noon on the silver Thames.

> Thro' POPE'S soft song though all the Graces breathe,
> And happiest art adorn his Attic page;
> Yet does my mind with sweeter transport glow,
> As at the root of mossy trunk reclin'd,
> In magic SPENSER'S wildy-warbled song
> I see deserted UNA wander wide
> Through wasteful solitudes, and lurid heaths
> Weary, forlorn; than when the fated fair,
> Upon the bright bosom of silver Thames,

> Launches in all the lustre of brocade,
> Amid the splendors of the laughing Sun.
> The gay description palls upon the sense,
> And coldly strikes the mind with feeble bliss.
>   Oh, wrap me then in shades of darksome pine,
> Bear me to caves of desolation brown,
> To dusky vales and hermit-haunted rocks![10] (lines 153–68)

To identify Pope with his ironic heroine, Belinda, is rather tendentious because it collapses the distance signalled by Pope's satire. But if we read the poem simply as a statement of preference for *The Fairie Queene* over *The Rape of the Lock*, there is no point in quibbling, nor are standards of taste here the real issue. What is more to the point is an examination of the evidence the poem provides for the grounds of evaluation. Warton's poem is intensely interesting because it reveals the contradictions at the very heart of the ideological construction we recognize as Romanticism, for the poem cannot sustain its own dichotomy between a sunny Classicism that is attractive but superficial – Pope, Belinda, "Attic" art – and a melancholy Gothicism that offers deeper pleasures – Spenser's Una, Milton's Penseroso. The poem itself gives evidence that Pope, master of classic forms, is also the primary revivalist and transmitter of Gothic gloom.

Structured as it is by opposing Mirth to Melancholy, Day to Night, and Spenser–Milton to Pope, the logic of the poem breaks down in several places. First of all, Pope is represented in the poem not just by Belinda, but also by his Eloisa and the Unfortunate Lady, both of whom are recruited to the side of pensive Melancholy. It is worth noting that these two figures were the ones Blake, too, recalled when representing Pope for a series of English authors (Figure 1).

The opening lines of Pope's *Elegy to the Memory of an Unfortunate Lady* read as follows:

> What beck'ning ghost, along the moonlight shade
> Invites my step, and points to yonder glade?
> 'Tis she! – but why that bleeding bosom gor'd,
> Why dimly gleams the visionary sword?[11]

The ghost appears with sword and bleeding bosom, we soon discover, because she is the spirit of a principled young woman who chose death rather than marry against her wishes in order to enrich her guardian. The speaker of Warton's "The Pleasures of Melancholy," apparently, saw the same ghost during his own midnight vigils:

Figure 1. *Alexander Pope*, by William Blake. The Unfortunate Lady is on the left side, and Eloisa is on the right.

> But when the world
> Is clad in Midnight's raven-color'd robe,
> In hollow charnel let me watch the flame
> Of taper dim, while airy voices talk
> Along the glimmering walls, *or ghostly shape*
> *At distance seen, invites with beck'ning hand.* (lines 44–9, my emphasis)

Eloisa, unlike the Unfortunate Lady, is named explicitly in the poem, but before turning to that passage it is useful to reread the much-admired set piece on Melancholy from Pope's *Eloisa to Abelard* (1717):

> The darksom pines that o'er yon rocks reclin'd
> Wave high, and murmur to the hollow wind,
> The wand'ring streams that shine between the hills,
> The grots that eccho to the tinkling rills,
> The dying gales that pant upon the trees,
> The lakes that quiver to the curling breeze;
> No more these scenes my meditation aid,
> Or lull to rest the visionary maid.
> But o'er the twilight groves and dusky caves,
> Long-sounding isles, and intermingled graves,
> Black Melancholy sits, and round her throws
> A death-like silence, and a dread repose:
> Her gloomy presence saddens all the scene,
> Shades ev'ry flower, and darkens ev'ry green,
> Deepens the murmur of the falling floods,
> And breathes a browner horror on the woods. (lines 155–70)

Here is Warton, twenty-eight years later:

> Few know the elegance of soul refin'd,
> Whose soft sensation feels a quicker joy
> From Melancholy's scenes, than the dull pride
> Of tasteless splendor and magnificence
> Can e'er afford. Thus Eloise, whose mind
> Had languished to the pangs of melting love,
> More genuine transport found, as on some tomb
> Reclin'd, she watch'd the tapers of the dead;
> Or through the pillar'd iles, amid pale shrines
> Of imag'd saints, and intermingled graves,
> Mus'd a veil'd votaress; than Flavia feels,
> As through the mazes of festive balls,
> Proud of her conquering charms, and beauty's blaze,
> She floats amid the silken sons of dress,
> And shines the fairest of the fair. (2nd ed., lines 92–106)

Warton's allusion to Eloisa embeds her within an opposition to a Belinda-like coquette, Flavia, while picking up verbal echoes from both poems. Notice that the thematic structure in this passage is the same as in the lines preferring Una–Spenser to Belinda–Pope. But, if we apply Warton's synecdochical method of associating characters with their authors, the explicit opposition Eloisa/Flavia in this passage signifies an implicit opposition of Pope to himself, Pope/Pope. Since this passage (Pope/Pope) occurs some fifty lines *before* the one in which authors are openly named and evaluated (Spenser/Pope), and since the thematic content of the two passages is identical, the difference between them, the substitution of Una for Eloisa in the second passage, is highly significant. For it is this substitution that allows Warton to displace Pope altogether. When the structure Pope/Pope becomes Spenser/Pope, the preference expressed between two characters in Pope has been transformed into a preference for Spenser over a Pope now wholly identified with one of his own satiric creations.

The internal contradiction by which Pope is dissociated from Eloisa, but identified with Belinda is the crucial, foundational move. For it is in the disjunctive space created by that substitution and displacement, and indeed by the subsequent dissociation of "Pope" from himself, that the ideology of what later will be called "Romanticism" grows and flourishes. It may be useful here to cite Freud on the mechanism of repression:

> In this connection it becomes comprehensible that those objects to which men give their preference, that is, their ideals, originate in the same perceptions and experiences as those objects of which they have the most abhorrence, and that the two originally differed from one another only by slight modifications. Indeed, . . . it is possible for the original instinct-presentation to be split into two, one part undergoing repression, while the remainder, just on account of its intimate association with the other undergoes idealization.[12]

Freud's formulation, that our ideals and those things we abhor were originally similar but have become split through repression, casts some light on the strange contradictions at work in Warton's poem. In *Eloisa to Abelard*, Pope drew upon Ovid's *Heroides* for a genre of the woman's lament, but he transposed it to the Gothic Middle Ages. Thomas Warton, however, separates out the Gothic and the classical strands in Pope, and then attributes what he idealizes, in this case Gothic, to someone else. This constitutive contradiction and displacement, of course, is a symptom of the repression of Warton's intense identification with Pope. The misrecognition that brings "Romanticism" into being is, at bottom, a response to the anxiety of Pope's influence.

What I suggest has happened is that an early reading of Pope's poetry has inspired the young Warton to become a poet himself. In place of Pope-as-muse, however, the role of muse is taken over by the more traditional gender for muses, specifically a female character in one of Pope's poems. Relevant here is the general observation made by a feminist critic of Joyce: "The woman in the text converts the text into a woman, and the circulation of this text/woman becomes the central ritual that establishes the bond between the author and his male readers."[13] Warton's identification with, his desire to be, Pope, is made quite clear in the way he adapts *Eloisa to Abelard* in the rest of the poem. Notice that after claiming that Pope's description of Belinda "coldly strikes the mind with feeble bliss," Warton turns away and cries, in lines I have cited above: "Oh, wrap me then in shades of darksome pine." The pines, of course, are those with which Pope surrounded Eloisa's convent in the other passage already cited: "The darksom pines that o'er yon rocks reclin'd." Thus Warton turns coldly from "Belinda" to rush into the arms of "Eloisa." In the continuation of these lines Warton's use of Eloisa is revealing.

Gothic settings are congenial to ghosts and phantoms, and these poems are no exception. Pope's *Unfortunate Lady* opens, as we noted, with an apparition; in *Eloisa*, too, the heroine's desire for Abelard produces in her the delusion of his presence. She rushes after the phantom, only to be returned abruptly to her forlorn condition:

> Sudden you mount! you becken from the skies;
> Clouds interpose, waves roar, and winds arise.
> I shriek, start up, the same sad prospect find,
> And wake to all the griefs I left behind. (lines 245–48)

Warton rewrites this incident, but in his version the "you" refers reflexively to the speaker who recounts his experience of waking from delusion:

> Sudden you start – the imagined joys recede,
> The same sad prospect opens on your sense. (lines 186–87)

The close verbal repetitions suggest that Warton writes from the place of Eloisa. The ghost he chases, however, is not Abelard, but one Sapphira, and the experience, unlike the painful awakening of Eloisa, is for Warton one of the pleasures of melancholy:

> These are delights that absence drear has made
> Familiar to my soul, ere since the form
> Of young Sapphira, beauteous as the Spring,
> When from her violet-woven couch awaked
> By frolic Zephyr's hand, her tender cheek

> Graceful she lifts, and blushing from her bower,
> Issues to clothe in gladsome-glistering green
> The genial globe, first met my dazzled sight. (lines 191–98)

According to the logic of the poem, Sapphira should not really be attractive to Warton because she so clearly personifies the L'Allegro chain of associations that he shuns (day, sunshine, greenness, spring-summer). Not just "beauteous as the Spring," she actually embodies the Spring's power for it is she who "[i]ssues to clothe in gladsome-glistering green / The genial globe." But the speaker had already told us: "I choose the pale December's foggy glooms" (line 74). Now we see that he was driven to melancholy by his love for Sapphira, that, indeed, one of its pleasures is the contemplation of her glad, green, spring-dayness from his retreat. Penseroso, so far from holding Allegr[a] in contempt, has been dazzled by her and nurses his wound in solitude; the Penseroso character is, in Warton's version, brought into being simultaneously with his desire for Allegra.

If we correlate this section with Warton's literary historical allegory, the contempt he displays for Belinda is the defensive reaction-formation of his desire for her. The explicit aggression against Pope–Belinda in the earlier passage suggests, in the light of this later one, a parallel between Warton and the Baron who plots to clip Belinda's lock, and whose only wish in battling her is to "die" upon his foe. For surely, Sapphira, as goddess and power of nature, is a pastoralized, or rather pasteurized, form of Belinda, launched forth on the Thames and shining brighter than the sun, in that her "toxic" elements have been neutralized.

This particular episode rehearses Eloisa's hallucinatory sorrow over Abelard's absence (and ultimately, of course, over the crucial absence signified by his castration), but with a difference, for now we have a male Eloisa contemplating in retreat a sublimated, idealized, and thus more acceptable image of Belinda, duly transferred from a social to a pastoral garden. The contradictions in Warton's text suggest that the poem accomplishes for him the first stages of a disengagement from Pope, while the fact that he retreats into Eloisa's role at all reveals the strength of the original attachment. The internal contradictions of the poem show him clearing a space for himself by creating a structure that fragments Pope, and then opposes part to part.

Warton's original identification with Pope, we may conclude, ultimately gave rise to an ambivalence that produced a series of corresponding images: the negative values attached to Belinda and her double, Flavia, little better than tarts, are matched symmetrically by the positive values attached to Eloisa, the holy, and Sapphira, the light of life. The text of Pope has been first feminized and then fragmented into a saint on one hand and a whore on the other.

"The Pleasures of Melancholy" is both useful and fascinating because it manifests the influence of Pope *before* it has been fully repressed and transformed. Here we see the very process by which the text of Pope is divided, alienated from itself, and assigned to "Pope" on the one hand, and to "Spenser–Milton" on the other. A more maturely "Romantic" poem would be self-conscious enough of its own origins to efface any explicit trace of Eloisa while retaining her poetic value in the name of "Milton" or "Spenser." But we must remember that Warton was only seventeen years old; in his revision of the poem ten years later, he did, in fact, edit out several verbatim echoes of *Eloisa*, including the "darksom pine" passage, but he could not eradicate her completely without destroying the fabric of the poem.

"Romanticism," therefore, originates in a two-fold strategy: arising from a charged reading of Pope, it differentiates itself by misrepresenting him on a doctrinal level – Pope is all Attic ease and sunshine – while transposing him into a less threatening, pastoral version of himself on the level of imagery. The doctrinal necessity of opposing Pope to Spenser, or to Milton, ensures that explicit references to Eloisa will eventually drop out. Thus, although Pope's mediation of the early Milton in *Eloisa to Abelard* arguably leads to the valorization of the Penseroso figure as the characteristic Romantic protagonist, Pope's role as transmitter of Gothic alienation (and this describes *Eloisa* more appropriately than it does Milton's poem) will nonetheless be gradually forgotten, even though it remains open to be read in Warton's poem. This is not the place to detail the reception of Pope's poem. Let it suffice for the moment simply to quote Gillian Beer: "The tradition of heroic epistle and, in particular, Pope's *Eloisa to Abelard*, offered a language of sensation, an iconography, a grandeur of scale, an emphasis on sequestration and an acceptance of women's extreme emotion which were all essential to the Gothic novelists."[14]

Both Wartons quickly become jealously possessive of Milton and begin to consider Pope as a usurper of the poetic tradition. They come to construct Pope as no more than the poet of witty rhyme and polished couplet whose dominance actually prevented Milton's "Il Penseroso" from being appreciated. They, of course, revived the "true" line, and thus, as Thomas said in his 1785 Preface to an edition of Milton's minor poems, "the school of Milton rose in emulation of the school of Pope."[15] An anecdote told by both brothers about the relation of Pope's *Eloisa* to Milton's *Penseroso* takes us to the heart of Romantic literary history.

According to the Wartons, Pope owed his knowledge of Milton's minor poems to their father, Thomas Warton the Elder, who brought them to his attention through Digby, a mutual acquaintance. Very shortly after, Pope's *Eloisa* appeared with passages, Thomas, Jr. claims, "pilfered from *COMUS* and the *PENSEROSO*. He was however conscious, that he might borrow from a book then scarcely remembered, without the hazard of discovery, or the imputation of plagiarism." Having made the accusation, Warton backs off a little: "Yet the theft was so slight, as hardly to deserve the name: and it must be allowed, that the experiment was happily and judiciously applied, in delineating the sombrous scenes of the pensive Eloisa's convent, the solitary Paraclete."[16] Whether Pope's troping upon Milton deserves the name of theft or not, it is curious that the charge comes from the writer who drew so liberally upon Pope when writing "The Pleasures of Melancholy." It is odd also that it appears in an edition of Milton, the overstuffed notes of which call our attention to "parallel passages" in authors ancient and modern. Warton returns to this story in his discussion of *Comus*, and manages to insinuate that it is an odd thing altogether that Pope's poem ever came into existence because it isn't like him: "It is strange that Pope, by no means of a congenial spirit, should be the first who copied *Comus* and *Il Penseroso*. But Pope was a gleaner of Old English poets; and he was pilfering from *obsolete* English poetry, without the least fear or danger of being detected."[17]

The problem with such a narrative, of course, is that it is false, not just in its larger claims, but also in the very details of the transmission. In actual fact Pope possessed an edition of Milton's minor poems (1645) at least as early as 1705, when he was seventeen, some twelve years before he wrote *Eloisa*, and before the Elder Warton is supposed to have mentioned the volume to Digby. We know this because William Trumbull, former Secretary of State under William III and Pope's neighbor, sent Pope a letter, dated 19 October 1705, thanking him for the loan of the book. Internal evidence, furthermore, shows that influences of "Penseroso" appear as early as Pope's first published work, *The Pastorals* (1709), as the Twickenham edition records. The Elder Warton, apparently, lent Pope a rare copy of *Gorbuduc* in the summer of 1717, but the sons' dissemination of the Milton story is clearly a self-serving myth.[18]

There are two conclusions I draw from these facts. First, Pope assimilated Milton's minor poems, transformed them, and transmitted that strain in his work. Second, the Wartons cannot give Pope credit for this; instead they transfer the source of proper taste to their father, while accusing Pope of being both an alien ("by no means of a congenial spirit") and a thief. While the Wartons are defenders of true poetry, Pope is the usurper who came to the early Milton only on the recommendation of the Elder Warton, and then stole from it shamelessly. This anecdote, in fact, encodes in miniature the paradigm of Romantic literary history operative in Francis Jeffrey and many others, according to which the Wartons revived Milton in opposition to Pope. Jeffrey simply repeats the Wartons, as others will repeat Jeffrey. Wordsworth recalls the anecdote when he comments on Milton's early poems, which, he says, "though on their first appearance they were praised by a few of the judicious, were afterwards neglected to that degree, that Pope in his youth could borrow from them without risk of its being known."[19] Gosse retells the same story in 1915, but adds, with extraordinarily ignorant complacency: "So far as I am aware, *Eloisa to Abelard* has never taken a high place among Pope's extreme admirers, doubtless because of its obsession with horror and passion."[20] Northrop Frye, one of the founders of modern criticism of the Romantics, gives evidence of the almost mechanical power of reproduction of Thomas Warton's allegory of Day and Night in "The Pleasures of Melancholy," and of the view of literary history it encodes, when he simply takes for granted the standard construction of Romantic literary history as it has updated itself and accommodated Wordsworth: "It is a datum of literary experience that when we cross the divide of 1798 we find ourselves in a different kind of poetic world, darker in color, so to speak, than what has preceded it."[21]

The denials that work themselves out in the Wartonian, which is to say, the "Romantic," version of literary history need, perhaps, no further elaboration. But some ironies are too rare, too significant, and too representative, to let pass. One of these involves, again, the Elder Warton, who, as it happens, was born in 1688, the same year as Pope. A few years after their father's death in 1745, the dutiful sons, pressed for funds, hit upon the idea of publishing a collection of their father's verse by subscription to friends and relatives as a kind of memorial. Occasionally, scholars have looked into the collection to discover clues to pre-Romanticism and have found them. But it is also possible to find there a poem like "The Ode to Taste," which pays glowing tribute to Pope. The opening stanza, addressed to Taste, reads as follows:

> Leave not Brittania's Isle; since Pope is fled
> To meet his Homer in Elysian Bowers,
> What Bard shall dare presume
> His various-sounding Harp?
> Let not resistless Dulness o'er us spread
> Deep Gothic night; for lo! the Fiend appears
> To blast each blooming Bay
> That decks our barren Shores.[22]

Pope, according to this stanza, was the last bulwark of Taste against the spread of Dulness' "Gothic night." Now that he is gone and no worthy successor has appeared to take up his instrument, Britain appears to be in a bad way, so much so that the loss threatens an apocalyptic breach with true standards. The poem, in fact, constructs Pope in the very terms he had fashioned for himself in *The Dunciad*. It is fair to assume he would have been pleased. Since Pope fled to Elysian Bowers in 1744, this tribute clearly had to have been written in the final year of the Elder Warton's life.

However, the most remarkable thing about this poem is that it was not written by the Elder Warton at all, but by Thomas, Jr., roughly about the same time that he wrote "The Pleasures of Melancholy." David Fairer, by examining the manuscripts, determined that, since the father's corpus was not large enough to make up a volume, his pious sons contributed about ten poems of their own, selflessly donating them in their father's name. Subsequent investigations by Christina Le Prevost led her to conclude that nineteen poems were certainly by the brothers, and fourteen others probably, leaving the father with less than a third of the volume, not even counting the fact that of those remaining some were revised by Joseph.[23]

Fairer concludes from his evidence that, since poems showing pre-Romantic tendencies were actually written by the sons, the Elder Warton can no longer be legitimately considered a lone pre-Romantic voice in Pope's generation. Unless we want to assimilate Pope to "Romanticism" and label certain of his poems "pre-", a move I advise against because it simply extends the imperialistic tendencies of "Romanticism," then my argument to this point means that we can no longer talk in such terms. Fairer does not deal with "The Ode to Taste" except to identify it as Thomas, Jr.'s, but his scholarship, together with Le Prevost's, adds evidence to my thesis that "Romanticism" begins in a love–hate relation to Pope that is ultimately a symptom of an internal split. When Warton assigned his ode to his father, he simply transferred his own earlier self, one cathected to Pope, to the previous generation, and then began a series of polemics against it.

More than any other single piece of writing, Joseph Warton's *Essay on the Genius and Writings of Pope* (vol. I, 1756; vol. II, 1782) established the criteria and provided the arguments for the Romantic, hence the Modern, construction of Pope. The argument is profoundly self-contradictory, yet, perhaps for that very reason, highly functional. For to understand Warton is to understand how Pope was constructed so as to embody a "modern" dilemma, the loss of the sublime. This is a problem which it has been long thought Wordsworth solved, but it is one that returns again as romantic poetry, and the sublime itself, are gradually demystified.

Warton's *Essay* needs to be understood against the background of his own struggle to achieve poetic subjectivity. The Advertisement to his *Odes on Various Subjects* (1746) is often cited as evidence of a shift in values, but is worth quoting again in full:

> The Public has been so much accustom'd of late to didactic Poetry alone, and Essays on moral Subjects, that any work where the imagination is much indulged, will perhaps not be relished or regarded. The author therefore of these pieces is in some pain least certain austere critics should think them too fanciful and descriptive. But as he is convinced that the fashion of moralizing in verse has been carried too far, and as he looks upon Invention and Imagination to be the chief faculties of a Poet, so he will be happy if the following Odes may be look'd upon as an attempt to bring back Poetry into its right channel.[24]

The oppositions set in motion here, such as moral/descriptive and didactic/imaginative, recur full-blown in the *Essay*. They are not reliable guides to literary history because there can be no purely descriptive poetry that does not in some way allegorize and moralize its landscapes. But what we are only recently in a position to recognize is the degree to which these divisions in Joseph Warton, which signify an internal division or dissociation of sensibility, represent a conversion experience.[25] The temporal progression implied by the word "conversion," however, is not fully accurate; the situation is better described as an ongoing tension between a Popean and a post-Popean Warton.

Christina Le Prevost's conclusions about Joseph Warton's poetic activity in the 1740s are unequivocal. Warton signed his name to poems, such as the *Odes* and "The Enthusiast" (1744), that departed from Popean poetics, while those that didn't, such as "Fashion" (1742), he either published anonymously, or, like the ghost-written volume of 1748, he simply attributed to his father. In Warton's early satiric phase, Pope is a figure of admiration representing high moral standards. Notes toward a satire on luxury and corruption include the following: "Pope is the only Poet who boldly lashes our [Vices] – Luxuries."[26] A fragment of verse reveals the terms in which Warton revered Pope, and perhaps also the extent of his identification with his hero:

> That name recalls a thousand Critics Hate,
> From Wrongs triumphant, & by Envy great!
> Come then, reviving Tibbalds rise around,
> And Dennis stare, & write, & shake the ground . . .
> While He regardless & Superior sits, . . .
> Nor [blushes as] 'listens to' the Scoffs of [meaner] 'lying' Wits.

Le Prevost comments: "It would appear that the judicious coolness, and, at times, dismissiveness with which he treats Pope in the famous *Essay* (1756) was a sequel to a period when he indulged in extensive imitation of him (as all these manuscripts show, indeed) and was also an extravagant and open admirer."[27]

Joseph's turn away from his Popean origins takes the same form as his brother Thomas's, but the tone is sharper, more accusatory. Having identified himself totally with Pope's satiric persona of the 1730s, that of the virtuous poet forced to confront the low standards of the Court, Joseph's disengagement was so violent as to lead him to argue that satire is merely a form of wit, and that thus Pope is not really a poet at all. The Dedication to the *Essay on Pope* throws down the challenge. The first paragraph, after a sentence of polite deference to the dedicatee, Edward Young, states:

No love of singularity, no affectation of paradoxical opinions, gave rise to the following Work. I revere the memory of POPE, I respect and honour his abilities; but I do not think him at the head of his profession. In other words, in that species of poetry wherein POPE excelled, he is superior to all mankind: and I only say, that this species of poetry is not the most excellent one of the art.[28]

The denial of "singularity" and "affectation of paradoxical opinions," of course, raises the very possibility that it is meant to defend against. The opinion that requires this proleptic defense, the demotion of Pope from the head of his profession, needs further to be prefaced by professions of respect and reverence. I defer for the moment the question of whether the 1750s really valued Pope above Shakespeare or Milton; I only point out that Warton clearly thinks this is the case. The criteria of demotion are crucial. Genre determines rank: Pope will be judged not according to his performance, which is superior, but to his *kind* of poetry, which is not. The next move will argue that the kind of poetry Pope writes is not really poetry.

Continuing, Warton quotes a remark of Dryden's on Donne, that he was "the greatest wit, though not the greatest poet, of this nation," and applies it by implication to Pope: "We do not, it should seem, sufficiently attend to the difference there is betwixt a MAN OF WIT, a MAN OF SENSE, and a TRUE POET. Donne and Swift were undoubtedly men of wit, and men of sense: but what traces have they left of PURE POETRY?" The opposition between "wit" and "poet" is extended further to that between "morality" and "poetry." "Poetry" is defined according to its origin in "a creative and glowing IMAGINATION . . . which so few possess, and of which so few can properly judge." The proportions, we are told, are twenty to one: "For one person, who can adequately relish and enjoy a work of imagination, twenty are to be found who can taste, and judge of, observations on familiar life, and the manners of the age." Evidence offered is the fact that Pope's Ethic Epistles "are more frequently perused, and quoted, than L'Allegro and Il Penseroso of Milton." Whereas Pope's appeal is wide, real poetry appears to be only for fit audience, though few. And what is pure, or real, or true poetry? It is a question of content: if you translate it into prose, it "will retain its lustre" like a diamond unset, or as he says a little later, "like Ulysses in his disguise of rags, still a hero." The essential point follows: "The Sublime and the Pathetic are the two chief nerves of all genuine poesy. What is there very sublime or very Pathetic in POPE?"[29] Therefore, Warton applies to Pope what Voltaire said of Boileau, that he is "LE POETE DE LA RAISON," prefacing the remark quite astonishingly with the confession that he chooses to quote Voltaire "because I am perhaps ashamed or afraid to speak out in plain English." The thought arises that Warton needed to resort to a foreign language in order to evade the censorship of his own superego. Be that as it may, here is the source of all those disparaging remarks, Arnold's standing out among them, about Pope, reason, and the eighteenth century. A contemporary reader, however, made a shrewd observation on this passage. Owen Ruffhead thought it unfair to refer to what Voltaire said of Boileau when one could refer to what Voltaire said of Pope, which Ruffhead goes on to cite: "the best poet in England, and at present in all the world . . . so amiable an imagination, so gentle graces."[30]

The final paragraph brings us to the crisis by dividing the English poets into four classes. In the first are "our only three sublime and pathetic poets; SPENSER, SHAKESPEARE, MILTON." In the second class are those who have the true poetical spirit in more moderate degree, but who "had noble talents for moral and ethical poesy," such as Dryden, Prior, Addison, and others. In the third class are men of wit and elegant taste and lively fancy like Swift and Donne, and in the fourth are "mere versifiers."[31] The final sentence of the Dedication states the purpose of the Essay: "In which of these classes POPE deserves to be placed, the following work is intended to determine."

From what has gone before, one might predict that Warton would place Pope in either the second or the third class. Since real poetry, however, is restricted to the first class only, whereas what follows are lesser alloys, it would seem not to matter whether one is in the second class or the fourth. Thus the line of argument that began by judging Pope as superior in his class, though not of the first, now implies that anything less than the first is not truly poetry. When the second volume eventually appeared in 1782, Warton, quite amazingly, placed Pope in the first class, if indeed with a sort of reduced status or second-class citizenship:

Where then, according to the question proposed at the *beginning of this Essay*, shall we with justice be authorized to place our admired POPE? Not, assuredly, in the same rank with *Spencer*, *Shakespeare*, and *Milton*, however justly we may applaud the *Eloisa* and *Rape* of the *Lock*; but, considering the correctness, elegance, and utility of his works, the weight of sentiment, and the knowledge of man they contain, we may venture to assign him a place *next* to *Milton*, and *just* above *Dryden*.[32]

Warton, in other words, has invented a unique space within which to contain the paradox that to him is "Pope": above the second class (Dryden), and "next to," or on a level with the first class (Milton), but not actually in it.

If this seems contradictory, the entire conclusion is composed of similar waverings. Pope's major fault, according to the indictment, is that he described modern manners which are not susceptible of sublime treatment, the line of argument to be taken up by Bowles and disputed by Byron. Yet in the body of the text *Eloisa* is both sublime and pathetic; here is Warton on the famous Melancholy set piece: "The figurative expressions, *throws*, and *breathes*, and *browner* horror, are I verily believe the strongest and boldest in the English language. The IMAGE of the Goddess MELANCHOLY sitting over the convent, and as it were expanding her dreadful wings over its whole circuit, and diffusing her gloom all around it, is truely sublime, and strongly conceived."[33]

Similarly, Warton had written of a passage in *Essay on Man*: "Whilst I am transcribing this exalted description of the omnipresence of the Deity, I feel myself almost tempted to retract an assertion in the beginning of this work, that there is nothing transcendently sublime in POPE."[34]

Pope possessed imagination, Warton tells us, but it was not his predominant trait. Yet, comparing the depiction of the Sylphs in the *Rape* to *A Midsummer Night's Dream*, we are told that, "by the addition of the most delicate satire to the most lively fancy, Pope, in the following passage, has excelled anything in Shakespeare, or in any other author."[35] Pope had "poetical enthusiasm," of course, but it was "withheld and stifled." Therefore, although he is "the great Poet of Reason, the First of Ethical authors in verse," which by Warton's definition is not poetical, yet he is "next to Milton." Though next to Milton, he owes his reputation to dropping names, such as Chesterfield and Walpole, which "failed not to make a poem bought up and talked of." Hence his kind of poetry "lies more level to the general capacities of men than the higher flights of more genuine poetry."

Warton's evaluations of individual poems are similarly telling. The *Pastorals*, usually thought to display precocious skill, are simply dismissed; the *Essay on Criticism* is a masterpiece, but it is not poetry; *The Dunciad*, the *Essay on Man*, and the *Moral Essays* will perish, tautologically, because they are not eternal. Only the *Rape of the Lock*, *Eloisa*, the *Elegy to an Unfortunate Lady*, and *Windsor Forest* will remain.[36] These last poems seem formidable examples of Pope's claims to poetry, at least in Warton's own terms. But when Warton comes to summarize Pope's poetical character, he identifies him almost entirely with the poems he doesn't like. If the *Rape* shows imagination, that is not the author's predominant characteristic; if *Eloisa* and *The Elegy* are pathetic, Pope isn't pathetic very often. Johnson observed ironically that this was like saying Milo was not really strong because he lifted the ox only once.[37]

Discussing the *Essay* in his anthology of 1819, Thomas Campbell observed wryly, "There is something like April weather in these transitions."[38] Ruffhead was sharper: "With what propriety then can he ask, – 'What is there transcendently sublime or pathetic in Pope?' – when he has himself, with real taste and candor, pointed out so many instances of both in the course of his criticisms on little more than one volume of our poet's verse."[39] The fundamental inconsistency between the stated criteria and the final evaluation was spelled out reluctantly by John Wooll, Warton's student, friend, and biographer:

But yet, notwithstanding my love and veneration for his memory . . . I must presume to hazard an opinion, that he has either placed Pope too high, or in his separate sections has not done him justice. I venture not to say on which side the mistake lies; but, if Pope is just above Dryden, he had more genius than Dr. Warton allows him; and, vice versa, if he has not more genius than is attributed to him; if he is more the poet of reason than of fancy, that situation is surely above his pretensions.[40]

The ambiguity of the book led to a double reception: some thought it commonplace, others revolutionary.[41] It could be taken as commonplace because, however much Pope was revered in his time – and Voltaire noted in the late 1720s that he found portraits of Pope in nearly every English house he entered – perhaps only a very few thought him equal to Shakespeare or Milton. Certainly there were enthusiasts like the anonymous biographer who wrote a year after Pope's death that he was "the *greatest Poet* this or any age produced, if we consider him in the several kinds of that art wherein he excelled."[42] But we need only recall Johnson, who was sympathetic with the whole line of development that produced Pope, but whose praise of Shakespeare and of Milton, whom he thought second to Homer only because Homer wrote first, goes well beyond his assessment of Pope's achievement. Ironically, Warton's attack on Pope places him above Dryden, whereas Johnson's sympathy produces an elaborate comparison that finally divides the palm by saying Dryden was the brighter genius, but Pope the more accomplished artist.[43]

It seems fair to conclude that Pope presented more of a threat to the poetic ambition of Joseph Warton than to the reputation of past classics. Warton overvalued his object in the first place, and then compensated by undervaluing it. The overestimation that places Pope at the "head of his profession" (as he certainly was if we speak of contemporary poetry) and then finally cuts him down to size by placing him "next to Milton" would not raise much comment. What seemed odd or singular was the definition of poetry that argued for Pope's exclusion. Boswell recorded this conversation between citizens at Child's Coffee House near St. Paul's on Saturday, 1 January 1763:

1 CITIZEN. Pray, Sir have you read Mr. Warton's *Essay on the Life and Writings of Pope*? He will not allow him to be a poet. He says he has good sense and good versification, but wants the warm imagination and brilliancy of expression that constitutes the true poetical genius. He tries him by a rule prescribed by Longinus, which is to take the words out of their metrical order and then see if they have the sparks of poetry. Don't you remember this?

2 CITIZEN. I don't agree with him.
1 CITIZEN. Nor I, neither. He is fond of Thomson. He says he has great force.
2 CITIZEN. He has great faults.
1 CITIZEN. Ay, but great force, too.
2 CITIZEN. I have eat beefsteaks with him.
1 CITIZEN. So have I.[44]

It is difficult to know how much Boswell may have retouched the dialogue, but, as it is given, the detail of the representation of Warton's thesis suggests a fascination that the off-hand dismissal doesn't fully negate. Nonetheless, the dialogue begins to suggest why Warton's book could be seen as revolutionary, for the full consequences of his position would take some sixty years to work themselves out. Warton's *Essay* fell into neglect only after the so-called Romantic poets were fully established, hence only after its ideological work had been accomplished. At the very end of the nineteenth century, the Wartons were rediscovered by scholars such as Phelps, Beers, and Courthope, who were looking for precursors to what they understood to be the Romantic movement. At the end of the twentieth century, at a time when conventional notions of Romanticism are under fire, the Wartons may prove interesting once again.

EDWARD YOUNG, THEORIST OF ORIGINALITY

The religious element in the Romantic paradigm, sometimes referred to as displaced theology, becomes explicit in the country clergyman, Edward Young. Young, we recall, is the man to whom Joseph Warton dedicated his *Essay on Pope*. Young and Warton, if they had not already become acquainted through the Elder Warton, certainly came into close contact when Young sent his son to the Winchester of which Warton was the Headmaster. Young's *Night Thoughts* of the early 1740s, moreover, which openly represents itself as an anti-*Essay on Man*, undoubtedly influenced the Warton brothers.[45] In this section, I focus on the history of Young's relation to Pope as a means of approaching the *Conjectures on Original Composition* (1759), an essay that has been celebrated as a monument to the romantic imagination. Indeed, if Warton constructs his rival as lacking feeling and sublimity, Young constructs his as lacking original genius.

It is easy to be ironic about Edward Young (1683–1765). Coleridge called him a "Preferment-hunter" and George Eliot called him "a sycophant and a psalmist."[46] Five years older than Pope, he lived twenty-one years longer. Longevity, as Wordsworth's life shows better than Young's, is perhaps the best revenge; at least it provides one with more opportunities. To understand Young, one must understand the age in which Addison could parlay good Oxford connections and a few obsequious but well-turned poems into a political career that would eventually make him Secretary of State. Johnson praised Pope for his independence: "he never exchanged praise for money, nor opened a shop of condolence and congratulation."[47] But then Pope, being Catholic, had absolutely no prospects for "preferment" and he knew it.

Young's ambitions were large. He assiduously played the preferment game, but continually lost because he had a talent for backing the wrong horse.[48] A poem dedicated to Granville produced no fruit as the Tories soon fell from power, and Granville himself was imprisoned in the Tower as a Jacobite. Later, he attached his hopes to the rising young nobleman, Philip Wharton, but these also were dashed as Wharton quickly sank from view, eventually dying in disgrace and exile at the age of thirty-two. In the 1730s he cultivated Frederick, the Prince of Wales, who became his son's godfather, even naming the boy Frederick. A few years later the Prince fell out with the King. Young's most recent defender hits the perfect note when she laments: "no one could have foreseen then that the connection with Frederick would become detrimental to favor at the royal court."[49]

Friends with Addison's disciple, Tickell, at Oxford, he became part of the circle at Button's Coffee House, presumably where he met Pope (he sent him a letter there), the young poet who at twenty-one had published the *Pastorals*, at twenty-three *An Essay on Criticism*, at twenty-four *Messiah* (which Addison had printed and praised in *The Spectator* as better than Virgil), at twenty-five *Windsor Forest*, and at twenty-six the enlarged version of *The Rape of the Lock*. Before he was thirty Pope would publish a collected edition of his *Works* (1717). His translation of Homer, undertaken for money, became the standard version in English for over a hundred years; in the opening pages of *Praeterita* (1885), Ruskin related how powerfully Pope's Homer affected him as a child. Young's attitude toward Pope was essentially duplicitous – he dared not make an open enemy of so powerful a writer, but he would undermine him if he could. His conduct in the war of the rival Homer translations is a case in point. Addison urged Tickell to translate Homer as a direct challenge to Pope, and probably helped him in the work. The two translations were published in the same week: Pope's distributed to subscribers on Monday, 6 June and Tickell's published 8 June. At Pope's request, Young distributed twelve copies to libraries at Oxford, and was quite pleased to be at his service. Yet in the subsequent debate over the merits of the books at Oxford, he did what he could to suggest that Pope's was inferior.[50]

From 1725 to 1730 Young wrote satires in which he made direct appeals to Pope to take up his pen against corruption. In 1725, he wrote in "The Love of Fame":

> Why slumbers *Pope*, who leads the tuneful Train,
> Nor hears that Virtue, which He loves, complain?[51]

After noting that Donne, Dorset, Dryden, Rochester, and Addison are dead, and Congreve, though alive, will not write, he continues to ask:

> Double distrest, what author shall we find
> Discreetly Daring, and Severely Kind,
> The courtly *Roman's* [Horace's] path to tread,
> And sharply Smile prevailing folly dead?
> Will no superior Genius snatch the quill,
> And save me, on the Brink, from Writing Ill?

In 1730, Young wrote two satires called "Two Epistles to Mr. Pope, Concerning the Authors of the Age," in which he identifies with Pope's position in the *Dunciad* of 1728, yet seems not quite sure if he is not a dunce himself. His deference to Pope as the pre-eminent poet of the age is omnipresent, as he continues to represent himself in a secondary role. Yet there is also the strain of accusation – Pope is not taking action as the times require. The opening of "Epistle I" reads:

> Whilst you at Twickenham plan the future wood,
> Or turn the volumes of the wise and good,
> Our senate meets; at parties, parties bawl,
> And pamphlets stun the streets, and load the stall.[52]

The situation is so bad that Young can contain himself no longer:

> O Pope! I burst, nor can, nor will, refrain;
> I'll write; let others, in their turn, complain.

The implication here that Young, by writing, may pollute the situation even more, giving others grounds for complaint, is made explicit a few lines later:

> For who can write the true absurd like me? –
> Thy pardon, Codrus! who, I mean, but thee?

His identification with those he attacks proceeds as he turns again to Pope:

> Pope! if like mine, or Codrus', were thy style,
> The blood of vipers had not stain'd thy file;
> Merit less solid, less despite had bred;
> They had not *bit*, and then they had not *bled*.

The psychology of this opening is strange indeed. The speaker's position is precarious and the tone keeps shifting. Young is an ally, sympathetic over attacks Pope has sustained in the wake of the *Dunciad*, yet also an accuser – why has not Pope done more? The double identification, with Pope on the one hand and with the dunces on the other, produces futher complications. For if it is so, as he claims, that Pope was attacked because he stood above the crowd, that "with *fame*, in just proportion, *envy* grows," then Young himself is possibly among the crowd of enviers, which may account for his confused position in the poem. In any case, "Pope" appears to be one of the constituent figures of Young's poetic identity, not only here, but also in the work that brought him real fame, *Night Thoughts*, where the same structure is repeated. At the close of "Night the First" he refers to Pope and to his *Essay on Man*:

> O had *He* prest his Theme, pursued the track,
> Which opens out of Darkness into Day!
> O had he mounted on his wing of Fire,
> Soar'd, where I sink, and sung *Immortal* man!
> How had it blest mankind? and rescued me?[53]

What had to have made Young's situation even worse is that when Pope did turn to Horatian cultural critique he picked up several hints from Young's poems but, as might be expected, did it better. Pope's use of Young's "Two Epistles to Mr. Pope" in "An Epistle to Dr. Arbuthnot" caused Warton to note that Pope had "heightened, improved, and condensed the hints and sentiments of Young." Thus Young was speaking from experience when he told Spence in 1759, the same year he attacked Pope in his *Conjectures*, that "Pope was so superior to all the poets his contemporaries in versification that if he met with a good line (even in a much inferior [poet]) he would take it (like a lord of the manor) for his own." The few remarks that give us Pope's notion of Young are revealing. According to Ruffhead, Pope thought Young passed a foolish youth, the sport of peers and poets, that he was a genius without common sense, but that he had a good heart which was suitable to his clerical duties. Ruffhead's account, which he got from Warburton, comes to us as hearsay, but it seems corroborated by a letter Pope wrote to Gay in the spring of 1714 in which he pokes fun at Young's literary vanity: "I have

contracted a severity of aspect from deep meditation on high subjects...
In a word, Y—g himself has not acquired more Tragic Majesty in his
aspect by reading his own Verses than I by *Homer's*."[54]

Herbert Croft, who wrote the by no means unsympathetic biography of Young at Johnson's request, commented on the impropriety of Warton's Dedication of his *Essay on Pope* to Young: "If Young accepted and approved the dedication, he countenanced this attack upon the fame of him whom he invokes as his Muse." Croft goes on:

Either the *Essay*, then, was dedicated to a patron who disapproved its doctrine, which I have been told by the author was not the case; or Young appears, in his old age, to have bartered for a dedication an opinion entertained of his friend through all that part of his life when he must have been best able to form opinions.[55]

What I would suggest is that Young and Pope were never really friends and that Young, who toadied to Pope while he was alive, quite naturally turned against him as soon as he was dead. The conclusion is fairly reasonable since Young spent most of his life in Pope's shadow, and his pretensions were by no means imaginary; indeed, some saw him as the next poet after Pope. When Young finally turned openly against Pope in his *Conjectures* (1759), he did so with great vehemence. The fire of the essay is described by Croft who says "it is more like the production of untamed, unbridled youth, than of jaded fourscore."[56] A reason might be that Young is settling a grudge that he had been nursing since his youth. Of Young's *Conjectures*, Edith Morley wrote that it is "the logical sequel to that of the Wartons, which preceded it," and that Young "endorses Warton's indictment against Pope (1756)."[57] For the same Young who admired Pope, the same Young who looked up to Pope in verse from among the crowd and scarcely distinguished himself from Codrus, now claims that Pope is an imitator. With Young begins the Romantic discourse of "originality" that is as contradictory and inconsistent as Warton's evaluation of Pope, but that proves nonetheless to carry the day.[58]

"Originality," as defined by Young, is actually a form of imitation: "*Imitations* are of two kinds: one of Nature, one of Authors: the first we call *Originals*, and confine the term *Imitation* to the second." Having acknowledged that "originality" is a relative term, always involving a relation of supplementarity to a prior source, whether "nature" or book, Young proceeds, only a few sentences later, to mystify originality as magic that creates *ex nihilo*: "The pen of an *Original* Writer, like *Armida's* wand, out of barren waste calls a blooming spring: out of that blooming spring an *Imitator* is a transplanter of Laurels, which sometimes die on removal, always languish in a foreign soil."⁵⁹ Only later will Young imply that magic, too, is an art, and that magicians also work by cause and effect, by observing, crucially, that magic accomplishes its effects by "means invisible."⁶⁰

The figure of transplanting recurs in the reflections of several writers on the nature of writing in this period. A related notion, the *translatio studii*, is explicitly thematized in many eighteenth-century "progress pieces." In this tradition, imitation is not slavish adherence to prior models, but rather a species of invention involving a complex, self-conscious game of ironic intertextuality.⁶¹ The source text, or more often texts, are evoked precisely in order to trope, translate, transplant, or graft them into a new context. Pope, needless to say, was a master of this mode in all its varieties, and preferred himself the metaphor "grafting" when discussing it.⁶² The successful transplant, moreover, subsumes the power of classical or biblical, or even vernacular authority by relocating it in the writer's present. Milton's epic remains the sublime example, but the numberless naiads and dryads inhabiting the banks and overhanging trees of the Thames or Windsor Forest from the sixteenth to the nineteenth centuries testify to continuing efforts to identify classical authority with the local, northern *genius loci*.⁶³ Not surprisingly, Wordsworth operates in this mode both early and late.

The contradictions in Young's essay – another example is the very strict distinction between genius and learning – seem to occur because Young is genuinely unaware that writing means transposition. Just as he represses his lifelong relation to Pope, so too his concept of originality requires a repression, or elision, or erasure of an "origin," an origin that itself derives from an even remoter source. Hence the very terms "original" and "imitation" are highly unstable: by Young's own definition, an original is first a species of imitation; but second, an original is recognized as such because it produces imitations. It is only logical to conclude, although Young avoids doing so, that originality is really only a superior form of imitation, an imitation, that is, that does not look like one (because it introduces an element of difference that transforms the text). Young's odd distinction between "real" and "accidental" originals strengthens this conclusion. "Accidental" originals are those imitations whose models, conveniently, have been lost, hence "[t]hey, on their Father's Decease, enter, as Lawful Heirs, on their Estates in Fame."⁶⁴

Whether the source is lost, or never detected, originality is figured by the death of the Father.

The central specimen of a modern imitator is, of course, Pope. Rather than focus, however, on the Horatian Imitations, which might hit too close to home since he had produced several of his own, Young represents to us the essence of Pope by the translation of Homer. Translation, it appears, is the logic of imitation taken to its debased extreme. Young's anxiety over the logic of supplementarity appears acutely in the figure of Patroclus. What can one expect from translations of Homer, he asks?: "Not *Homer's Achilles*, but something, which, like *Patroclus*, assumes his name, and at its peril, appears in his stead."[65] The attack on Pope that follows brings forth a rich association of metaphors of the "other," including papist idolatry, satanic fall, and effeminacy. For instance, Pope's translating Homer into rhyme, an "effeminate decoration" (that Young had used throughout his career), is like putting "Achilles in petticoats a second time."[66]

What I want to focus on for the moment is the religious analogy, for here Young explicitly opposes a Protestant inner light to a Catholic regard for tradition, but applies them to literary history. Young makes the analogy between imitation and catholicism by way of the third term, blind worship. The figure appears first in the distinction between "the well-accomplished Scholar, and the divinely-inspired Enthusiast." The scholar, "up to his knees in Antiquity," treads in "the sacred footsteps of great examples, with the blind veneration of a bigot saluting the papal toe."[67] A little further on Young applies the analogy directly to Pope: "His taste partook of the error of his Religion; it denied not worship to Saints and Angels; that is, to writers, who, canonized for ages, have received their apotheosis from established and universal fame. True Poesy, like true Religion, abhors idolatry; . . . nor looks it for any inspiration less than divine."[68]

This attack on Pope's religion is a particularly low blow for Young to throw because, as Pope's contemporary, he would have known how often Pope's enemies, some of them paid by the government, used the same strategy. Moreover, in placing Pope on the side of the "scholar" and not of the "poet," Young had to repress completely the fact that the Queen Anne's "wits," such as Swift, Pope, Gay, and Arbuthnot, were the poets who took as their enemy the pedantry of scholars like Bentley and Theobald. The question of divine inspiration, however, is an important defensive maneuver in the attempt to establish personal authority. Let me cite Johnson to contextualize such a claim:

Speaking of the *inward light*, to which some methodists pretended, he said, it was a principle utterly incompatible with social or civil security. "If a man (said he), pretends to a principle of action of which I can know nothing, nay, not so much as that he has it, but only that he pretends to it; how can I tell what that person may be prompted to do? When a person professes to be governed by a written ascertained law, I can then know where to find him."[69]

Johnson's objection to the "inner light," typically post-Civil War in its fear of self-authorization, raises specifically the issue of the absence of the text, the written law. Young tropes upon this social–religious–political context in several ways. Drawing upon the dichotomies law/spirit and catholic/protestant, he displaces the argument into the realm of poetry. Self-authorization, strictly disciplined in the political sphere, becomes in a safer, aesthetic zone, the sign of "genius." Genius, as he says, is "that God within" that gives rules to nature. Proclaiming a gospel of anti-intimidation, "reverence yourself," Young's enthusiasm consists of worshipping an internalized ideal, "the Stranger within," an ideal that somewhat earlier in his life, we cannot help but noticing, he associated with the figure of Alexander Pope. Now, however, poetry has nothing to do with Pope, textuality, learning, or poetic tradition. The once revolutionary threat of inner-light politics (never a serious interest of Young the social climber) is appropriated for its emotional intensity into the purely aesthetic retreat of a "lettr'd recess," where, paradoxically, letters are conceived of as secondary and derivative.[70] But by displacing "enthusiasm" into a bracketed world of garden retreats and late-night reading, Young taps for literature, defined as anti-Popean, the energies of religion.

This is a reactionary gesture that leads ultimately to ever grander idealizations. It is a very short step from here to Wordsworth's representation of himself as bringing the good news of natural revelation. The advantage of such a move is the power it opposes to science and the other forces of the modern world – poetry on this plan recovers magic, spirit, lost transcendence. But it is very different from Pope's shrewd observation at the opening of *Windsor Forest*: "The groves of Eden, vanish'd now so long, / Live in description and look green in song." Young's claims forsake Pope's sophisticated awareness of the nature of his power and its limitations. For Young the poet is unabashedly a magus, weave a circle round him thrice. Ironically, the celebration of "genius" and the rejection of the influence of prior texts takes place from within textuality itself as Pope becomes the inescapable, demonic, effeminate, other. But then the representation of "Pope" as Other is at the root of "Romanticism."

INSTITUTIONAL SETTINGS: WINCHESTER, OXFORD, THE CHURCH

Dissatisfaction with Pope, a cornerstone of "Romanticism," dovetailed literary oedipal dynamics with broader cultural problems, for many writers in the mid-eighteenth century express the feeling that truly great poetry can be produced only in a more primitive society. "Primitive" in this context signifies not just Homer, but also the sixteenth and early seventeenth centuries. Johnson, for instance, states in his 1765 Preface that England in the time of Shakespeare was only just "emerging from barbarity." The smoothness and polish supposedly initiated by Denham and Waller was, in this view, improved upon by Dryden and perfected by Pope. Thus, the eighteenth century's sense of itself as having reached a certain plateau accounts for its sense of historical self-consciousness and perspective, but also for a civilized discontent that could only increase. Ironically, to the more fully bourgeois nineteenth century, the eighteenth century, constructed by some as an age of reason, could look to others both rough and obscene. Scott, for example, trying to contextualize Dryden, wrote of "the comparative rudeness of his age."[71] Be that as it may, Horace Walpole, to choose one example among many, focused the larger problem for poetry when he observed that epic poetry, traditionally the vehicle of sublime thought and expression, "is not suited to an improved and polished state of things."[72] In this climate, Pope's very perfection came to seem an ambivalent accomplishment. Refinement, once attained, could seem confinement.

I consider these issues more fully in the next chapter, but I raise them here as they touch upon the Wartons. Joseph Warton's expression of the problem is encoded in his comments on *An Essay on Criticism*: "In no polished nation, after criticism has been much studied, and the rules of writing established, has any very extraordinary book ever appeared."[73] Yet the turn away from the polished manners and moral ambiguity of the social world to the contemplation of a purer nature involves, as John Sitter has said, a "flight from history." Sitter finds the turn from history and politics a general characteristic of mid-eighteenth-century poetry, as opposed to the novel, for example, which turns outward. "Retirement," the virtuous space from which Pope attacks public corruption, becomes in the Wartons full retreat. Poetry becomes a refuge from the "crushing presence" of history as Pope and Swift's "literature of opposition" is replaced by "a new agreement with the reader in which poetry will be opposed not to a particular politics but (ostensibly) to all politics."[74]

Sitter draws back from arguing for an anxiety of Pope's influence, even though he has gathered much evidence in that direction and has shown that Pope is frequently represented as a father in mid-century poetry. But, perhaps because he correlates the notion of the autonomy of art in poets like the Wartons with Romantic theories of art such as those of Frye and Bloom to which he is opposed, Sitter misses seeing the extent to which Bloom's theory, when properly historicized, applies to the post-Popean generation. Hence I argue that mid-eighteenth-century poetry flees not just from history, but also from recent *literary* history in the person of Pope. Flight, Freud explains, is a response to external stimuli, whereas repression is the internal counterpart.[75] The transvaluation of Augustan values Sitter describes, often expressed by these poets without full control over their allusive implications, further suggests a struggle that is not successfully resolved.[76]

We need to place the flight from history and politics, together with the rise of the doctrine of the autonomy of art, in a larger social and economic context. William Dowling argues that the "flight from history" must be understood in terms of a changed understanding of what "history" meant. Drawing upon Pocock's analysis of the role played by the discourse of civic virtue in the rhetoric of opposition to Walpole, Dowling distinguishes between the Augustan situation and the one that immediately follows it. Swift and Pope had "a sense of poetry as having the power to work change upon the world, and in specific terms having this power because of its preservation of an idea of the virtuous republic in a time of cultural crisis and moral disarray."[77] Yet this sense collapses as it comes to be seen as clearly on the losing side. England did not appear to be approaching an apocalypse as a poem like the *Dunciad* prophesied, but rather appeared to be increasing in strength and prosperity. Therefore, the sense of "history," as Dowling puts it, "as a field of symbolic action, of poems as events with enormous consequences in the domain of the real," vanishes with the Augustan collapse. What takes its place for poets is a conception of history as a realm of depoliticized imaginative ideals in a Gothic past appealed to as a refuge from the noisy commercialism of the present.

Another context for the changing role of the artist is the shift brought about by science. Douglas Lane Patey argues convincingly that the new aesthetic is an effect of the Ancient/Modern debate which separated out "art" from "science." Art, which once had been defined as any rule-governed production, now was seen to be addressed exclusively to the senses rather than the understanding, and its appreciation became a matter of "taste."[78]

The causes that bring about these suddenly changed understandings of "history" and "art" also bring about poetry's loss of instrumentality, which is illustrated in the sequence moving from Dryden's very active political role as Charles II's Laureate, to Pope as a kind of Opposition Laureate (the phrase is Sitter's), to Goldsmith, whose attack on the destructive effects of luxury capital in *The Deserted Village* (1770) had no apparent political impact: "the political argument of the poem could either be ignored or dismissed, with the implication that political economy had now taken over the cognitive functions of poetry with respect to social and economic questions."[79] The doctrine of art's autonomy follows very closely upon these changes, whether as the defensive reaction of the elite artist to the pressures of the mass market, so that the loss of influence on the world is now claimed as a virtue, or whether it is that the artist, as the man of no specific occupation, and hence interest, assumes the ideology that had once been part of the role of the disinterested "gentleman."[80]

But having opened up the issue to broader currents we need as well to make finer distinctions, for those who share a similar politics, or a similar cultural dilemma, often clash, for other reasons altogether, over aesthetic doctrine. For example, both Goldsmith and Johnson were opposed to empire and unfettered capitalism – Johnson wrote of "the true spirit of unfeeling commerce" in the *Life of Addison* – yet both follow Pope's aesthetic line, while a similar rejection of commerce by the Wartons produces a poetry that first identifies with Pope's critiques, and then apparently rebels against them. It is the Wartons who trumpet virtuous retreat, not Johnson. The larger contexts I have identified do not in any way obviate or refute the evidence I have put forward for an anxiety of Pope's influence. Whereas an epochal break is routinely asserted to have taken place in the eighteenth century, one can just as easily argue for continuity among change, especially when talking about cultural works that do not so easily become obsolete. Pope lived through changes, both in the marketing of books and in the general economy of England, and responded to them in ways that later generations continued to find meaningful. The relation between *The Dunciad* and Wordsworth's vision of London in *Prelude* Book 7, for instance, has often been commented on.[81] All this is to say that the highly emotional differentiation from Pope that we have seen in the Wartons and Young is not a necessary consequence of broadscale historical change. Marilyn Butler contextualizes Romanticism as part of the provincial country's assertion of its power in opposition to London as arbiter of taste.[82] We can pursue this generalization more fruitfully, I think, if we look to the institutions in the provinces, such as the university and the Church, that shaped the Wartons' and Young's discursive experience, for surely their defensiveness belongs as well to the institutions within which they were educated, lived, and worked.

The psychological dynamic I have isolated in the Wartons and Young, a dynamic I identify with "Romanticism" itself, occurs in a specific setting and in relation to a specific set of circumstances, even though it will eventually be widely disseminated. The question of setting answers a legitimate question: why did the swerve from Pope take the particular form of a return to Milton and Spenser? Why, for instance, didn't it return to Dryden? Well, a "return-to-Dryden" movement did in fact take place. That very logic touched off a two-years-long dispute in *The Gentleman's Magazine* (1789–91), in which the Dryden party accused Pope of polluting the pure spring of his master's poetry.[83] The claim, to some extent derived from Johnson, was that Dryden's "negligence" was more pleasing than Pope's perfection. Nor was the "Dryden Revival" without significant adherents, as the examples of Scott and Keats testify.[84] Yet the emotional appeal of Milton was clearly stronger. The institutional contexts in which the Wartons and Young flourished may suggest why Milton's solitary, pensive figure was so attractive and became so quickly valorized in Romantic poetry.

The poets who composed poetry as a "flight from history" were intimately connected with Oxford. The Elder Warton (1688–1745) was educated there, and served two five-year terms as Professor of Poetry from 1715 to 1725. Both sons were educated at Oxford and Thomas, Jr., who spent his entire adult life there, has been described recently as its "most representative figure" of the eighteenth century.[85] Oxford's almost total isolation in the eighteenth century was the result of its politics. Royalist in the Civil War, and predominantly Jacobite after the defeat of James II in 1688, Oxford began a long period of isolation from the political establishment after the Whig–Hanover succession was assured in 1714, an isolation that would be broken when Thomas Warton was appointed Laureate by George III in 1785. The Elder Warton, it has even been suggested, was appointed Professor of Poetry, in the year of the failure of the first Jacobite rebellion in 1715, purely on the basis of his strong Jacobite sympathies. Thomas, Jr., as if to show the tenacity of feudal sentiment, attacks Puritanism as late as his edition of Milton in 1785 because it destroyed the aesthetic delights associated with the Gothic cathedrals. Milton's appreciation of music and art, duly noted, separated him from those Puritans who were no better than barbarians. Note the intimate relation between aesthetic taste and politics in Warton's observations on the twin Penseroso/Allegro poems:

> No man was ever so disqualified to turn puritan as Milton. In this and the preceding poem, he professes himself to be highly pleased with the choral church-music, with Gothic cloysters, the painted windows and vaulted iles of a venerable cathedral, with tilts and tournaments, and with masques and pageantries. *What very repugnant and unpoetical principles did he afterwards adopt! He helped to subvert monarchy, destroy subordination, and to level all distinctions of rank.* But this scheme was totally inconsistent with the splendours of society . . . which belong to a court . . . The delights arising from these objects were to be sacrificed to the cold and philosophical spirit of calvinism, which furnished no pleasures to the imagination.[86]

An attack on Oxford's position was launched in 1748 by William Mason in "Isis." Thomas Warton's reply in "The Triumph of Isis" proclaims, in Fairer's paraphrase, "The Muse scorns political power," allying itself instead with the higher world of "poetic imagination." A student miscellany of 1750–51 similarly took isolation to be virtue, claiming that since the poetical muses had been banished from the court ever since the days of Queen Anne, they could now sing in the woods "with the same native wildness and unrestrained vivacity as they did in the *other golden age.*"[87]

Before Oxford, Thomas Warton (1728–90) was educated by his father, who had become the Vicar of Basingstoke and Headmaster of its school, but Joseph (1722–1800) was educated at Winchester, together with his classmate, friend, and rival poet, William Collins, before both continued to Oxford. Joseph eventually took holy orders, becoming his father's curate, before returning to Winchester first as Usher, and then Headmaster, remaining there until the 1790s. Set in the cathedral town, Winchester, both isolated and conservative – it was dubbed in 1908 "the most conservative institution in the world" – has been described as a school where clergymen sent their sons, who themselves became clergymen.[88] Since Wykeham built both Winchester and New College, Oxford, in the fourteenth century the usual arrangement was for graduates of Winchester to proceed to New College: "Of the Winchester scholars who survived to adult life, the great majority lived and died either as fellows of New College (and of Winchester itself), or as parish clergy, often in obscure country livings."[89] Edward Young (1683–1765), too, is a product of Winchester, Oxford, and the Church. After Winchester, Young remained at Oxford until his mid-forties, when, having at last taken orders, he accepted an Oxford-controlled benefice at Welwyn. True to tradition, his father completed the course of Winchester–Oxford–Holy Orders before him, just as Young's son would do after him. It is worth noting, as a footnote to the institutional history of Romanticism, that English conversation among the boys at Winchester was forbidden. Among Gothic architecture, supposed resting place of Arthur's Round Table, only Latin was permitted.[90]

The larger network of Winchester–Oxford affiliates includes Christopher Pitt (1699–1748), Joseph Spence (1699–1768), and Bishop Lowth (1710–87), these last two, like Thomas Warton and his father, also Professors of Poetry at Oxford. Pitt's translation of the *Aeneid* was chosen by Joseph Warton for his edition of Virgil because, he claimed, it was better than Dryden's. Spence succeeded Warton, Sr., to the Professorship of Poetry. Lowth, famous for his *Lectures on Hebrew Poesy*, was born in Winchester, was related to Pitt through his mother's father, and was the executor of Spence's will. And of course all of them were on intimate terms with the younger Wartons. Sydney Smith, clergyman, London wit, and co-founder of the *Edinburgh Review*, is a later product of the same institutional track.[91]

The Wartons' feudal sympathies would seem to have much in common with Pope who was constantly accused of Jacobitical treason. But as aspiring poets their differentiation from Pope took the form of an assertion of the values of their immediate environments, the academic retreats of Winchester College and Oxford. Pope's urban-centered world produced the poetry of political protest against Walpole's reign, while Oxford and Winchester celebrated the lament of the private consciousness. This turn, however, involved a form of self-mutilation, for in turning against Pope they were not only denying earlier selves, they were refusing to admit the continuity in values between satiric attack and elegiac lament. The specific form this takes in Joseph is the attack on satire, for the renunciation of politics in poetry is at the heart of his critique of Pope. Warton had said in his conclusion, for example, that Gray's *Bard* was more sublime than anything in Pope. From a greater distance, Ronald Paulson observed that "Gray's elegies on the Bard . . . are the mourning and funereal version of satiric projection in Pope's *Dunciad* and Swift's *Verses*," while Robert Folkenflik thought it ironic that Warton seemed not "aware of the role of the poet in Pope's later poetry."[92]

Oxford's most recent historian of this period, David Fairer, directly related Oxford's position to the shift in taste: "The shift from Addisonian poise and responsibility towards the nostalgic delights of Warton and his followers is not merely a shift in Oxford's relationship with the 'world,' but part of the wider movement from Augustan to Romantic."[93] Yes, the Wartons are only part of larger cultural changes that include a growing commercial economy and the turn away from public service to a more private concept of virtue. But, having said that, one could also put it the other way round. Oxford's isolation was a chief determinant of the shift, not simply part of a wider movement, in the sense that it is the Winchester–Oxford group that explicitly formulates the discursive - structure later disseminated more broadly, expressing as it does the dissatisfaction with modernity in elegies for personal loss. Young's *Conjectures*, it is important to note, had an immediate and profound effect upon the early Schiller and Goethe. The poetry of the 1740s had a similar effect upon Cowper at Olney and Weston, whose first public appearance was also his last. Working in Pope's shadow, these writers insist upon the virtue of isolation, not simply as the response to the corruptions of public life, but also as necessary to the revival of a purer, more lyrical poetry that is supposedly the very opposite of Pope's public posturing. Hence a dissociation sets in as Pope's sublime and pathetic poems are put aside and he comes to be constructed as the poet of modern manners which are not inherently poetical. Hence, too, the insistence on the Penseroso figure, again dissociated from Pope, at the heart of the "true" poetry, and the ironic necessity of dealing so unkindly, so unchivalrously one might say, with forlorn Eloisa.

The discursive formation we call "Romanticism" was thus determined in part by large-scale social and economic changes, in part by the academic–clerical sensibility of educational institutions on the margins of public life, and in part by the need to clear ambivalent space within a poetic scene dominated by Popean syntheses of the tradition. The continuity of this paradigm and its values can be traced in detail in mid- and late-eighteenth-century poetry, but it is perhaps enough for the moment to note that Cowper was overwhelmed in 1790 when informed of Joseph Warton's high opinion of *The Task*: "The Poet who pleases a man like him, has nothing left to wish for."[94] Perhaps more revealing is Southey's elaboration of Cowper's view of Pope: ". . . his dislike of Pope amounted to hatred. He is said to have wished him alive, not only that he might have a struggle with him for preeminence, but that he might endeavor to break his heart . . . He disliked Pope's manner as a poet, and his character as a man, and had formed the intention of attacking both."[95]

Cowper's overcharged emotion becomes comprehensible, I suggest, only when we understand how much *The Task* (1785) owes to Pope. Let me elaborate briefly. *The Task* is notoriously variable in its tone. It begins with a mock-epic tribute to a sofa that recalls Pope's *Rape of the Lock*, assumes Miltonic tones and pretensions as it proceeds, and veers away again. A recent critic of the poem, one who has studied it in depth, observed that Milton and Horace were the major influences, and that what Cowper took from Horace was lyric, satire, an example of meditative retirement poetry, "ease" and "self-deprecation." But the mention of Horace brings certain poems of Pope immediately to mind, and indeed several pages later we are told that the "comic, familiar style" derives from Swift and Sterne, as well as from *The Rape of the Lock* and "a general debt to Horace in Pope's *Imitations*."[96] Thus I would sharpen the point, and argue that Milton and Pope are Cowper's two most important models. Pope, after all, was his nearest and most famous example in England of a poet in retirement from a corrupt political and commercial culture. What he took from Pope specifically in the poems mentioned was the tone of jesting while actually being perfectly in earnest, an urbane self-deprecation that does not preclude a commitment to Miltonic seriousness.

Blank verse, we must recall, presented a special problem to the eighteenth-century poet, because it was understood to be so close to English conversation as to be unfit for the dignity of poetry unless elevated by an especially noble subject: "Poetry may subsist without rhyme, but English poetry will not often please; nor can rhyme ever be safely spared but where the subject is able to support itself."[97] Cowper's great success is to have written a blank verse that is personal, familiar, yet elevated nonetheless. The result of his synthesis of Milton and Pope is to have produced a mode capable of investing quotidian concerns and objects – such as the building of a greenhouse and the cultivation of a cucumber – with an almost redemptive significance without falling into bathos. This is the key lesson learned from Pope, but it is worked out in a blank verse that was directly bequeathed to Coleridge in his Conversation poems; Coleridge simply carries on "where Cowper left off."[98] Cowper repaid Pope, as we have seen above, with murderous hatred. He spent years translating Homer into blank verse in an attempt to displace Pope's translation, but the project was a failure.

If Cowper is another example, the most direct continuity in the transmission of the Warton paradigm manifests itself in the education and career of Rev. William Lisle Bowles (1762–1850), the man Byron called a "maudlin priest," and whom Coleridge, actually echoing criteria from a passage in Warton's *Essay on Pope*, praised in *Biographia Literaria* as the first, together with Cowper, to unite head and heart.[99] Bowles was trained under Joseph at Winchester before becoming Thomas's protégé at Oxford. His edition of Pope of 1806 continued that strange tradition of desire and aversion, inaugurated by Joseph's own edition of 1797, in which Pope's harshest critics are simultaneously the editors and preservers of his work. Byron responded to Bowles's edition with the following:

> A fulsome editor is pardonable though tiresome . . . But a detracting editor is a parricide. He sins against the nature of his office, and connection. He murders the life to come of his victim. If his author is not worthy to be remembered, do not edit at all: if he be, edit honestly, and even flatteringly . . . But to sit down "mingere in patrios cinere" [to piss on one's father's ashes] as Mr. B. has done, merits a reprobation so strong, that I am as incapable of expressing it as of ceasing to feel it.[100]

Byron's use of the word "parricide" proves to what extent Freudian models are appropriate to, and not imposed upon, this material. The debate between Bowles and Byron, joined in by others, has been named the Pope Controversy. James Chandler's recent survey of the documents concludes that the construction of Pope as a French alien by his attackers has much to do with the war between Britain and France, and the subsequent emphasis of British nationalism. He quite explicitly takes a cautious position in not wishing to locate the causes in a poetic competition with Pope.[101] There is no question that a polemical construction of what constitutes "Englishness" is a key weapon in the Pope Controversy, as it had been in other aesthetic quarrels: Jonson said that Spenser "writ no language," Addison said something similar about Milton, and Wordsworth thought Byron departed from pure English, just as Byron had his admirers who thought that only he wrote English.[102] Nonetheless, I argue the necessity of taking the bolder position because the construction of Pope as an alien, as I have shown, takes place much earlier in the struggles of Bowles's teachers for poetic independence.

What seems to me undeniable, however, is, with Macaulay and Arnold leading the way, the eventual triumph and predominance in the nineteenth and twentieth centuries of the Wartonian legacy.[103] One of the ironies of literary history, as I noted at the beginning of this chapter, is the way "Wordsworth" began to be substituted for "Cowper" in the oppositional structure of "Romanticism." Perhaps the first to do this was Leigh Hunt, who began his review of Keats in 1817 by rehearsing the Wartonian narrative in brief. Of late, he says, "something which was not poetry has made way for the return of something which is." After deriding Dryden and Pope, he states: "It has been thought that Cowper was the first poet who re-opened the true way to nature and a natural style; but we hold this to be a mistake ... It was the Lake poets (however grudgingly we say it, on some accounts) that were the first to revive the true taste for nature."[104] Once again, a true successor has replaced a pretender, but this time it is Cowper who is ousted and the epochal break moved forward to accommodate the revision. This view would not take hold until Wordsworth's popularity grew greater, but, as we saw, it was fairly standard by the 1850s. An altogether unexpected turn of the screw, though, is Bagehot's opinion in 1855 that "Cowper belongs, though with some differences, to the school of Pope."[105] Thus the poet who was thought the first to have succeeded in the rebellion against Pope, the one who hated him so passionately, now is viewed to be one of his party.

The writings of the Wartons and Edward Young are fashioned both by sensibilities formed in service of the university and the Church, and by the imperative to distance themselves from Pope, who is close to their values yet sufficiently different to qualify as a heretic. The fact that their "Romanticism" has much more in common, as far as essential values are concerned, with Pope than it does differences, and the fact that these writers express, at one time or another, the greatest admiration for Pope, makes the insistence upon difference all the more violent. As it emerges, a central tenet of "Romantic" literary history is the opposition of "Milton" to "Pope," and the representation of that opposition in terms of absolute values. A different reading would suggest that Pope's role has been seriously undervalued, and that one of the things that needs to be understood is the way Pope mediated and transformed Milton for the "modern" eighteenth century. The opposition between them, as I hope I have shown, is the result of a misprision on the part of poets who originally identified strongly with Pope, but then turned into bitter rivals and pressed "Milton" into their service as an ally. My reading of these relations is supported even further by some lines of Gray. In "Stanzas to Mr. Bentley," Gray praises the sister art of Bentley, who had illustrated Gray's poems with his drawings. Gray wishes that his own lines might "catch a lustre" from Bentley's flame, for if they could,

> The energy of Pope they might efface,
>   And Dryden's harmony submit to mine.
> But not to one in this benighted age
>   Is that diviner inspiration giv'n,
> That burns in Shakespeare's or in Milton's page,
>   The pomp and prodigality of heav'n.[106]

These lines describe the dilemma of the post-Popean generation quite accurately. For Gray is saying that he could overcome Pope–Dryden *only* if he were Shakespeare–Milton. We so much take for granted the superiority of Shakespeare and Milton that we find it hard to imagine that poets were once so intimidated by Pope–Dryden that they turned to the earlier poets as a way of putting them down.

Gray's "Stanzas to Mr. Bentley" was written five years after William Collins' "Ode on the Poetical Character" appeared in 1746, and may be used as a gloss on the ending of Collins' poem. For there the speaker of the poem is represented as "retreating" from "Waller" in order to pursue access to Milton's Eden, a figure for inspiration, but access is denied. The pathos of the poem derives from the failure of the poet to attain transcendence, to achieve the incarnation of the poetical character, to be, in fact, Milton. But to retreat from Waller means the poet must have been where Waller was; and what is the motive for the "retreat"? The retreat from Waller is conventionally interpreted as the sign of Collins' rejection of the Augustan line supposedly initiated by Waller and Denham and leading to Dryden and Pope. But "retreat" implies temporary defeat, not rejection. Collins, in my view, expresses the dilemma Gray does, but with much greater complexity. What we must remember is that Collins and Joseph Warton were friends and schoolmates not only at Winchester, but also at Oxford, that their first published poems were sent to London together under the same cover, and that their Odes were not published in the same volume only because of a publisher's decision. But, whereas the Wartons turn to Milton unproblematically, Collins knows, it is what his poem is about, that to go from "Pope" to "Milton" is to go from the frying pan into the fire. Cowper, as we saw, solved this problem in a rough way and opened up new possibilities for the poetic subject.[107]

CHAPTER TWO

Refinement, Romanticism, Francis Jeffrey

It is not difficult to extend my thesis about the eighteenth-century origin of Romanticism forward into the early nineteenth century, and not only because the writings I analyzed in the previous chapter were so influential in forming the aesthetic tastes of the following generations. Pope's poetry continued to be read and thus continued to present similar problems, not to the common reader, but to the ambitious writer. From the evidence, one can only conclude that Pope's poetry is the most powerful, or perhaps I should say "problematic," influence on English poetry for roughly eighty years after his death in 1744. Milton's influence is crucial, and has been amply documented, but its context is accurately understood as an auxiliary in the central battle to overcome Pope.[1] Thomas Warton, who should know, said in 1785: "the school of Milton rose in *emulation* of the school of Pope."[2] This chapter substantiates, and works out some of the implications of, the fact that Pope occupies for the late eighteenth and early nineteenth century a double, or paradoxical role: he represents modernity (a fallen condition), yet he also enjoys the status of a classic, or ancient.

Theories of Romanticism, as Herbert Lindenberger has recently written, are ultimately always theories of modernity, even when a later version of modernity defines itself by its very distance from Romanticism.[3] In the English literary tradition the "fall" into modernity becomes increasingly associated with Pope's mode, and Pope's mode is most frequently constructed as one of "refinement," an interpretation that was certainly plausible, but which necessarily excluded *The Dunciad*, a poem that according to Joseph Warton contained some of Pope's best lines, but that nonetheless lacked decorum and propriety.[4] Commenting more recently on that poem's dark vision, Harold Bloom, who has written not often enough on Pope, relates it directly to Milton's "darkness visible."[5]

Nonetheless, from the Restoration on, English writers saw themselves as refining upon a rich but disorderly language and literature. In general it can be said that the eighteenth century considers the pre-Restoration period to be primitive, rude, even barbaric; the line of improvement was conventionally thought to begin with Waller. Atterbury, in 1690, wrote of Waller that "the tongue came into his hands like a rough diamond: he polished it first . . . He undoubtedly stands first in the list of refiners." Erskine-Hill glosses this statement by pointing out that to "polish," in this context, is "to make manifest a latent value and beauty"; to call Waller a "refiner" is to refer "to the actual process of refining, extracting from dross what is essential and valuable, taking a noble and durable metal from the ore."[6] Later generations thought that the refiners, from Waller through Pope, had stabilized the language, but the poets, in the midst of the work, struggled with its instability. Waller lamented, "we write in sand." Pope, in his 1717 Preface, and Gray, in a letter to West, made similar complaints. Yet no sooner had the "Augustans" stabilized, improved, and polished the language than nostalgia for supposedly earlier freedoms began to surface. Northcote, in the early nineteenth century, reveals his sense of a lost paradise of freedom in language that "modernity" does not allow:

Don't you think Shakespeare and the writers of that day had a prodigious advantage in using phrases and combinations of style, which could not be admitted now that the language is reduced to a more precise and uniform standard, but which yet have a peculiar force and felicity when they can be justified by the privilege of the age?[7]

The settling of the language into a certain regularity very quickly began to be perceived as a discouragement to enterprise. W. J. Bate reads Young's assertion of originality quite appropriately in the context of the mid-eighteenth century's anxiety that advancing civilization destroys the conditions necessary for great art.[8] The increasing number of models of excellence, it was felt, tended to depress ambition in the same degree that they raised admiration. Another way of putting it was that refinement attenuated the necessary boldness of an original impulse. Joseph Warton, for instance, noted the "timidity and caution which is occasioned by a regard to the dictates of art."[9] Francis Jeffrey's observation of 1803 encoded this very idea in a diachronic narrative of eighteenth-century literary history: "The gradual refinement of taste had, for nearly a century, been weakening the force of original genius."[10] Hume's warning in 1742 appears apt: "The *excess* of refinement is now more to be guarded against than ever."[11]

Bate's book, however, as intelligent as it is and as useful as it has been, does not convey any sense that despair over advancing refinement and civilization is directly related to Pope's achievement. In fact, he seems to go out of his way not to notice this particular implication of his thesis.[12] But both Hume and Jeffrey (writing sixty years after) are addressing the same phenomenon: "refinement" is code for "Pope." This is explicit when Thomas Campbell, speaking of Pope as a contemporary influence in 1808, asks in the *Edinburgh Review* "whether a slight return to negligence, might not be preferable to the very acme of smoothness which [Pope] has chosen."[13]

More recently, James Engell registers the association of refinement with Pope, but his impressive erudition is organized according to the perspective of Romantic literary history. He concludes, accordingly, that refinement "finally becomes questioned, dissected, and diminished." "Unlike originality," which is "open-ended," refinement "looks backward." Thus he asks rhetorically, "can the stick be whittled forever?"[14] My view is rather that we must look behind the explicit statements from which Engell and others draw their conclusions to see that, in spite of the polemic against Pope, refinement remains a necessary virtue, a fact integral to a central romantic dilemma, for "original" poets find that they can do nothing with Pope, but also nothing without him. In what follows, I bring out the Popean features of this dilemma by reconstructing the force of Pope's reputation in the early nineteenth century, and by analyzing in particular the Romantic literary history of Francis Jeffrey.

The contemporaneity of Pope in the first decades of the nineteenth century is well illustrated by the following anecdote. Charles Lamb and Henry Crabb Robinson went to the Lyceum on 30 March 1811 to see a play called *The Siege of Belgrade*. When the two leads, a Mr. Dignam and a Mrs. Bland, came on stage together, Lamb turned to Robinson, saying, "And lo! two puddings smoked upon the board."[15] An obscure moment in history flashes forth: two friends sit in the dark at the playhouse, one drops a casual witticism; the other, later in the evening, records it in his diary. We infer from the remark, clearly an allusion, that the now-forgotten actors in the now-obscure play were slightly overweight and perhaps, too, slightly middle-aged playing roles more suited to youth. Few readers of Robinson's unannotated diary today, however, will recognize the source of the quotation, the source that both Lamb and Robinson simply take for granted as a given in their particular cultural space. Lamb's nimble mind recalled one of Pope's famous set pieces from "The

Epistle to Bathurst" (1733), the tale of Balaam, "a Citizen of sober fame," whom the Devil decides to tempt: "But Satan now is wiser than of yore, / And tempts by making rich, not making poor." Lamb alludes to one of the lines that describes the complacent Balaam, fortunes on the rise, depicted by Pope in colloquial terms:

> Sir Balaam now, he lives like other folks,
> He takes his chirping pint, and cracks his jokes:
> "Live like yourself," was soon my Lady's word;
> And lo! two puddings smok'd upon the board. (lines 357–60)

Lamb's playfulness presupposes not only a wide dissemination, but also a detailed knowledge, of Pope's writings that is difficult for us to recover today when a reading of Pope cannot be assumed even among professors of English literature outside of very strict period divisions. Yet, for the nineteenth century, Pope was inescapable, as thoroughly naturalized a part of English culture as Shakespeare or Milton. Diaries, letters, poetry, prose of any sort: all testify to Pope's influence. D'Israeli referred to this phenomenon when he spoke of lines of Pope "that circulated as the coin of the people, and are still proverbial."[16] Later in the century, George Eliot still admired "those felicitous epithets . . . those pregnant lines, by which Pope's Satires have enriched the ordinary speech of educated men."[17] Newman lectured in 1854, juxtaposing names in a not unorthodox series: "Whether we will or no, the phraseology and diction of Shakespeare, of the Protestant formularies, of Milton, of Pope, of Johnson's Table-talk, and of Walter Scott, have become a portion of the vernacular tongue, the household words, of which perhaps we little guess the origin, and the very idioms of our familiar conversation."[18] Examples might be multiplied, but the point would remain the same: nineteenth-century writers were intimate with Pope, even or especially those who condemned him, but because of that condemnation, the twentieth-century critic of the nineteenth century is for the most part ignorant of Pope as a pervasive cultural presence.

An exchange of letters between two men close to Wordsworth who might be called general readers, Edward Quillinan and, once again, Henry Crabb Robinson, reveals more specifically the degree of influence Pope exercised over men who lived well into the nineteenth century. Quillinan, born in 1791 (twenty-one years after Wordsworth), a man who loved and admired Wordsworth as both man and poet, and who eventually married Dora, the poet's daughter, writes to Crabb Robinson in 1843:

I will not reveal to you, for you could not comprehend, my *idolatry* of Pope from my boyhood, I might also say from my infancy, for the first book that ever threw me into a rapture of delight was Pope's Iliad . . . My admiration of Pope, the man, the son, the friend, as well as the poet, in no degree diminished as I grew older, & is as vivid now as ever.[19]

Stung by Macaulay's attack on Pope in a review of Addison in the *Edinburgh Review* of July 1843, Quillinan's panegyric in defense runs on for more than two pages. In reply, Robinson urges Quillinan to "keep within bounds": "After all, Pope is or rather *was* as great a favorite with me as any one English poet." Notice that before catching his heresy in time, and then swiftly assigning it to the past, Robinson had almost written, "Pope is as great a favorite with me as any one English poet." He goes on,

Perhaps I knew once more of him than of any other English classic. Referring to an early period in my life, before I had heard of the Lyrical Ballads, which caused a little revolution in my taste for poetry there were 4 poems which I used to read incessantly. I cannot say which I then read oftenest or loved the most – They are of a very different kind And I mention them to shew that my taste was *wide* They were – The Rape of the Lock, Comus, the Castle of Indolence & the Traveller – Next to these, were all the Ethic Epistles of Pope – And with respect to these, they were so familiar to me that I never for years looked into them – I seemed to know them by heart.[20]

Incidentally, one of the "Ethic Epistles" that Robinson "seemed to know by heart" included the line that Lamb quoted to him in the playhouse. Perhaps more to the point, the example of Quillinan shows that Robinson's renunciation of Pope was by no means a necessary consequence of an admiration for Wordsworth. The example of Robinson shows that those who gave over Pope at this stage, and they were in the minority, still knew Pope by heart, and still thought of him as an "English classic." John Wilson viewed this phenomenon ironically in his *Noctes Ambrosianae* dialogue in *Blackwood's Magazine* for March 1825: "*North* [to the Shepherd]. Stop, James – you will run yourself out of breath. Why, you said, a few minutes ago, that you did not care much about Pope, and were not at all familiar with his works – you have them at your finger ends."[21]

Those who commented on these things associated Pope's name almost automatically with Milton and Shakespeare. In this golden age of anthologies – Bell's (1776–82), Johnson's (1779–81), Anderson's (1795), Chalmers' (1810), etc. – editors' prefaces were, not surprisingly, strategic sites from which to pronounce canonical judgments. Robert Anderson, who for the most part accepted the Wartonian view that Pope was the poet of society, or "artificial" nature, and thus relatively inferior, expressed his understanding of Pope's position in these terms in 1795: "The compositions of Pope are perhaps a greater accession to English literature, than those of any other poet of our nation, except Spenser, Shakespeare, and Milton."[22]

From the perspective of 1819, Sydney Smith, in a letter recommending reading to his son, focuses on the essentials: "Consider what it is most needful to have, what it is most shameful to want":

> For the English poets I will let you off at present with Milton, Dryden, Pope, and Shakespeare; and remember, always in books keep the best company. Don't read a line of Ovid till you have mastered Virgil; nor a line of Thomson till you have exhausted Pope; nor of Massinger, till you are familiar with Shakespeare.[23]

In 1823, Hazlitt speculated that the present age was an age of criticism for the simple reason that a surplus of great art already existed: "When we have Shakespeare, we do not want more Shakespeares: one Milton, one Pope or Dryden, is enough . . . Do we not neglect the standard authors to hunt after mere novelty? This is not wisdom, but affectation or caprice."[24]

In conversations recorded in the 1820s, James Northcote, who painted Coleridge among many others, gave Hazlitt a reading list organized by ages. Up to the age of six, one should read *Jack the Giant-Killer*; from six to twelve, *Pilgrim's Progress* and *Robinson Crusoe*; from twelve to twenty, Fielding and *Don Quixote*; and from twenty to thirty, "Milton, Pope, Shakespeare." Hazlitt once asked him about Wordsworth's chance for immortality:

> No; the world can only keep in view the principal and most perfect productions of human ingenuity; such works as Dryden's and Pope's, and a few others, that from their unity, their completeness, their polish have the stamp of immortality upon them, and seem indestructible like an element of nature. There are few of these: I fear your friend W— is not one.[25]

Hazlitt observes in reply that Wordsworth, whom he calls "one of the Illustrious Obscure," has been hurt in the competition for immortality by not being popular in his own lifetime. Northcote's authoritative pronouncement comes to us across the years loaded with a heavy freight of irony. But the very fact that it could be made in the 1820s serves to undermine the still widespread perception that everything changed in 1798.

Romantic ideology, as defined by McGann in his book on the topic, is a construction that reproduces the values of Wordsworth and Coleridge.

In relation to Pope I would call it an intensified, or extreme form of Wartonianism. But, with the exception of readers such as Quillinan or Northcote or Byron, undoubtedly representative of a certain portion of the readership, a moderate form of Wartonianism exemplified by Hazlitt and others seems to have been very widely diffused. The moderate position does not rank Pope in the highest class, but recognizes his status as a classic, and appreciates his virtues.

Hazlitt, for whom Pope is a standard author, expresses his own version of Wartonianism succinctly in the anthology he edited in 1824: "*POPE* is at the head of the second class of poets, *viz.* the describers of artificial life and manners. His works are a delightful, never-failing fund of good sense and refined taste, he is a model of elegance every where, his style is polished and almost faultless in its kind."[26] In an essay on Pope, however, he explicitly repudiates the extreme line associated with both Warton and his student Bowles. Quoting passages from "Arbuthnot" and "Jervas," Hazlitt asks, echoing Johnson: "And shall we cut ourselves off from beauties like these with a theory? . . . and go about asking our blind guides, whether Pope was a poet or not. It will never do." What is most amazing in its implications, though, is Hazlitt's final sentence: "If I had to choose, there are one or two persons, and but one or two, that I should like to have been better than Pope!"[27] Hazlitt, regardless of his critical estimation of Pope's works, is not alone in his time in identifying with Pope almost to the point of preferring to be Pope rather than himself. Moreover, the reaction-formation against this powerful pull of identification was, as we will see, as integral to the time as Quillinan's idolatry and Hazlitt's more reserved admiration. Byron implies the centrality of Pope's position when he complains of "the unjustifiable attempts at depreciation begun by Warton and carried on to and at this day by the new School of Critics and Scribblers, who think themselves poets because they do *not* write like Pope."[28]

By virtue of its wide circulation, *The Edinburgh Review* was without question the most influential organ of opinion of the early nineteenth century. Founded by Francis Jeffrey, Sydney Smith, and Henry Brougham in 1802, the number of subscribers in 1808 was 9,000 with an estimated readership of many times that number. These figures need to be understood in relation to the total number of literate people, estimated in 1812 at just over 200,000, of which 30,000 constituted the highest ranks of society.[29] No competitor emerged until 1809 when Walter Scott and others founded the *Quarterly Review*. By 1818 both journals reached a peak monthly circulation of about 14,000 each; the

Edinburgh, moreover, was also sold as a book, two numbers to a volume. Its form, Sheldon Halpern noted, "set the pattern for critical periodicals to this day."[30] Marilyn Butler's assessment of Jeffrey seems accurate: "His influential position assured that from 1802 to 1817 he was the leading critic of the age."[31]

For the great majority of students of the Romantic poets, though, Jeffrey is the villain who wrote the infamous opening sentence of the review of Wordsworth's *Excursion*: "This will never do!" This romantic consensus on Jeffrey is well illustrated by two quotations. Halpern places Sydney Smith's position on contemporary literature by comparing him to Jeffrey: "Smith was not an anti-Romantic in the way that Jeffrey was, actively fighting the literary principles of Wordsworth and his followers; but he was a non-Romantic."[32] Halpern, predictably, identifies Wordsworth with Romanticism itself; to be against him, quite simply, is to be anti-Romantic.

Another example is Lindenberger's description of the several phases of Romantic reception, the first an initial failure:

a failure that resulted from the application of early critical criteria inappropriate to their particular mode of writing – in short what we might call the "this-will-never-do" phase or the "Keats-and-the-reviewers" tragedy. From here we move on to their eventual triumph – not simply their acceptance within the literary canon, but even more fundamentally, the institutionalization of certain of their guiding ideas within anglophone culture as a whole.[33]

Lindenberger wants to view this narrative from a slightly ironic distance, but he nonetheless feels that "this account is probably not too far off the mark." The fact that a relatively narrow version of "Romantic" values has been thoroughly institutionalized, however, works against romantic critics radically reassessing those very values. In this case, we need to understand Jeffrey from a different perspective than the one dictated by the "eventual triumph" of Wordsworth.

René Wellek, as far back as the 1950s, read through Jeffrey's essays and pronounced his position a "moderate romanticism," but it is clear from my examples that Wellek's assessment has not been widely influential.[34] Jeffrey, it appears, fulfills a certain epistemic role beyond which he is not considered to be interesting. Wellek's account, moreover, is handicapped by making a sharp distinction between "Romantic" and "Neoclassical" poetics, and ascribing Jeffrey's limitations to the latter.

The problem is that Jeffrey has been judged according to his own value judgments, most centrally his pronouncements on Wordsworth.

Hence Wellek devotes much space to showing why Jeffrey couldn't appreciate the Lake poet. Alternatively, Jeffrey has been evaluated for his "intrinsic" abilities, by both Wellek and Ian Jack for example, and found not up to the level of Johnson, or Coleridge, or Arnold, as a critic.[35] Weighing in on the other side, Bate claims he was "certainly one of the shrewdest minds of the time and in our own century one of the most underrated."[36] For or against, the crucial point is that evaluation drives literary history. Jeffrey is interesting, I would claim, not because his pronouncements are "right" or "wrong." Johnson, too, made many pronouncements that look "right" or "wrong" to later generations. Nor is the issue whether he had, or had not, a first-rate mind. The key point for literary history is the amount of influence he exercised from his central position in literary culture. In that sense, Jeffrey has been most assuredly underrated, for while the bald fact of his ascendancy has been recognized, it takes its place within an organization of knowledge that deplores his power to deprive Wordsworth of his due.

Francis Jeffrey's construction of literary history is essentially Wartonian, and thus deserves special attention, for, ironically, Jeffrey, the enemy of Wordsworth and, putatively, of Romanticism, had a much more decisive influence on the spread of Romantic literary history than Wordsworth, at least in this second formative stage, and thus, even more ironically, helped pave the way for Wordsworth's later successes. Because Wartonianism always involves some sort of transference to Pope, through a reading of Jeffrey we can be precise about the kind of pressure Pope applied on aspiring poets.

Writing in 1816, Francis Jeffrey, almost an exact contemporary of Wordsworth's, reflects back on his youth in the 1790s:

By far the most considerable change which has taken place in the world of letters, in our days, is that by which the wits of Queen Anne's time have been gradually brought down from the supremacy which they had enjoyed, without competition, for the best part of a century. When we were at our studies, some twenty-five years ago, we can perfectly remember that every young man was set to read Pope, Swift, and Addison, as regularly as Virgil, Cicero, and Horace. All who had any tincture of letters were familiar with their writings and their history; allusions to them abounded in all popular discourse and all ambitious conversation; and they and their contemporaries were universally acknowledged as our great models of excellence, and placed without challenge at the head of our national literature.[37]

The wonder for Jeffrey is not that the change has taken place, but that the essentially mediocre Queen Anne writers were able to hold the field for so long: "they may pass well enough for sensible and polite writers, – but scarcely for men of genius." The great change, stimulated by the Wartons, occurred by means of a re-evaluation of the Elizabethans: "The Whartons [sic], both as critics and as poets, were of considerable service in discrediting the high pretensions of the former race [the Queen Anne writers], and in bringing back to public notice the great stores and treasures of poetry which lay hid in the records of older literature."[38] Jeffrey's sense of satisfaction over his own contribution to what the Wartons began breaks through in an 1820 review of Keats with whom he was enchanted: "That imitation of our older writers, and especially of our older dramatists, to which we cannot help flattering ourselves that we have somewhat contributed, has brought on, as it were, a second spring in our poetry; – and few of its blossoms are either more profuse of sweetness, or richer in promise, than this which is now before us."[39]

The very sharp contrast between the native, northern genius of the Elizabethans and the imported, continental refinement of Dryden and Pope is the central recurrent opposition in Jeffrey's frame of reference. In 1812, reviewing Madame de Staël, he agrees with her that north and south are radically different:

We rather think she is right in saying, that there is a radical difference in the taste and genius of the two regions; and that there is more melancholy, more tenderness, more deep feeling and fixed and lofty passion, engendered among the clouds and mountains of the North, than upon the summer seas or beneath the perfumed groves of the South.[40]

Jeffrey disagrees with de Staël, however, over the causes, which she assigns exclusively to climate. He attributes the northern character rather to the independence of the tribes, and to Protestantism, which allowed everyone to read the "gloomy and awful poetry" of the Bible. One supposes it never occurred to Jeffrey that the melancholy poetry of the Bible, so congenial to the northern, Protestant genius, was actually composed in the luxurious warmth of the eastern Mediterranean.

Be that as it may, a year earlier than the de Staël review, Jeffrey set forth a Romantic literary history all of a piece with his racial and geographic one. In a review of John Ford in 1811, Jeffrey spoke of the Elizabethans in the most hyperbolical terms available. They are simply the best, ever:

The aera to which they belong, indeed, has always appeared to us by far the brightest in the history of English literature, – or indeed of human intellect and capacity. There was never, any where, any thing like the sixty or seventy years that elapsed from the middle of Elizabeth's reign to the period of the Restoration.[41]

The literature of this period, according to Jeffrey in another review, absorbed a little classical learning but "it was intrinsically romantic [i.e. Gothic, northern European] – serious – and even somewhat lofty and enthusiastic."[42] The Restoration, however, brought in "a French court" with "new corruptions and refinements."[43] It was here that "the wings of our English Muses were clipped and trimmed" in favor of "what was called a classical and polite taste," and English culture was reduced "to a province of the great republic of Europe."[44] Following upon the Restoration, Pope's era corrects the indecency of the court wits, polishes and improves the language, but still labors under the alien French influence. Jeffrey's view of Pope is a version of Joseph Warton's: "Pope is a satirist, and a moralist, and a wit, and a critic, and a fine writer, much more than he is a poet . . . He is much the best, we think, of the classical Continental school; but he is not to be compared with the masters – nor with the pupils – of that Old English one from which there has been so lamentable an apostasy."[45] Given such an opinion, we are not at all surprised to discover that Jeffrey, in his review of Campbell's *Specimens*, says he will not enter into detail on the question of Pope, but rather inclines to support Bowles.

Jeffrey's narrative essentially repeats the eighteenth century's self-understanding of its role as a refiner of the tradition. The key difference is that Jeffrey thinks it was a bad thing. In Dryden, he says, the struggle took place between the genius of the French and English schools: "But the evil principle prevailed!"[46] But refinement, as we shall see, appears to be a necessary evil, as a deeper look at the contradictions that Jeffrey inherited from his critical precursors will reveal.

The condemnation of Pope's tradition, ironically, went together with a recognition that refinement, both in verse and in manners or sentiments, was an essentially positive "modern" value. Isaac Reed, prefacing a 1780 edition of Dodsley's *Old Plays* (1744), represents general opinion when he states: "The polish of modern fashions ill agrees with the barbarity of ancient manners."[47] Reed refers to the fifteenth and sixteenth centuries, but a similar sense of incongruity between ancient and modern manners, and hence of impropriety in Homer became an issue in modern translation. Pope adapted Homer to polite taste quite successfully, but then criticism complained that his version wasn't Homer.

The contradiction between the value of refinement and the value of nature or origin accounts for a perennial dilemma. Goldsmith's observation describes a paradox: "The more polite every country becomes, the fonder it seems of investigating Antiquity."[48] The dilemma an artist faced in a politer world was diagnosed astutely by Wimsatt: "The main paradox of the romantic mind was that it yearned for a primitive or direct nature, yet was compelled to do this through the medium of its own historical awareness and introspective virtuosity."[49] In literary historical terms, closeness to nature undiluted by civilization, if this was how incongruously the courtier Spenser and the city dramatist Shakespeare were constructed, was simply no longer possible, even if "nature" was defined in terms of greater linguistic license. For if the "romance" tradition of the Elizabethans was considered the standard of great poetry, and the civilized refinement that followed it identified with a French falling off, there was still no going back. The only way forward was to combine the two in a synthesis.

According to Jeffrey, in fact, it was precisely this synthesis between ancient and modern that constituted Walter Scott's particular virtue. Here is the opening of his review of *The Lay of the Last Minstrel* (April, 1805):

> We consider this poem as an attempt to transfer the refinements of modern poetry to the matter and the manner of the ancient metrical romance. The author, enamoured of the lofty visions of chivalry, and partial to the strains in which they were formerly embodied, seems to have employed all the resources of his genius in endeavouring to recall them to the favour and admiration of the public; and in adapting to the taste of modern readers a species of poetry which was once the delight of the courtly, but has long since ceased to gladden any other eyes than those of the scholar and the antiquary. This is a romance, therefore, composed by a minstrel of the present day; or such a romance as we may suppose would have been written in modern times, if that style of composition had continued to be cultivated, and partaken consequently of the improvements which every branch of literature has received since the time of its desertion.[50]

What exactly the refinement of old romances entailed Jeffrey tells us directly: "It was his duty, therefore, to reform the rambling, obscure, and interminable narratives of the ancient romances – to moderate their digressions – and to expunge altogether those feeble and prosaic passages, the rude stupidity of which is so apt to excite the derision of a modern reader." What should be retained, however, is "the force and vivacity of their minute and varied representations," "the energy and conciseness," and "the lively colouring and accurate drawing by which they give the effect of reality to every scene they undertake to delineate."[51]

Jeffrey's criteria are representative, not at all eccentric to the early nineteenth century. Unfortunately, the attack on Pope has too often blinded later generations to the sorts of real continuity that exist between two supposedly antithetical literary periods. Again, individual value judgments are misleading – we must look instead to the framework of values that binds writers together even though they appear to disagree over particulars. Bishop Percy, we recall, had "improved" the ancient ballads in order to make them accessible to modern taste, much as Pope had modernized Homer.

The term "chaste," again applied both to versification and sentiments, was another way of figuring "refinement." Joseph Trapp, the first Professor of Poetry at Oxford, set Virgil against Ovid in these terms: "By this comparison of *Ovid* and *Virgil*, how tedious seem the Trifles, and how nauseous the Repetitions of the former; how various the Description, how diffusive, and yet how chaste the Elegance of the latter?"[52] Homer and Virgil, moreover, were frequently compared by critics, Pope and Johnson among them, in terms of the oppositions nature/art, sublimity/elegance. Virgil, in this scheme, borrowed his material from Homer, but improved upon his supposed roughness. Joseph Warton compared Homer to the wilderness of Mt. Atlas, and Virgil to the Capitoline in Rome in his "Preface Dedicatory" to Virgil's *Works*, but he also gave Virgil credit for sublimity; his style "is remarkable for perspicuity and purity, for harmony, brevity, and sublimity." Virgil succeeded in forming the ideal style, for he "is clear without being tame, and is lofty without being tumid in his expressions."[53] Homer's faults Warton attributes to the rudeness of his age, "but what Homer wants in *refinement*, he amply makes up in *nature*."[54]

The poetic values of the eighteenth century construct themselves, quite naturally, in relation to Virgilian elegance, for if "nature" was a basic value (no matter that it was constructed in multiplicative and contradictory ways), yet the age considered itself sophisticated. Johnson, for example, defended Pope's Homer by an appeal to Virgil. Pope's translation necessarily had to take into account not only differences in language and meter, but also "the change which two thousand years have made in the modes of life and the habits of thought"; Virgil, much closer to Homer in time and language, "found, even then, the state of the world so much altered, and the demand for elegance so much increased, that mere nature would be endured no longer." Hence, Johnson concludes, "what was expedient to Virgil was necessary to Pope."[55]

With the refinement of English poetry considered to be accomplished by Pope, we are not surprised to find Anna Seward speak of "the chastity of the heroic couplet" in connection with "the elegant style of Pope."[56] Pope, himself, had used the trope of chastity in an episode of *Windsor Forest* (lines 161–218) that meditates on the transformation of nature into art and its lesson for politics. In the complex allegory that structures the poem, Queen Anne, who has just brought peace, is opposed to the barbaric war-monger, William. In this particular episode, she is "chaste" (line 163), associated first with Diana, the virgin-hunter goddess, and then with Diana's nymph, Lodona, who was "chased" by Pan, but metamorphosed into the "chaste current" (line 209) of the Lodon river for her trouble.

If "refinement," "elegance," "chastity," and "polish" became code words associated with Pope's aesthetic, another way to define this Popean virtue was by the name of "good sense." Joseph Warton said of Pope that "*good sense* and *judgment* were his characteristical excellencies," and Johnson followed him with a famous passage describing Pope's poetical character:

> Of his intellectual character, the constituent and fundamental principle was Good Sense, a prompt and intuitive perception of consonance and propriety. He saw immediately, of his own conceptions, what was to be chosen, and what to be rejected; and, in the works of others, what was to be shunned, and what was to be copied.
>
> But good sense alone is a sedate and quiescent quality, which manages its possessions well, but does not increase them; it collects few materials for its own operations, and preserves safety, but never gains supremacy. Pope likewise had genius; a mind active, ambitious, adventurous, always investigating, always aspiring; in its widest searches still longing to go forward, in its highest flights, still wishing to be higher; always imagining something greater than it knows, always endeavouring more than it can do.[57]

Hazlitt, too, in the passage quoted earlier, spoke of Pope's "never-failing fund of good sense and refined taste." Jeffrey, for his part, cites "good sense" as a characteristic Augustan virtue. In response to the "gross indecency" of the Restoration, Jeffrey writes, the Queen Anne period not only improved the language, but suffused "through the whole of its irony, its narration, and its reflection, a tone of clear and condensed *good sense* which recommended itself to all who had, and all who had not any relish for higher beauties."[58] Hence, again taking his cue from Warton but expanding the hint from one poet into an age, Jeffrey concludes that circumstances favored "an age of reason, rather than feeling or fancy."

Wordsworth and Coleridge do not, indeed cannot, reject these virtues constantly associated with Pope. Wordsworth's argument with Pope, rather, is that he betrayed himself. The early *Essay on Criticism*, Wordsworth feels, "has furnished proofs that at one period of his life he felt the charms of a sober and subdued style, which he afterwards abandoned."[59] Wordsworth's own commitment to refinement is explicit in his criticism of what he calls the "natural and sensual school," which includes first Chaucer, and then Burns: "Crabbe, too, has great truth, but he is too far removed from beauty and refinement."[60] Part of the task of creating the taste by which he is to be enjoyed, we are told, requires "overcoming the prejudices of *false* refinement."[61] Wordsworth's delicacy is such that he deplores an inappropriate metaphor in "so chaste a writer as Cowper."[62] Wordsworth, moreover, appeals to "good sense" to shore up his argument about the decorum of "natural" language: "there are few persons, *of good sense*, who would not allow that the dramatic parts of composition are defective, in proportion as they deviate from the real language of nature."[63]

Coleridge, similarly, participates in the aesthetic of refinement. Indeed, the first excellence of Wordsworth's poetry that Coleridge lists is

> an austere purity of language both grammatically and logically; in short a perfect appropriateness of the words to their meaning. Of how high value I deem this, and how particularly estimable I hold the example of the present day, has already been stated: and in part too the reasons on which I ground both the moral and intellectual importance of habituating ourselves to a strict accuracy of expression.[64]

The attainment of such a style, he goes on, is "arduous work," and can only be acquired "as the result of watchful good sense, of fine and luminous distinction." Good sense, in fact, finds a respectable place in the theory of imagination. Working from Johnson's dialectic between good sense and genius in the "Life of Pope," Coleridge makes the distinction between good sense and "Imagination" in *Biographia Literaria*: "GOOD SENSE is the BODY of poetic genius . . . IMAGINATION the SOUL."[65] In a letter, Coleridge defines the value of good sense with more precision: "Poetry must be *more* than good sense, or it is not poetry; but dare not be less, or discrepant. Good sense is not, indeed, the superstructure; but it is the rock, not only on which the edifice is raised, but likewise the rock-quarry *from* which all its stones have been, by patient toil, dug out."[66]

If it is fair to say that Pope, especially after Johnson, is identified with "good sense," then "Pope" is an inseparable component of modern poetry, the rock, in fact, to use Coleridge's image, upon which it is built and from which it is quarried. Even for those who attacked Pope, those who no longer associated him as Warton did, at times, with sublimity, the assimilation and absorption of this more pedestrian virtue was a necessary requirement. Johnson's and Coleridge's managing of the issue reveals the implicit ambivalence of "refinement" and "good sense" as poetic values: they are necessary, but not sufficient.

The writers that follow Pope struggle with problems posed by the ambivalent nature of "refinement" itself. Can one be inspired, forceful, and yet refined at the same time? There was danger on both sides: one could be faulted for being too refined, but also for not being refined enough. As an example, the two writers Jeffrey praised highly for breaking with Pope's mode, Burns and Cowper, he also faulted for lacking refinement, Burns in his morals and Cowper in his versification.

The double bind of modern refinement issued in a polemical distinction between a "true" and a "false" version. Just as Longinus defined a true and a false sublime, and Addison a true and a false wit, so too there was a true and a false refinement. We find it as early as Swift, and a little later in Hume, who abhors "false delicacy and refinement."[67] Joseph Warton praised the naturalness of the diction of Dryden and Pope, who dared to introduce "common and familiar Words and Objects" in poetry, and censured their critics for a "fastidious Delicacy, and a false Refinement."[68] Wordsworth, of course, will accuse Pope of "false refinement." The distinction between a true and a false refinement in itself, however, shows the extent to which the later eighteenth century and the early nineteenth century accepted refinement as a value.

Practically speaking, the distinction proved useful because it allowed one to turn the tables on one's adversary: his virtue could be defined as a vice because of its excess. Hence D'Israeli observes how Pope was faulted for being perfect: "Pope carried his art to such perfection, as far as poetry is an art, that the very excellence proved injurious to his poetical character; it inspired despair, and his baffled rivals fancied they had broken the provoking spell by declaring it to be *nothing but Art!*"[69]

A major contributing factor to this development was the mediocrity of Pope's imitators. Perhaps no one was more unfortunate in his imitators than Pope, or perhaps his own perfection really was part of his downfall. Cowper put the problem this way as part of his defense of his own "roughness":

I know that the ears of modern verse-writers are delicate to an excess, and their readers are troubled with the same squeamishness as themselves. So that if a line do not run as smooth as quicksilver, they are offended ... For this we may thank Pope; but unless we could imitate him in the clearness and compactness of his expression, as well as in the smoothness of his numbers, we had better drop the imitation, which serves no other purpose than to emasculate and weaken all we write. – Give me a manly, rough line, with a deal of meaning in it, rather than a whole poem full of musical periods, that have nothing but their oily smoothness to recommend them.[70]

Following this passage, Cowper adduces the metaphor of the hair of the plum that should not be rubbed off for the sake of polish, proving unwittingly how relative his own idea of roughness actually is. He goes on, furthermore, to show that he is quite conscious of the importance of clear and smooth language: "I always write as smoothly as I can, but I never did, never will, sacrifice the spirit or sense of a passage to the sound of it."[71] But then, by Cowper's own description, Pope didn't either. The problem with those who have come after him is that they can't match Pope's compactness of meaning, even though they have acquired from him a certain musical competence. The result is emasculation, something that Pope's example has done to them, but also by a kind of transfer something that Pope has done to the language of verse. Thomas Campbell also complained that Pope was hampered by his imitators: "In order to do justice to Pope, we should forget his imitators, if that were possible." Pope's verse exploited by his followers he compares to "the most beautiful air ... played or sung by vulgar musicians."[72]

Gilbert Wakefield, a political radical and an admirer of Pope's, defended him in these terms in 1796:

That satiety, of which some complain in the poetry of Pope, must be explained in part from his consummate propriety of expression, his suavity of numbers, and that inculpable perfection which pervades the whole body of his compositions; and, in part, from the sickly fastidiousness and hasty misconception of the censurer himself ... It is not the insipidity of viands, but their luscious juices and exquisite flavour, that makes them cloy, and renders palatable even the neutrality of vulgar fare. It was neither the flatness nor poverty of the Archangel's conversation, but his energy of conception and his *charming voice*, that wearied our first parent, and opprest his sense,
 – strain'd to th'height,
In that celestial colloquy sublime.[73]

Wakefield's conception of Pope as the angel Raphael is the other side of the coin to Young's conception of Pope as the fallen Satan in his *Conjectures* (1759). Either way, Pope aroused strong feelings. Wakefield's defense of Pope from those who complain of "satiety" refers to the kind of revealing comment made by William Morfitt in the *Gentleman's Magazine* in 1790: "For my own part, I cannot read 200 pages of Pope together, without satiety."[74] The downright silliness of such a statement was not lost on another correspondent, M. F., who wrote:

> Mr. Morfitt complains of his satiety by the time he has read 200 pages of Mr. Pope; but I cannot consider this as decisive against the excellence of the poetry . . . Sure I am, I never could read 200 pages of *any author, on any subject, poetry or prose*, without a desire of relieving the attention by a walk, or business of some kind.[75]

It appears that even those who criticized Pope had a very high threshold of tolerance for what they perceived to be his faults.

The instability of the value "refinement," or, rather, the lack of consensus over who gets it right, creates further ironies from our more detached perspective. For Jeffrey, for example, it was precisely Wordsworth who was an example of affectation or false simplicity. Wordsworth is among those who failed to make the proper synthesis between old and new that Scott had made; the fault is to imitate the old without assimilating the refinements of the new:

> Southey, and Wordsworth, and Coleridge, and Miss Baillie, have all of them copied the manner of our older poets; and along with this indication of good taste, have given great proofs of original genius. The misfortune is, that their copies of those great originals are liable to the charge of extreme affectation . . . Their style is more remarkably and offensively artificial than that of any other class of writers.[76]

What for Jeffrey constitutes artificiality?

> . . . so much of the mawkish tone of pastoral innocence, and babyish simplicity, with a sort of pedantic emphasis and ostentatious glitter, that it is difficult not to be disgusted with their perversity, and with the solemn self-complacency, and keen and vindictive jealousy, with which they have put in their claims on public admiration.

It is only fair, nonetheless, to quote further, for Jeffrey feels that the "lake school," with all the faults of affectation, demonstrates fertility, force, feeling, and imagination strong enough to class them with a much higher order of poets "than the followers of Dryden and Addison, and justifies an anxiety for their fame, in all the admirers of Milton and Shakespeare."[77]

I have made the claim that "Romanticism" always involves a complicated relation to "Pope." In focusing on the various uses of the term "refinement," I have tried to show that Pope's example is continually present to the later eighteenth and early nineteenth century, the period that has been styled High Romanticism, and that supposedly has left Pope behind. But it is possible to go further. Jeffrey, by a reading similar to Wellek's, is Romantic, because he promotes, more effectively than others given his position, a version of Wartonian literary history, but did he also suffer a version of the anxiety of Pope's influence? It is not crucial to demonstrate this, but it would be interesting to do so because it would link Jeffrey emotionally, not just doctrinally, to the Wartons, to Young, to Cowper, to Wordsworth, and to the construction of Romanticism generally. In fact, I believe a case can be made that Jeffrey betrays the anxiety about Pope that the poets display.

In the following passage Jeffrey speaks of the despair caused by "them," meaning the Queen Anne's men, of whom Pope is the preeminent representative:

It was hopeless to think of surpassing them in that style; and, recommended as it was, by the felicity of their execution, it required some courage to depart from it, and to recur to another, which seemed to have been so lately abandoned for its sake. The age which succeeded, too, was not the age of courage or adventure. There never was, on the whole, a quieter time than the reigns of the two first Georges and the greater part of that which ensued.[78]

The Elizabethans, as we have seen, are mythologized in a way that suggests they function for Jeffrey as a compensation for a perceived loss in the present. They existed, according to this view, in a prelapsarian Eden. They were "Giants" whose characteristics were "great force, boldness, and originality; together with a certain raciness of English peculiarity, which distinguishes them from all those performances that have since been produced among ourselves, upon a more vague and general idea of European excellence."[79] The Reformation liberated them from tradition, while the paucity of writers and readers meant that there was not much competition; furthermore, no common standard of style or language enforced conformity. All these factors together led writers to depend on their own resources "without fear or anxiety."[80] The situation of the late eighteenth century was quite the reverse. Pope was the blocking agent, the writer who delayed the return to the true, native, national religion. If not for "the fine talents of Pope," we would have returned "to our original faith half a century ago."[81] The slight irony carried by the adjective "fine" sums it all up. Pope's achievement demands admiration, yet it is also the very symptom of decline.

It is not at all far-fetched to speculate that Jeffrey himself harbored poetic ambition in his youth. His subsequent failure and personal intimidation by the Augustans surfaces in his review of Burns, one of those originals who did break courageously through. Here Jeffrey laments "the effects of regular education, and of the general diffusion of literature, in repressing the vigour and originality of all kinds of mental exertion": "Among well educated people, the standard writers of this description [poets] are at once so venerated and so familiar, *that it is thought equally impossible to rival them, as to write verses without attempting it.* If there be one degree of fame which excites emulation, there is another which leads to despair."[82] He then pictures a young man of fancy and learning as the type *least* likely to succeed precisely because his head is filled with all the passages of excellent ancient and modern authors:

He is perpetually haunted and depressed by the ideal presence of those great masters, and their exacting critics . . . Thus, the merit of his great predecessors chills, instead of encouraging his ardour; and the illustrious names which have already reached to the summit of excellence, act like the tall and spreading trees of the forest, which overshadow and strangle the saplings which may have struck root in the soil below – and afford efficient shelter to nothing but creepers and parasites.[83]

One or two great souls a century are able to overcome such intimidation, but the natural tendency, and general effect, of education "is to repress originality, and discourage enterprise; and either to change those whom nature meant for poets, into mere readers of poetry, or to bring them out in the form of witty parodists, or ingenious imitators." Or, we might question, to turn them into critics with a particular axe to grind?

Burns was able to escape this fate, which was so clearly Jeffrey's, because he was not a gentleman, but lived in rustic circumstances:

Since that time [of Elizabethan Giants], although books and readers, and opportunities of reading are multiplied a thousand fold, we have improved chiefly in point and terseness of expression, in the art of raillery, and in clearness and simplicity of thought. Force, richness, and variety of invention, are now at least as rare as ever. But the literature and refinement of the age does not exist at all for a rustic and illiterate individual; and, consequently, the present time is to him what the rude times of old were to the vigorous writers which adorned them.[84]

Jeffrey, in his view of Burns, participates in a widely disseminated fiction, but one that suits a particularly appealing elegiac view of one's own position. The depiction of Burns as primitive and untouched is a projected myth, for, on his own evidence, Jeffrey knows better. Earlier he spoke of Burns's reading in these terms: "His taste for reading was encouraged by his parents and many of his associates; and, before he had ever composed a single stanza, he was not only familiar with many prose writers, but far more intimately acquainted with Pope, Shakespeare, and Thomson than nine tenths of the youths that now leave our schools for University."[85]

Jeffrey, one of the discontented civilized, embodies in his own self-consciousness the theses proposed by Bate and Bloom on the repressive effects of culture on those who think of themselves as having arrived late. Jeffrey's example, which is by no means isolated or unique, shows us, however, that the repressive force is closely associated with Popean refinement and elegance, and specifically not the towering presence of Milton and Shakespeare, who are understood as giants, certainly, but as products of a more primitive and unrestricted era. The thesis that "Pope" was the central problem is reinforced by the following observations of D'Israeli on the Pope Controversy:

> Whenever any class, or any form of literature has touched its meridian, Art is left without progressive power; there are no longer inventors or improvers; excellence is neutralised by excellence, and hence a period of languor succeeds a period of glory. At such a crisis we return to old neglected tastes, or we acquire new ones which in their turn will become old; and it is at this critical period that we discover new concurrents depreciating a legitimate and established genius whom they cannot rival, and finally practising the democratic and desperate arts of a literary Ostracism.[86]

Quite clearly, from at least one perspective of 1820, Pope is the "established genius" who, because of the crisis caused by his having brought art to its "meridian," now suffers the illegitimate attacks of lesser talents. According to D'Israeli, the recourse to older tastes is a direct consequence of such a crisis, which is exactly how Thomas Warton explained the rise of the "school of Milton." Warton and D'Israeli agree on this point, even though they stand on opposite sides of the issue, and interpret the dynamic differently. But those who defended Pope, like Byron, took for granted what we call the Freudian psychology. Byron, we remember, called Bowles a "parricide."

The psychology of the "father complex" that Freud would later formulate, and Bloom apply to literary history, seems irrefutably part of the way in which early nineteenth-century writers saw their own relation to Pope, regardless of whether their personal response to it was positive or negative. It is no part of my argument to enter into the question of which aesthetic is ultimately "right" or "wrong" because I consider that a fruitless undertaking. And, in fact, one of the unavoidable conclusions is the extent to which the disputants share much common ground as to basic values, and that "Pope" was simply subsumed into the later aesthetic, just as Thomas Warton subsumed Pope's "Eloisa," while transferring the credit from Pope to Milton. What I do feel is important, however, is the recognition that an entire context for understanding the eighteenth and early nineteenth centuries has been lost because of the partisanship that the controversy evokes.

I have focused, for the most part, on what appear to be aesthetic issues. The underlying continuity between the eighteenth and the nineteenth centuries can be described in aesthetic terms, but it may be useful to turn to the broader social context as a means of understanding the inevitability of that continuity.

The aesthetic value of "refinement," it appears, is essentially a counterpart to social changes on the one hand and to technological progress on the other. Susan Staves addresses the social context of Pope's popular reception by noting the way that "Pope created a new poetry suited to a new class, a class which may be called the 'class of the polite,' or the 'class of the refined.'" She explains:

Refinement was not simply an aesthetic virtue, it was also a social virtue. A person of refinement was a person of sensibility and humanity, someone far removed from coarseness or brutality. On the one hand, refinement was a critique of older aristocratic styles of behavior, including resort to physical violence. On the other hand, refinement, by definition not accessible to the vulgar, was the upwardly mobile virtue of the formerly vulgar bourgeoisie. The new class of the polite was more inclusive than the old aristocracy, comprising all those who could manage to describe themselves as ladies and gentlemen: aristocrats, certainly, if they did not disqualify themselves by brutal behavior; gentry, if they were willing and able to be presentable in society; professional men, barristers, solicitors, even well-bred attorneys and newly fashionable doctors; merchants, bankers, artists – and the wives of all these gentlemen who were willing to go to the theater to see *Cato* or to converse with their friends about Mr. Newton's theories as related by *The Spectator*.

The crucial distinction, Staves goes on, becomes the one between the polite and the vulgar, not between the aristocrat and the commoner. The quality of Pope's verse that appealed to this broad "class of the refined" was "the civilized colloquialism of his diction" that overcame the traditional distinction between high and low styles by establishing an "urbane middle style."[87]

Technological progress, on the other hand, assured that refinement as a social value would be closely tied in with the gradual taming of the environment. Sidney Smith, at the age of seventy-three in 1844, listed nineteen changes that had occurred in England since he was born in 1771 (a year after Wordsworth). They included macadam highways, wooden-paved streets in London, gas lighting, cheap and maneuverable cabs, umbrellas and waterproof hats, medicines, the penny post, banks for the savings of the poor, and the ubiquity of the police force making a walk across London safer than it had ever been.[88]

The value of such social changes has been debated by recent critics. The effect of standardized, or refined language, John Barrell observes, was double: it allowed some people to rise through education, but it existed, and continues to exist, as a barrier to keep others out.[89] As true as this is, it is hard for me to see the trend toward levelling distinctions based on birth as a pernicious force. The explicit call for a society based on the tolerance of differences began, perhaps, with the need for religious toleration, but it is the virtue of our own moment that we have moved such ideals to the center of our political consciousnesses.

The poetry that Wordsworth rebelled against has been likened by M. H. Abrams to a "literary *ancien régime*."[90] The analogy suggests a decadent aristocracy that we are well rid of. But, whatever the effects of the French Revolution, the key revolutions in England took place in the seventeenth century. Living with the consequences of those upheavals, Pope opposed himself to the fanaticist claims of religious enthusiasm as well as to the vulgarity of aristocratic rakes. Technically perfect, his style was urbane, sophisticated, and accessible. He managed to appeal to the values of the landed aristocracy, but made those values widely available to the literate middle classes. In fact, the landowners were in the forefront of economic development, so that, unlike in France, the upper and middle classes were natural allies.[91] It was for all of these reasons that Pope maintained his ascendancy for so long. If we take the long view, Pope's poetry, however much diminished from its once dominant influence, would begin to lose its hold altogether only when the Greek and Latin classics, upon which so much of its framework of reference depends, ceased to be the common property of the majority of readers. At this point, and only here, could Pope be represented as part of an *ancien régime*. He had mixed and parodied the high genres in colloquial language, hence his almost novelistic modernity, but once the old generic codes became obscured, he himself became part of what Bakhtin calls the "absolute past" of epic, closed off from contemporaneity. One might say that the classics simply became refined out of existence as subjects closer to home began to be taken seriously. Yet the high genres encoded structures of feeling that could, and would be transformed. Wordsworth's role in refining upon Pope in this way was central.

Refinement had both social and formal dimensions. Thus, even as the substance of Pope's poetry lost its social context, refinement in the sense of formal propriety continued to seem important. As late as 1882, Popean refinement could be explicitly evoked as a standard of taste. An anonymous writer in *Cornhill Magazine* praised Tennyson, the present Laureate, for combining the virtues of two systems, "the elegance and finish of the Twickenham school, with the deeper insight, higher aspirations, and more subtle sympathies of the Lake school of poetry."[92] Even beyond Tennyson, however, into the twentieth century, effects can be traced. One example: Wallace Stevens' college notebook shows that "elegance," defined as "perfection of style," was illustrated by his teacher, Barrett Wendell, by reference to Pope.[93]

CHAPTER THREE

Wordsworth's Pope

The history I have been recounting is one of rivalry between males. Such a story may be criticized as narrow and exclusive. Yes, but that is precisely the point. To analyze how this dynamic has operated in literary history is not to endorse its values or to suggest that this is the only story. But in the case of Romanticism, with its emphasis on originality and its condescension to Pope, it is a story worth telling. The mechanism of the oedipal confrontation, as Neil Hertz describes it in the context of Kant's mathematical sublime, allows for a reduction of diversity into a definable conflict. It clarifies things: hence, the "*wish* is for the moment of blockage, when an indefinite and disarrayed sequence is resolved (at whatever sacrifice) into a one-to-one confrontation, when numerical excess can be converted into that supererogatory identification with the blocking agent that is the guarantor of the self's own integrity as an agent."[1] Translated into a particular historical context, this statement reads: it is not an accurate reconstruction of literary history to say that Pope is the only important influence on Wordsworth, or even that all influences are "oedipal," for a great diversity of factors both poetical and more broadly historical are in evidence; but it is true to say that Wordsworth, like others before him, focused his hostilities on a constructed "Pope" that helps him define himself and that he saw himself as displacing. The succession thus takes place by identifying the "enemy," and by sharpening and reducing the image of this precursor into a convenient point of departure. The early attachment to that figure, the debt of pleasure one owes to that work and its continuing effects, will be silently passed over. The choice of Pope was inevitable for the later eighteenth century given his achievement, which Stuart Curran describes in terms of the pastoral, but which may be taken for the impact of the whole. Pope, he notes, is the central figure for "exhausting the possibilities of classical imitation and for transforming the Renaissance Christian pastoral to the requirements of modern civilization."[2] To write modern poetry after this required the poet to operate the same procedure of transformation on Pope that Pope had accomplished with the Renaissance.

The first poem we have that Wordsworth wrote is a school exercise at Hawkshead in 1784–85, which, in his own words, is "a tame imitation of Pope's versification, and a little in his style."[3] He must have been reading Pope at a very young age indeed; when he thought of writing poetry, he thought naturally of Pope. Having begun with Pope, however, Wordsworth came to the Wartons at an early stage in his development. Bowman, the Headmaster of Hawkshead, put the Wartons in his hands, and his reading was by no means superficial.[4] Wordsworth's translations of the *Georgics* show lines influenced by Joseph Warton's criticism of Pope's adaptions of the same passages.[5] Wordsworth's later criticisms of Pope are not simply repetitions, but actually intensifications of the Wartonian view. Gradually, Wordsworth leavened Pope with Goldsmith and many others in the poems written by the undergraduate at Cambridge. These poems have been studied, most recently by Paul Sheats, Edwin Stein, and Bruce Graver.[6] I will not focus on the details of Wordsworth's stylistic development other than to note in passing two interesting points. First, in his collected works Wordsworth designated everything he wrote up to the age of twenty-seven as Juvenilia.[7] Second, the development of his mature style shows how, stylistically, ontogeny recapitulates phylogeny: he begins with Pope and works his way through eighteenth-century developments until he discovers his own voice. Not that he leaves anything behind; as Edwin Stein's detailed tracking shows, the eighteenth-century poets remain with Wordsworth as points that continue to orient him. The lesson to draw is that "originality" is not a power creating something from nothing, but rather a power that works transformations from within a system of discourse. Originality is relational; it is a process of transference, or transplanting. Wordsworth's great success, part of the unique power of his mature style, is to assimilate previous poetry so fully to his own voice that he effaces it as origin while adding depth and strength to his own verse. I cite Curran once again:

At his best, Wordsworth always seems beyond the reach of art: spontaneous, fresh, neither bound by old traditions nor vestured in the fashions of his time. Still, it is reasonable to suppose that the art that successfully poses as pure originality may be the most sophisticated there is. That art Wordsworth possessed in abundance.[8]

But while work on the early poetry registers Pope's influence, it would be a mistake to assume that Wordsworth simply outgrew Pope with his early style. In this chapter I will look at Pope's influence on the mature work, particularly its impact at the moment of breakthrough in 1798–99. If Wordsworth's peculiar greatness begins to appear in *Tintern Abbey*, and in the two-part *Prelude* of 1799, then the recognition of Pope in these works becomes particularly significant. Wordsworth's greatness, I claim, is not to be found in his rejection of Pope's "classicism," so much as in his successful use of it. Before turning to specific readings, however, I must establish the general case for Wordsworth's anxiety of influence, for it is not enough to document, as I have done in the previous chapter, the pervasive anxiety over Pope that affects many writers from the 1740s through the 1790s. We must see this pattern at work in Wordsworth himself.

We are familiar with the terms of Wordsworth's condemnation of Pope from the Preface to *Lyrical Ballads*, the *Essay on Epitaphs*, the Essay, Supplementary to the Preface of 1815, and from comments in various letters. For Wordsworth it is a question of nature versus artifice. Pope's "false refinement," accordingly, is condemned through metaphors of seduction, witchcraft, disease, corruption, and poison. Commenting, for example, on an epitaph written by Lord Lyttelton for his daughter, Wordsworth writes:

Lord Lyttelton could not have written in this way upon such a subject, if he had not been seduced by the example of Pope, whose sparkling and tuneful manner had bewitched the men of letters his Contemporaries, and corrupted the judgment of the Nation through all ranks of society.[9]

Elsewhere he notes of a collection of eighteenth-century epitaphs that "there is scarcely one which is not thoroughly tainted by the artifices which have overrun our writings in metre since the days of Dryden and Pope," and goes on to speculate that we do not recoil in horror from this debasement of poetry because literature has "cooperated with other causes insidiously to weaken our sensibilities, and deprave our judgments."[10] In a letter to Walter Scott, the moral evil of "artifice" is viewed as a poison: "It will require yet half a century completely to carry off the poison of Pope's Homer."[11]

The very excess of these pronouncements raises, or at least should have raised, critical suspicion. Wordsworth's rhetoric fits the pattern of Warton, Young, Cowper, and Bowles, for whom the motive in attacking Pope was never disinterested. If Wordsworth was to create the taste by which he was to be enjoyed, he had simultaneously to subvert the prevailing taste, which as late as 1815, apparently, still enjoyed Pope. In the Essay, Supplementary of that year, Wordsworth complains of Pope's translation of "the celebrated moonlight scene in the Iliad" that "there is not a passage in descriptive poetry, which at this day finds so many and such ardent admirers."[12] Lawrence Lipking, however, has shown very convincingly that Wordsworth's fragment of January 1798, later titled "A Night-Piece," is a re-working of the Homeric passage based on Pope, even echoing key words. Set in context, Lipking shows how "the title itself issues a challenge."[13] We no longer see these kinds of connections, or see them intermittently, because we have been trained not to look. Wordsworth's Pope, the "Pope" depicted in Wordsworth's polemics, has become our Pope. The ultimate success of Wordsworth's polemic against Pope, however, has long obscured his real debt, for before the maturing Wordsworth came to see Pope as a threat to his own reputation, there was a time when he, too, admired Pope greatly. Like many of his contemporaries, like Lamb and Crabb Robinson for instance, he had most of Pope by heart. When accused of unfairly denigrating both Dryden and Pope, Wordsworth could reply with the curious non sequitur that he didn't disparage them because he had memorized them: "I have been charged by some with disparaging Pope and Dryden. This is not so, I have committed much of both to memory."[14]

Hazlitt, in *The Spirit of the Age*, also protested that Wordsworth had been unfair, even hinting that the motive was jealousy: "It is mortifying to hear him speak of Pope and Dryden, whom, because they have been supposed to have all the possible excellencies of poetry, he will allow to have none." When, in 1839, Wordsworth read this passage in Barron Field's manuscript, he burst out in indignation (for the second time) in the margin: "Monstrous again – I have ten times the knowledge of Pope's writings & of Dryden's also, that ever this writer had – to this day I believe I could repeat with a little previous rummaging of my memory several 1000 lines of Pope – But if the beautiful the pathetic & the sublime be what a Poet should chiefly aim at how absurd is it to place these men among the first Poets of their Country – admirable they are in treading their way but that way lies almost at the foot of Parnassus."[15]

Wordsworth's outburst (at age sixty-nine) expresses pure romantic literary history derived from its source in Joseph Warton, even to the specific denial to Pope of the sublime and the pathetic. The ambivalence of the pattern here – "I haven't criticized them, I have memorized them, they are second rate" – also fits exactly what we have seen in the Wartons and others, and suggests an interpretation along the lines of an anxiety of influence extending well beyond any specific echoing of lines or conscious borrowings. It must be admitted that the opening sentence of the third "Essay on Epitaphs," in which Wordsworth acts in the double capacity as defense attorney for "Nature" and as prosecutor of Pope, does sound vaguely parricidal:

> I vindicate the rights and dignity of Nature; and as long as I condemn nothing without assigning reasons not lightly given, I cannot suffer any Individual, however highly and deservedly honoured by my Countrymen, to stand in my way. If my notions are right, the Epitaphs of Pope cannot well be too severely condemned.[16]

Pope stands in Wordsworth's way, but Wordsworth feels slightly ambivalent about knocking Pope down: the poet who must be "severely condemned" is also a writer "highly and deservedly honoured." The same division of sentiment appears in that letter to Scott in which, just before observing that it will take fifty years to be rid of Pope's poison, Wordsworth first confesses "a very high admiration of the talents both of Pope and Dryden," and then concedes that "ultimately, as from all good writers of whatever kind, their Country will be benefited greatly by their labours." At which point a judicious balance must be restored: "But thus far I think their writings have done more harm than good." In cooler moments, of course, Wordsworth's judgment conforms to the general opinion: "The Poetic Genius of England with the exception of Chaucer, Spenser, Milton, Dryden, and Pope, and a very few more, is to be sought in her Drama."[17]

Ambivalence of this sort is explained in precise terms by the psychiatrist Murray Bowen, whose theories owe much to Freud, but whose practice breaks with traditional psychoanalysis by bringing the parents themselves into the therapeutic process. According to Bowen, although we are all emotionally fused in varying degrees to our parents, the attempt to differentiate ourselves in adolescence proceeds in an orderly or disorderly fashion according to the degree of differentiation established in early childhood. Emphatic denial of attachment during adolescence, what Bowen calls "emotional cut-off," should be read as an indication of undifferentiation: "the intensity of the denial . . . is a remarkably accurate index of the degree of unresolved emotional attachment to the parents."[18] In Bowen's terms, "Pope" represents for Wordsworth a literary "family of origin." The rhetorical extravagance of Wordsworth's denials of Pope's value, the attempt at the emotional cut-off of a writer whose thousands of lines still hold the memory of the seventy-year-old poet, signals that Wordsworth is actually more emotionally fused to Pope than he could ever possibly admit. Wordsworth's strategy for dealing with this early fusion takes the form of keeping it in the past. Those thousands of lines of Pope's poetry, however, despite repression, will help determine and shape Wordsworth's poetry, for they played a significant role in the growth of the poet's mind. Before looking directly at that influence, I turn first to note the ironic presence of Pope in the Essay, Supplementary.

THE ESSAY, SUPPLEMENTARY TO THE PREFACE, 1815

Stung by the effect that Jeffrey's criticisms, most recently of *The Excursion*, were having on the sale of his poetry, Wordsworth prefixed the Essay, Supplementary to the 1815 edition of his poems. Ironically, however, for an Essay that attacks the taste associated with Dryden, Pope, and Johnson, three echoes of Pope serve to reinforce the main argument. Two of these are especially significant.[19] When, speaking of Percy's collection of ballads, Wordsworth writes that "Dr. Johnson, 'mid the little senate to which he gave laws, was not sparing in his exertions to make it an object of contempt,"[20] he calls upon his readers' knowledge of Pope's *Epistle to Dr. Arbuthnot*, where Atticus is portrayed as one who,

> Like *Cato*, give[s] his little Senate laws,
> And sit[s] attentive to his own applause. (lines 209-10)

Thus Wordsworth achieves his satiric effect here by drawing a parallel between Johnson and Pope's portrait of Addison as literary dictator. The drama is double: while overtly attacking Pope and his allies, Wordsworth covertly draws upon Pope's satiric authority by means of allusion.

The same strategy is employed in the attack on Macpherson: "All hail, Macpherson! hail to thee, Sire of Ossian! The Phantom was begotten by the snug embrace of an impudent Highlander upon a cloud of tradition."[21] In the first sentence, the editors point out, Wordsworth echoes Shakespeare, troping upon the witch's address to Macbeth, and thus raising the specter of usurpation. But in the second sentence, as prelude to a discussion of plagiarism, Wordsworth echoes Pope's treatment of a plagiarist in Book II of *The Dunciad*. There the prize for the footrace that Dulness fashions out of air, which will be embraced vainly by the winner, Curl, is made to look like the plagiarist, James Moore Smythe:

> Never was dash'd out, at one lucky hit,
> A fool, so just a copy of a wit;
> So like, that critics said, and courtiers swore,
> A Wit it was, and call'd *the phantom* More. (lines 47-50, my emphasis)

Thus when Wordsworth labels Ossian "the Phantom" he casts Macpherson in the role of a dunce, and assumes for himself the cultural authority of Pope's persona in *The Dunciad*, that of the isolated prophetic voice who decries the degenerated culture of his day.[22]

These few explicit echoes illuminate the broader insight that Wordsworth's polemical strategy, complex as it is, is informed in many ways by the techniques and values of Popean satire. Jonathan Wordsworth reinforces my sense that this is so when he suggests of the famous "language-as-counter-spirit" passage that "in its way the force let loose resembles the apocalyptic dulness of *Dunciad*, Book IV, but it is felt as a personal fear."[23] The seizure of the high moral ground, the tone of prophetic indignation, the equation of art and morality, the depiction of literary enemies as agents of degeneration – all these characteristics place Wordsworth's polemics in the tradition of Tory satire that demonizes its object.[24] Here, however, Satan, Sin, and Death are Dryden, Pope, and Johnson for, in an astonishing reversal, Pope himself is now a dunce, someone who pandered to the public because he was seduced by an over-love of immediate popularity (a temptation, by the way, to which Wordsworth was not exposed). Pope was "someone who bewitched the nation by his melody, and dazzled it by his polished style, and was himself blinded by his own success."[25] Pope now is cast in terms of his own satiric creation, the Wizard of *Dunciad* IV (lines 516f.), the Magus of Dulness who, in Pope's own note to the passage, is described as putting the country to sleep with his "*Cup* of *Self-love*," misleading the nation through his own narcissistic self-aggrandizement.

If I am right, however, about Wordsworth's youthful love for Pope, one should expect some measure of sympathetic connection, however hidden, and indeed it is there. For if the Essay argues that original poets are not immediately popular because the taste of the public is not prepared for them, it follows that Pope was popular because he was not original. But that is not Wordsworth's claim. Pope *was* an original, but chose to lower himself, which he could not have done had he "confided more in his native genius." Thus Pope's story, as told by Wordsworth, is the tragedy of a great poet who made the wrong moral choices, the issue of which was a vicious style. In a letter to Alexander Dyce, Wordsworth again imputes to Pope a knowledge of the better path. Commenting first on Thomson, Wordsworth is led to the judgment that Thomson, Collins, and Dyer "had more poetic Imagination than any of their Contemporaries, unless we reckon Chatterton as of that age – I do not name Pope, for he stands alone – as a man most highly gifted – but unluckily he took the Plain, when the Heights were within his reach."[26]

The drama becomes complicated further by the Essay's implicit claim that a taste for Pope's poetry, or poetry associated with Pope, is a sign of regression. The Essay's opening sentence sets the foundation of the argument:

> With the young of both sexes, Poetry is, like love, a passion; but, for much of the greater part of those who have been proud of its power over their minds, a necessity soon arises of breaking the pleasing bondage; or it relaxes of itself; – the thoughts being occupied in domestic cares, or the time engrossed in business.[27]

The only reliable critics are those who continue to cultivate poetry "*as a study*," for only they pass beyond the passions and delusions of youth to form accurate judgments based on reasoned principles. The majority of readers, however, whatever advance their understandings make in practical affairs, "have not, at this art [poetry], advanced in true discernment beyond the age of youth":

> If, then, a new poem fall in their way, whose attractions are of that kind which would have enraptured them during the heat of youth, the judgment not being improved to a degree that they shall be disgusted, they are dazzled; and prize and cherish the faults for having had power to make the present time vanish before them, and to throw the mind back, as by enchantment, into the happiest season of life.[28]

No wonder, then, that "such Readers will resemble their former selves also in strength of prejudice, and an inaptitude to be moved by the unostentatious beauties of a pure style."

Let me draw the threads together. If it is true that Wordsworth, like so many of his generation, was, in his own terms, "beguiled" into an admiration for the poetry of Pope at a time when passion predominated; if Pope was an early model for the fourteen-year-old poet at Hawkshead; and if Pope is thus identified with a "former self," then the Essay, Supplementary can be read as dramatizing an internal conflict, a conflict in which the identity of the mature poet is constituted by his denial of his youthful self. Whatever Pope was then, now he is an evil other, whose self-love compromised his genius, and whose poetry, dazzling and enchanting, appeals to the blind passions of youth, and therefore represents the danger of regression in maturity. Ironically, the denial is accomplished rhetorically by evoking the terms of Popean satire.

FORMING THE HEART

The question of unformed youthful poetic judgment is handled more sympathetically in the scene that ends Book V of *The Prelude* (1805). The young boy wakes for the first time to the "charm / Of words in tuneful order" finding them "a passion and a power" (lines 577–79).[29] The distinction between poetry and nature begins to blur as we see the boy and a friend so enthralled by verse that they recite it at dawn in the public road "as happy as the birds / That round us chaunted" (lines 589–90). In retrospect, the older man comments:

> Well might we be glad,
> Lifted above the ground by airy fancies
> More bright than madness or the dreams of wine.
> And though full oft the objects of our love
> Were false and in their splendour overwrought,
> Yet surely at such time no vulgar power
> Was working in us, nothing less in truth
> Than that most noble attribute of man –
> Though yet untutored and inordinate –
> That wish for something loftier, more adorned,
> Than is the common aspect, daily garb,
> Of human life. What wonder then if sounds
> Of exultation echoed through the groves – (lines 590–602)

Curiously, the poetry that the mature man, in this passage, sees as intoxicating, false, and overwrought, is redeemed, nonetheless, because it has a power like nature's to stimulate the boys' imaginations and lift them above themselves. The poet goes on to claim,

> in the humblest sense
> Of modesty, that he who in his youth
> A wanderer among the woods and fields
> With living Nature hath been intimate,
> Not only in that raw unpractised time
> Is stirred to ecstasy, as others are,
> By glittering verse, but he doth furthermore,
> In measure only dealt out to himself,
> Receive enduring touches of deep joy
> From the great Nature that exists in works
> Of mighty poets. (lines 609–19)

The passage appears to be structured by opposing ecstasy at glittering verse to the deep joy in nature caused by great poetry, but actually the relation between them is inclusive, for the youth intimate with nature responds to both; one pleasure is simply deeper, more refined than the other. The real opposition here is between "others" (line 614) and "himself" (line 616). It is not so much that there is no nature in "glittering" verse, but that Wordsworth has a finer sensibility than others, and has therefore advanced beyond the seductions associated with Pope, whereas others have not. Responding to the adjectives "false," "overwrought," and "glittering," R. D. Havens surmised that this poetry was Dryden's and Pope's, and I agree.[30] But in recovering his experience and observing that no vulgar power was at work, Wordsworth the autobiographer grants a more beneficial power to "artificial" poetry than Wordsworth the polemicist ever allows. This episode, in fact, completely undermines the sharp distinction between nature and artifice advanced in the polemical writings by implying that there are only degrees of art, and that the better the art the more it approximates nature.

Moreover, the specific content of this episode – intoxicated youth remembered from the perspective of sober maturity – manifests the general structure of Wordsworth's relation to Pope: youthful admiration followed by ambivalent critical distance. The same structure informs such poems as *Tintern Abbey* and "There was a boy," in which there is a similar desire for continuity and renewal. I turn first to *Tintern Abbey*.

In the third and last section of the poem, the pivotal phrase "the language of my former heart" signals the displacement of the poet's youthful response to nature onto the "Sister." Let me repeat the passage for context:

> Nor, perchance,
> If I were not thus taught, should I the more
> Suffer my genial spirits to decay:
> For thou art with me here upon the banks
> Of this fair river; thou, my dearest Friend,
> My dear, dear Friend, and in thy voice I catch
> The language of my former heart, and read
> My former pleasures in the shooting lights
> Of thy wild eyes.   (lines 111–19)

But if the poet catches in her voice the language of an earlier self, I catch in his voice the language of Pope. Pope uses the phrase "the language of the heart" twice, once in the very widely known *An Epistle to Dr. Arbuthnot*, and once in the Horatian Imitation, *To Augustus*. In *Arbuthnot*, Pope pays tribute to the natural virtue of his biological father in these terms:

> Un-learn'd he knew no Schoolman's subtle Art,
> No language, but the Language of the Heart. (lines 398–99)

In *To Augustus*, a literary historical progress piece, he condescends to a poetic father, Cowley, in this way:

> Who now reads Cowley? if he pleases yet,
> His moral pleases, not his pointed wit;
> Forgot his Epic, nay Pindaric Art,
> But still I love the language of his Heart. (lines 75–78)

I do not wish to deny the drama occurring on the surface of *Tintern Abbey* – the man returns to a place five years later and reflects upon the changes in himself. Nor am I unaware of the presence of other poets. But it is clear that Pope is there in a significant way as well. The change of "five years" is an emotional chronology, not a historical-biographical one; after his experiences in France Wordsworth in 1793 was hardly an unexperienced youth wedded to the forces of nature. The structure of feeling in the poem is precisely a structure to which the content of Wordsworth's shifting relation to Pope fits as well as any other. For if the poem compresses together many sources into a single structure, the emotional content of Wordsworth's relation to "Pope" is significantly there in the very phrasing of the poem. That Wordsworth echoes a precursor, who with that very phrase describes *his* fathers, suggests a psychological subtext too rich to ignore. In terms of the notion "the child is father to the man," the phrase "the language of my *former* heart" alerts us to the uncanny presence of Pope as "father," or former self. If this phrase, by echoing Pope, refers obliquely to Pope, as I think it does, then the landscape of the poem associated with that former self is also literary, and the distinction between nature and art is blurred. In one sense, then, the language of the heart is the language of the poetry that one has by heart.

Walter Scott recalled a time, roughly age fourteen for him, when, he said, "to read was to remember." In this phase, this seed-time, the reader assimilates the text directly, identifies with it, without the intervention of the critical or philosophical mind. Reading then is swift, not yet come to be slow, tortured, and full of questionings. In *Tintern Abbey*, the cataract haunts the former self of the speaker "like a passion" at the time when nature was "all in all." This situation transposes easily to the case of the youthful reader. The cataract, or echoing waterfall, is a recurring trope for literary history in eighteenth-century progress pieces such as Gray's. The passionate response corresponds with the several places that Wordsworth identifies true poetry with passion. For the purposes of interpretation, the structural homology of the responses to both nature and poetic text allows for their mutual substitution. Hence, if we read "Pope" in place of "Nature," the emotional ambivalence of *Tintern Abbey* becomes symptomatic, among other things, of the repression of Wordsworth's youthful passion for Pope. As Wordsworth's memorization of Pope suggests, that poetry was internalized until it was "[f]elt in the blood, and felt along the heart" (line 28). Its influence was nourishing, and is still cherished, but, with the arrival of the philosophic mind (i.e. mature ego), it is, with regret, outgrown.

Yet, the narrative of maturity, the putting aside of the things of childhood, hardly does away with the sense that the former self is still present, even though it must be denied, and projected onto the Sister who now becomes the text in which is read "the language of the former heart." The anxiety of discontinuity, of being cut off from former sources of strength and consolation, is resolved by the appearance of the Sister. In keeping with the reading that separates out and identifies what has been repressed in the fusion of nature and poetry, we may recall what the ending of *Prelude* V says of poetry:

> There darkness makes abode, and all the host
> Of shadowy things do work their changes there
> As in a mansion like their proper home. (lines 622–24)

Here, in *Tintern Abbey*, the Sister's mind "Shall be a mansion for all lovely forms" (line 141), suggesting once again, by the common term "mansion," that these "forms" are both natural and textual. By means of projection, it appears, the "Sister" has become a receptacle for a split-off portion of Wordsworth's poetical memory. Why should this be so? First note that Onorato refers to Dorothy's role as a "fostering maternal presence."[31] We can speculate that the "father" (Pope) was transformed by repression first into a "mother" (Nature), and then into a younger sister. As in Bloom's explication of the term transumption, early has been made late.[32]

BOYS AND ECHOING OWLS

I have to agree with critics who have noted that Wordsworth's descriptions of nature are embedded with literary history.[33] One reads descriptions of natural phenomena, that is, and hears the still, sad music of textuality. The same is true of another poem, "The Boy of Winander," which was quarried out of the 1798 Goslar notebook, printed separately in the 1800 *Lyrical Ballads*, and finally incorporated into Book V of *The*

Prelude. The incident depicts the death of naive pastoral consciousness, but it also encodes that consciousness as a spot of time by representing it as an object of meditation for the older poet. The poet who stands mute above the grave of the boy contemplates, in effect, his lost childhood, a time when, as in *Tintern Abbey*, consciousness was indistinguishable from the natural world.

Signifying the bond of consciousness with nature in this poem, the owls answer the boy's mimic hootings, a naturalized version of the pastoral response topos. But as the naturalization of that classical immigrant might suggest, the "echoes loud, / Redoubled and redoubled" (*The Prelude*, Book V, lines 402–403) in this passage belong not merely to the owls; the prophetic line of the tradition is represented as well as it is redoubled through Pope's *Messiah*. I am thinking in particular of the point at which a version of apocalypse occurs, the gently traumatic moment in which the natural world no longer reinforces the child's desires, and the owls cease to respond:

> Then sometimes in that silence, while he hung
> Listening, a gentle shock of mild surprise
> Has carried far into his heart the voice
> Of mountain torrents.   (lines 406–409)

In Pope's *Messiah*, a startled shepherd sees and hears signs of the approaching divinity:

> The Swain in barren Deserts with surprise
> See Lillies spring, and sudden Verdure rise,
> And Starts, amidst the thirsty Wilds, to hear
> New Falls of Water murm'ring in his Ear. (lines 67–70)

Characteristically, Pope's conflations of classical and biblical material in this passage are quite complicated. The poem purports to be a rendering of Virgil's "prophetic" Fourth Eclogue from the point of view, as it were, of Isaiah, a combination praised by Addison, who printed it in his *Spectator*, and who thought that the inmixture of scripture made it superior to Virgil. But Pope's syntheses go well beyond his explicit sources. First, he combines two separate biblical tropes: one, the image of the desert suddenly blooming because of God's presence; and two, the "sound of many waters," which is one of the prophet's figures for the voice of the Lord. He further adds a sentient witness, the swain, drawn, apparently, from a conflation of similes in *Iliad* 4 and *Aeneid* 2 that also depict rushing waters. Here is Pope's translation of Homer describing the joining of battle:

> As Torrents roll, increas'd by num'rous Rills,
> With Rage impetuous down their ecchoing Hills;
> Rush to the Vales, and pour'd along the Plain,
> Roar thro' a thousand Channels to the Main;
> *The distant Shepherd trembling hears the Sound:*
> So mix both Hosts, and so their Cries rebound.
>
> (lines 516–21, my emphasis)

Pope's note to this passage alerts the reader to Virgil's transposition of it to *Aeneid* 2, where the simile is used to image Aeneas' shock at seeing his Troy burning and embattled below. Dryden's translation removes the element of hearing, so I quote Wordsworth's version (yes, Wordsworth's), which reproduces the rhyme in Pope's *Iliad*:

> High on a rock, the unweeting Shepherd, bound,
> In blank amazement, listens to the sound.[34]

By bringing these classical similes under a biblical influence and transferring them to the landscape of *Messiah*, Pope effects a shift in tone: the swain hears not "torrents" that figure the violence of war, but "falls" that prefigure a joyful apocalypse, the coming of the Messiah. Wordsworth displaces the tradition once again. His naturalized version in the Boy of Winander passage combines both destruction and apocalypse, or rather hints at the destructive element in revelation. Wordsworth's own variations on the prophet's "sound of many waters" recur at key moments in his poetry: in the cataracts of *Tintern Abbey*, or on Mount Snowden, or in the Blind Beggar episode, or in the Immortality ode. In "There was a boy," the trope appears to signify the ambivalence of transcendence, for at the very moment in which the illusion of nature as a nurturer of narcissistic desire is broken, this traditional trope for super-nature appears, an appearance which, eerily enough, seems to foreshadow the boy's death.

What I am suggesting, of course, is that Wordsworth's Boy of Winander is a romantic revision of Pope's swain. Wordsworth has personalized the situation, actually stepped into it himself and become the swain. The only verbal echo that remains undistorted is the word "surprise," but the moments represented in both passages – a listener struck by the distant sound of rushing water – are remarkably similar. There is no question about Wordsworth's familiarity with *Messiah*, for in his Appendix on Poetic Diction (1802) he cites it as having vicious diction "throughout." Wordsworth, it is true, could also have been influenced directly by the Bible, by Homer (in Pope's translation?) or Virgil, and perhaps all these make a contribution; but what John Hollander has felicitously called "the resonance of context" points again to *Messiah*.[35] For the boy in *The Prelude* V is juxtaposed to the "monster birth / Engendered by these too industrious times" (lines 293–94), an example of utilitarian education. The boy, a saving exception of education by nature, is precisely like an oasis in a "barren desart" of spiritual death. The crisis occurs because the pastoral reciprocity with nature does not survive the maturing of consciousness, so that its archaic existence as memory, or as poetry, is all that keeps it alive. With *Messiah* as subtext, the parable of Winander reads: amidst this desert, there was a boy (the description of whose experience of nature inscribes a figure associated by Pope with the approach of the Messiah), but the boy is dead.

Pope's presence just below the surface of "There was a boy" leads to further speculations about Wordsworth's relation to his precursor. The ironic treatment of the monster birth, for example, owes a debt to Pope's satire on education in *Dunciad* IV. Thus the juxtaposition of the boy and the monster birth for the sake of contrast brings into a small compass *Messiah* and *The Dunciad*, a positive and a negative apocalypse, the two conceptual poles of Pope's poetic world.[36] The way these texts are absorbed into *The Prelude* illuminates a more general Wordsworthian strategy. For if Wordsworth avoids apocalyptic self-consciousness by binding the imagination to nature, as Geoffrey Hartman has taught, he uses this same strategy of anti-self-consciousness to sublimate the "sovran voices" of literary history, a cataract of sounds received unawares into the heart.[37] I have read "There was a boy" in terms of its partial origin in Pope's *Messiah*, but, on another level, it is possible to construe its emotional structure as an allegory of Wordsworth's shifting relation to Pope: from pastoral harmony, to apocalyptic self-consciousness, to death by repression, to ambivalent elegy. Irreverent grave-diggers seeking the buried self of Winander would be shocked to encounter the face of Pope.

DIDO

In *Tintern Abbey* the pathos of the self dying into an uncertain rebirth, the kind of transformation particularly appropriate to the transition that was 1798, is reinforced by Wordsworth's identification with the tragic figure of Dido. In his letter to Scott of 1808, Wordsworth briefly commented on Dryden's translations: "As a Translator from the antient classics he succeeds best with Ovid." Since Wordsworth favored the Ovidian translations it is no wonder a particularly emotional line from the Ovidian Epistle "Dido to Aeneas" should stick in his mind. Near the close of the poem, the dying Queen turns to her sister, Anna, and addresses her thus: "Anna soror, soror Anna." Dryden's translation reads: "But thou, Dear Sister, and yet dearer Friend." The line is barely altered as Wordsworth/Dido addresses his/her Sister: "thou, my dearest Friend, / My dear, dear Friend, and in thy voice I catch / The language of my former heart." In these three lines Wordsworth put together, barely disguised, a line from Dryden and one from Pope, two poets, in his critical estimation, who are "harmful" influences on English poetry. The semantic content of the lines is related to their original contexts: pathos over a final separation, and filial affection.

Dido also figures centrally in the relation between Pope and Wordsworth embedded in the question "Was it for this?", which, as is well known, appeared in the Goslar notebook of 1798, and later became the enigmatic opening line of the 1799 *Prelude*. The context provided by the so-called "Glad Preamble" of the 1805 *Prelude*, which pushes the 1799 opening back some 200 lines, allows us to see that the "this" is the fallen state of the poet without inspiration, casting about for his theme. The question, made up of four of the most common monosyllables in the English language, is deceptively deep, as its pivotal position in the 1805 *Prelude*, and its originating role in the 1799 text, might suggest.

Jonathan Wordsworth noticed that Pope had used exactly the same phrase in *The Rape of the Lock*, and thus initiated a *TLS* correspondence asking readers to write in with other instances, with particular interest in any classical sources. In *Borders*, Wordsworth cites this correspondence, and concludes: "No striking classical source has come to light (in *Aeneid*, ii.644, for instance, the questioning is not developed), but it seems likely that one exists."[38] What I find of most interest in Jonathan Wordsworth's analysis of this passage is that, of all the possible examples, he chooses one from Milton that does not even fit the same verbal pattern. In a classical instance of Romantic literary history at work, Jonathan Wordsworth ignores Pope, and affiliates Wordsworth with Milton in these terms:

If ever there was a case of the anxiety of influence, it must be this. We can't know whether the *Samson* echo was conscious, but it beautifully catches the sense of Milton's presence looking over the ephebe's shoulders as he writes.[39]

One of the ironies here is that the passage in Pope leads us to the classical source in Virgil that Pope parodies, and that Milton, no doubt, had in mind as well. Unlike many things in Virgil, I can locate no previous instance in Homer. That classical source leads us back, once again, to the queenly figure that Wordsworth evoked in *Tintern Abbey*, the tragic figure of Dido.

Book 4 of the *Aeneid* can be read separately as a tragedy of a woman's struggle between passion and duty. In the final scene, abandoned by Aeneas, dishonored (and weakened politically), Dido decides to commit suicide, but without disclosing her intention asks her sister, Anna, to gather together all of Aeneas' effects in order to burn them in a gesture of apparent scorn. Then she climbs upon the pile and kills herself with a sword. Anna, in panic, rushes to the dying Queen, addressing her in these words as translated by John Ogilby in 1654:

> Her frighted sister, hearing, to the place,
> Beating her breast, disfiguring her face,
> Full of amaze and horror, breaks through all,
> And to the dying by her name did call.
> Did I this Pile for this, O sister, raise?
> For this design made I these altars blaze?

Deceived by Aeneas, Dido in turn deceives her sister but only in order to protect her, momentarily, from the truth. Anna's response to the truth expresses her own tragic recognition. At the close of the seventeenth century, in 1697, Dryden translated Anna's words like this:

> Was all that pomp of woe for this prepar'd;
> These fires, this fun'ral pile, these altars rear'd?
> Was all this train of plots contriv'd, said she,
> All only to deceive unhappy me?

The infelicity of that last line should not prevent us from focusing on the shifting verbal arrangement, which receives its final form, like so much else in the late Renaissance tradition, from Pope, in this case the parody of this scene in *The Rape of the Lock*. Virgil closes Book 4 by having Jupiter send Iris to cut a lock of Dido's hair which will separate her soul from her body and end her torment. The association of the lock was, no doubt, what led Pope to portray Belinda in terms of Dido (Figure 2).

Thus he opens his Canto IV with a direct translation of the first line of *Aeneid* 4. While readers have long noticed that particular echo, the phantasmagoric Cave of Spleen episode which follows appears to have prevented anyone from noticing that the scene in which Thalestris attempts to comfort Belinda is a reworking of the Death of Dido scene. The cut lock in Pope signifies, as Thalestris makes clear, not an actual death, but

Figure 2. "The Death of Dido," by Franz Cleyn, from *The Works of Virgil*, translated by John Dryden (1697), p. 327.

a social death for Belinda, and Anna's sense of tragic recognition is transposed here into Thalestris' sense of futile labor: was it for this fate that you spent so much time at the beauty parlor?

> Was it for this you took such constant care
> The bodkin, comb, and essence to prepare?
> For this your locks in paper durance bound,
> For this with tortur'ing irons wreathed around?
> For this with fillets strained your tender head,
> And bravely bore the double loads of lead?
> Gods! shall the ravisher display your hair,
> While the fops envy and the ladies stare! (IV.89ff.)

Belinda's reply to Thalestris parodies Dido's dying speech, and if we have not yet got the subtext, Pope alludes to it openly at the beginning of Canto V. Pope found his phrase by refining upon Dryden's translation of Anna, and in turn, his phrase influenced later translators such as Christopher Pitt. The phrase is overdetermined by the time it reaches Wordsworth. He could surely have Milton's Satan or Samson (more appropriately) in mind; but then why use Pope's phrasing, one linked so clearly to a particular Virgilian moment? The speaker of *The Prelude* suffers from a falling off, and turns back upon himself in almost elegiac accusation:

> Was it for this
> That one, the fairest of all rivers, loved
> To blend his murmurs with my nurse's song,
> And from his alder shades and rocky falls,
> And from his fords and shallows, sent a voice
> That flowed along my dreams? For this didst thou,
> O Derwent! travelling over the green plains
> Near my "sweet Birthplace", didst thou, beauteous stream,
> Make ceaseless music through the night and day. (I.272ff.)

There are several things to notice here: first, the way the literary context has been assimilated thoroughly to an autobiographical incident, suggesting again the merging of text and significant experience. Wordsworth here is both Anna *and* Dido. He addresses to himself the very words that Anna addresses to her sister. The mundane self of the poet gently accuses his more queenly, poetic self of betraying him. And it is precisely here, in the displacement of Pope–Virgil by internalization that he recovers his inspiration and his theme. Pope's straight use of Dido's tragic plea from Ovid's (and Dryden's) *Heroides* in *Eloisa* is not in sight; but, like Thomas Warton in "The Pleasures of Melancholy," there is a very close relation between Eloisa and Belinda as opposites, for Wordsworth's language recalls Belinda, but reverses the emotional valence of Pope's parody of Dido by recovering Virgil's pathos, and appropriating the situation of the tragic heroine to the situation of the poet at the turn of a very difficult century.

Another thing to notice is the way that a very important part of what is represented here is the generative and nurturing force of sounds that echo in the memory; the river "sent a voice" and made "ceaseless music," and the murmuring echoes (in this passage Pope and Virgil) are close to the point of origin, both physical and poetic. The sound patterns of anaphora and assonance, too, contribute to the sense of echoing: "alder shades and rocky falls . . . fords and shallows." The chiastic interlocking echo of the s's and f's further suggests such masters as Pope and Virgil. Note further that the sense of betrayal is extended to the river, almost as though the river itself were at fault, when he says, "For this, didst thou, / O Derwent!" The ambivalence and the identification associated with the oedipal crisis are present. The continuity that has been broken, causing the crisis of poetic self-confidence, is both the psychological continuity of the adult's sense of the child's "naturalness," and the continuity and naturalness of the river of poetic tradition. The recovery, I want to speculate, is caused, only apparently paradoxically, by a thorough repression that allows the narrative of origins by the side of the Derwent to displace the actual poetic origins in the "classical" tradition. The substitution of nature (in this case, a river) for Pope's language, as in *Tintern Abbey* and "The Boy of Winander," became the origin of what later generations, forgetting the Wartons and Cowper for instance, would identify as "Romanticism" proper. If Romanticism as we know it originates with the repression of Pope, it is also true that romantic pathos and sublimity are translated displacements of classical structures of feeling.

I recognize the difficulty of separating out one stream from the river of the poet's mind. The structure I have defined no doubt includes others – may, in fact, stand for Wordsworth's relation to everything he later came to think of as "artificial" in the poetry of his boyhood. But, as the echoes of Pope attest, the return of the repressed was inevitable, and that return may even have been essential to Wordsworth's imaginative integrity. If we keep Bowen's phrase, "emotional cut-off," in mind, a passage in *Prelude* XI ("Imagination, How Impaired and Restored") takes on new significance:

> Thus strangely did I war against myself;
> A bigot to a new idolatry,
> Did like a monk who hath forsworn the world
> Zealously labour to cut off my heart
> From all the sources of her former strength. (lines 74–8)

Using the metaphor of the wizard who dissolves in an instant "those mysteries of passion" which have made "one brotherhood of all the human race," the narrator tells us that the result is that "an emptiness / Fell on the historian's page, and even on that / Of poets, pregnant with more absolute truth." In this book we are told of the renovating virtue of "spots of time" by which "our minds / Are nourished and invisibly repaired" (lines 264–65). Though Wordsworth denounces Pope in prose, the poetry suggests a healing continuity in which Pope's verse, too, assumes the renovating virtue of a spot of time, for example as the buried self of Winander associated with a paradisal moment of youth.

At the age of seventy-two, Wordsworth wrote that "old men's literary pleasures lie chiefly among the books they were familiar with in their youth; and this is still more pointedly true of men who have practised composition themselves."[40] The return to Pope, and to the eighteenth-century forms of his youth, however, took place openly, and much earlier, in Wordsworth's translation of the first three books of *The Aeneid* into heroic couplets in the early 1820s. I opened de Selincourt's edition (IV.316) and chose almost at random:

> This by no doubtful signs Tritonia thew'd,
> The uplifted eyes with flames coruscant glow'd,
> Soon as they plac'd her Image in the Camp;
> And trickl'd o'er its limbs a briny damp;
> And from the ground, the goddess (strange to hear!)
> Leapt thrice, with buckler grasp'd, and quivering spear. (II.213f.)

This translation was a task imposed from within; it was not, for instance, commissioned by a bookseller, but was "an experiment begun for amusement," and appears to have been abandoned because of Coleridge's criticism that he was wasting his powers.[41] In a letter to Lonsdale, Wordsworth explained that he chose the heroic couplet, even though Virgil's hexameters are better suited to blank verse, and even though he is persuaded that Milton formed his blank verse "upon the model of the Georgics and the Aeneid." Blank verse, he explains, is not suitable because the religion, warfare, and manners of the people "are too remote from modern interest to allow it. We require every possible help and attraction of sound in our language to smooth the way for the admission of things so remote from our present concerns."[42] In other words, Wordsworth agrees completely with Pope and Johnson on this issue; so why did he attack Pope fifteen and twenty years earlier for poisoning the language with a vicious style in his translation of Homer? Even here, Wordsworth insists that his heroic couplets are freer than Pope's: "I ought to say a prefatory word about the versification, which will not be found much to the taste of those whose ear is exclusively accommodated to the regularity of Pope's Homer. I have run the couplets freely into each other, much more even than Dryden has done."[43]

Even before the *Aeneid* translation, in which he revels nostalgically in the poetic diction of his youth, Wordsworth showed signs that his resistance to the eighteenth century was beginning to weaken. Crabb Robinson objected to revisions in the 1815 edition of the poems, just as Barron Field was to object to similar changes in the 1827 edition:

And, first, I think I have detected a little disposition in your alterations, to mitigate that simplicity of speech, which you taught us was the true language of the heart, and to make some tardy sacrifice at the shrine of poetic diction; and thus, after having "created the taste by which you have been enjoyed," in a small measure deserting your disciples.[44]

It is convenient to assimilate this observation to the pattern of the revolutionary-turned-conservative, the political and the aesthetic running parallel. This would be a mistake. In the first place, if we accept Chandler's thesis that Wordsworth is already Burkean in 1798, then Wordsworth is *already* politically conservative when he writes the poetry that has been taken conventionally to be an aesthetic revolution. The political and aesthetic spheres do not always coincide so we should be wary in general of claims that draw analogies between poetic forms and politics. Secondly, revolutions in taste themselves need to be put into broader perspectives. Pope thought of himself as moving away from the seventeenth century in the direction of greater naturalness, and we have seen that contemporaries thought him at times colloquial. Wordsworth's "naturalness" needs similarly to be seen in perspective, for, along the lines of Coleridge's critique, there is much in his poetry that is very far removed from the everyday speech of our own time.

Keeping these things in mind, I will suggest another view, which is that Wordsworth did not really abandon Pope and then return to him, because Pope was always there, from his very first poem, to the epigraph of *The Borderers* that cites *To Cobham* ("It may be reason, but it is not man"), to the very important and interesting tropings of Pope in

1798–99, to the allusions in the Essay, Supplementary of 1815, and most clearly in the *Aeneid* translation. Barron Field made a shrewd observation when he said, "Mr. Wordsworth's genius has a kindredness with that of Pope's poetry, though an antipathy to that of his style. The human heart and character is the great province of both poets, and not mere descriptive landskip – nor 'arms and the man' – not 'the dragon's wing, the magic ring.' "[45] In closing, we may ask what most of all defines this relation, what, at the end of the day, did Wordsworth absorb, what was the lesson he learned? The answer, I speculate, can be found in a remark about Pope in the Preface to *Lyrical Ballads* that seems to have been overlooked. Talking about the power of verse as opposed to prose, Wordsworth turns to Pope as an illustration: "We see that Pope, by the power of verse alone, has contrived to render the plainest common sense interesting, and even frequently to invest it with the appearance of passion." This is a left-handed compliment, of course, which is what we might expect. But it is used, ultimately, as a defense of Wordsworth's humble subject matter. He continues: "In consequence of these convictions I related in metre the Tale of Goody Blake and Harry Gill, which is one of the rudest of this collection." It seems clear, moreover, that what he means by "verse" in this passage is very similar to what he refers to in the following sentence as "the power of the human imagination." In the Fenwick note to "The Thorn," we recall, Wordsworth defined imagination as "the faculty which produces impressive effects out of simple elements."

CHAPTER FOUR

Mirror and lamp

The continuity between Romantic values and academic critical practice in the second half of the twentieth century is an established commonplace. The details of these effects have been the subject of many articles and several books. Some continue to affirm that connection as healthy, and others wish to question it, but in either case the discussion often arouses fundamental passions, a sure sign that fundamental interests are at stake. In this chapter, I will question the nature of criticism's relation to Romantic literary history by focusing on M. H. Abrams' influential work, *The Mirror and the Lamp: Romantic Theory and the Critical Tradition* (1953). The sort of continuity Abrams argued for in that book, and which the book itself helped to establish, is well described by the editors of a recent collection of essays as "the end product of a line of critical argument Wordsworth himself had begun."[1] More than that, I agree with the assessment that this book laid the foundation for the modern study of Romanticism as it "began a long, slow, process of institutional recuperation fully consolidated only in the early 1960s."[2] Forty years after publication it is still in print. Moreover, its premises continue to be operative in those who have never read it, as well as in those who feel they have outgrown it, for the distinction it sets up between mimesis and expression (read "Classic" and "Romantic," or "Pope" and "Wordsworth") is part of every student's initiation into Romantic periodization in any survey course, particularly one that uses the Norton anthology. Its fate is what Johnson observed of Dryden's criticism: "Learning once made popular is no longer learning: it has the appearance of something which we have bestowed on ourselves, as the dew appears to rise from the field which it refreshes."[3]

In this chapter I set myself two tasks: first, to conduct a critique of Abrams' general argument; and second, to contextualize that argument in its moment of appearance in the mid-twentieth century. The second task is more difficult, for it involves posing a series of speculative questions. If Abrams' outlook is the "end product" of a line beginning with Wordsworth, then that line stretches back, as I have shown, to mid-eighteenth-century misrecognitions of Pope, meaning that Abrams is essentially Wartonian. The question then becomes, in what ways does Romantic literary history function for Abrams and the generations that follow him? Or more specifically, in what ways does Romantic literary history function allegorically in the twentieth century, what is "Pope" an allegorical counter for? For my assumption is that we are dealing with allegorical constructions that collapse the historical distance that exists between now and then.

Abrams' work, of course, has been criticized before. Ralph Cohen's review put the issue quite succinctly: "to identify a whole body of philosophical thought with a single metaphor is unnecessarily reductionist."[4] Others, however, have praised him for doing just that, for that is what has made the book so useful. More recently, Jonathan Culler's deconstructive critique assumes that Abrams is wrong on procedural grounds, that if you have a bold opposition such as mirror/lamp you must be dealing with a fiction, and shows that the two oppositions coincide in each other.[5] I agree with Culler, but it is not enough to oppose to Abrams a different set of values or a different method of criticism, or as others have done, throw doubt on the thesis by pointing out important mirror metaphors in the early nineteenth century. What must be written is a counter-narrative, drawing upon the same sources Abrams himself used, and presenting an alternative version of intellectual history enabling us to see a different possibility. The outline of a such a counter-narrative I sketch in the following pages.

MIMETIC/EXPRESSIVE

Abrams' argument is familiar, but let me review its essentials. It begins by defining critical orientations from Plato to the present according to their relation to the artist, the audience, the world, and the work itself. Theories are "mimetic" if their focus is the imitation of the world; "pragmatic" if their concern is the effect of the work on the audience; "expressive" if they focus on the poet's feelings and personality; and "objective" if they deal exclusively with the work of art. The thesis of the book is that there was a revolutionary shift from "pragmatic" to "expressive" at the end of the eighteenth and beginning of the nineteenth century. Yes, "pragmatic," for Plato and Aristotle, we are told, represent the "mimetic" approach, whereas the "pragmatic" orientation predominated from Horace up to the end of the eighteenth century.[6] The "expressive" explanation of art held the field from Wordsworth and Coleridge until "objective" theories, cutting the work off from both the poet and the audience, began to displace them in the mid-twentieth century.[7]

The only way that so reductive a narrative of intellectual history can be maintained is by operating two related kinds of de-contextualization: first, one must isolate statements within pieces of writing, selecting them out as representative of the whole work; and second, one must ignore historical and cultural forces that might account for differences of emphasis within a tradition of textual transmission.

Why, for instance, should one identify Plato and Aristotle exclusively with the mimetic orientation? The whole point of Plato's criticism of Homer in the *Republic*, one might easily argue, is that the influence of the Homeric heroes and gods on its audience is both powerful and undesirable, which suggests that Plato's approach is equally "pragmatic," according to Abrams' definition. The discussion of Homer, we recall, takes place in the context of deciding what is the proper education for the guardians of the ideal state. I do not argue that we should therefore categorize Plato as "pragmatic," for that would be to validate a similar reduction. My whole point is that such univocal categorization introduces procrustean distortions. If we want to employ such terms at all, we might ask, what is the relation of "pragmatic" to "mimetic" in Plato?

Aristotle's *Poetics* offers similar resistances to Abrams' history of criticism, for the treatise would seem to partake almost equally of "mimetic," "pragmatic," and "objective" assumptions. A tragedy is an *imitation* of an action, with the stated purpose of bringing about a catharsis of pity and fear in the *audience*, while the most effective means of doing so is the construction of the proper kind of plot, which is defined by *objective* criteria. Because Aristotle is defending poetry implicitly against Plato's attacks, he argues that the effects of tragedy are socially useful, and that art itself, so far from being a debased representation two removes from a metaphysical reality, is a skill that requires the highest genius. The "expressive" element, or the reference to the author, is given less emphasis, but it is present in the assumption that to make a tragedy requires a nobler character than to make a comedy: "Poetry now diverged in two directions, according to the individual character of the writers. The graver spirits imitated noble actions, and the actions of good men. The more trivial sort imitated the actions of meaner persons."[8]

If in Abrams' survey Plato and Aristotle are subsumed under "mimesis," Horace is said to inaugurate the pragmatic emphasis. Proof is the line that tells us that poetry must both please and instruct. But Horace's *Ars Poetica* conveys much advice, much of it admonitory, to a young nobleman ambitious to be a poet. As such, its approach cannot be represented by a single line. In fact, Horace rehearses a very wide range of artistic wisdoms that had been traditional since Aristotle. The inseparable relation between the construction of a good plot (objective) and that plot's effect on the audience (pragmatic) is a case in point. A crucial and recurring topic of discussion is the character of the author, so that the link between the character of the author and the quality of the work of art is quite explicit. For instance, Horace compares the character of the Greeks to the Romans to the disadvantage of the latter; the Greeks strove for fame and glory, not money, and "when this interest in commercial gain has stained the soul, how can we expect to have poems worthy of being preserved in cedar oil and kept in cypress cases?"[9] So far from being able to characterize ancient Greek and Roman thinking about art by a single orientation in a certain era, it looks as though the interrelation between what Abrams calls pragmatic, mimetic, and objective is consistently assumed, with the expressive present but given less emphasis.

Abrams' treatment of Sidney is similarly skewed. Sidney belongs to the "pragmatic" camp, as does all theory from Horace up to the Romantics, we are told, because he is so obviously concerned with the moral effect of poetry. But Sidney, of course, is responding to Stephen Gosson who has put forward a Christianized version of Plato's philosophical denunciation of poetry. Sidney's defense, therefore, must respond by demonstrating poetry's moral effects, but he goes further to claim for poetry and the poet divine origins. He defends not only the activity but also the character of the poet who engages in it. The essay includes all of the elements that are present in Greek and Roman criticism, but it adds to them the characteristic concerns of the Christian Neoplatonist.

The actual texture of Abrams' exposition appears less reductive than it actually is because every statement is hedged about with numerous qualifications. Abrams, it would appear, knows that his reading may seem one-sided, but he is confident that his generalizations are nonetheless true. I suggest, on the contrary, that the qualifications are so numerous as to render the generalizations purely a priori constructions. What is advanced is essentially an untenable generalization that is made to look reasonable by acknowledging the various qualifications of the thesis. Consider, for example, the following sentences on Aristotle:

I have chosen to discuss Aristotle's theory of art under the heading of mimetic theories, because it sets out from, and makes frequent reference back to the concept of imitation. *Such is the flexibility of Aristotle's procedure, however,* that after he has isolated the species "tragedy," and established its relation to the universe as an imitation of a certain kind of action, and to the audience through its observed effect of purging pity and fear, his method becomes centripetal, and assimilates these external elements into attributes of the work proper. *In this second consideration of tragedy as an object in itself...*[10]

Here, rather than construe the several aspects of Aristotle's theory as interrelated parts of a single view, Abrams, having isolated the mimetic, credits Aristotle with "flexibility" for including the others, and considers the discussion of plot to be in some way subsidiary to the element that has been isolated artificially in the first place.

At another point, here introducing the development of the expressive theory of poetry, Abrams states: "For convenience of exposition, I shall proceed topically, positing separately and in sequence developments that were in fact concomitant and interdependent."[11] What follows is a return to another tag line from Horace, this time as representative of expressive rather than pragmatic theory, and then the subsequent introduction of Longinus, whose treatise and influence had not been mentioned at all when it was claimed that criticism from Horace up to the Romantics had been "pragmatic." We need only substitute "poetry" for "sublimity," Abrams asserts, in order "quite to assimilate much of *Peri Hupsous* to the romantic pattern."[12] This is unsound. First of all, Longinus is very much aware of the pragmatic effect of writing on the audience which is why he opens his rhetorical treatise with a discussion of the false sublime. The true sublime is known by its effects, for "as if instinctively our soul is uplifted by the true sublime." Second, the reference to the author's soul is very similar to the connection between the work and the character of the author in the classical tradition; sublimity is "the echo of a great soul." Third, the emphasis on objective treatment is perhaps the driving force behind the work for to achieve the effect of the sublime requires art and technique:

A lofty tone, says one, is innate, and does not come by teaching; nature is the only art that can encompass it. Works of nature are, they think, made worse and altogether feebler when wizened by the rules of art. But I maintain that this will be found to be otherwise if it be observed that, while nature as a rule is free and independent in matters of passion and elevation, yet she is wont not to act at random and utterly without a system.[13]

Pope, no doubt, was thinking of this passage when he said, in a poem that praises Longinus, *An Essay on Criticism*, that art was "nature methodized." Longinus, it would seem, followed the classical pattern of thinking "organically" in terms of artist, form, and effect.

If this is "romantic," as Abrams says, then Romantic doctrine is best seen as a late version, under specific conditions, of classical humanism. And if that is so, then its divergence from the early eighteenth century will be a local matter of emphasis and self-conscious differentiation, based again on different local conditions. A constant distinguishing feature of "Romanticism," as I have argued throughout, is its particular relation to Pope's poetry. In terms of theory, the key relation is Johnson. Having asserted an epochal break between mimetic and expressive in the space between Johnson and Wordsworth, it is then odd to see Abrams detail how much of Wordsworth's theory is identical in terms and modes of argument to Johnson's.[14] It is even odder to read much later that the pragmatic orientation, "which denies that the judgment of poetic value ought to be severed from the consideration of the effects on the reader . . . continued to be affirmed by poets and critics right through the romantic period."[15] The difference, we are told, is that Johnson expected art to preach, whereas Wordsworth expected it to reform the feelings indirectly. Just in passing, let me remark that this is a "difference" that overrides many important distinctions and ignores similarities. Who will deny that Wordsworth himself is often intolerably preachy? Can we generalize from Johnson's remarks on Shakespeare's *drama* to make his prescription into a description of the actual practice of *lyric* poetry in his century? For, although Abrams' putative subject is the theory of criticism, a history of literature in which "feeling" replaces "reason" in the early nineteenth century is implicitly running parallel to his argument throughout. I think we are on much firmer ground with William Levine's description of the intertextual relations between Johnson and Wordsworth and Coleridge. Change occurs, but not as a radical break. Rather, "Wordsworth and Coleridge are part of an enterprise that absorbs, modifies, and co-opts the *Lives*."[16]

In a disarming way, then, Abrams offers us a procedure – "positing separately and in sequence developments that were in fact concomitant and interdependent" – that is totally unhistorical and that therefore distorts his historical material in a fundamental way. But these are merely preliminaries to his central claim about the "mirror" and the "lamp." We may overlook the paradoxes and blatant contradictions if, in the main, he has got it right.

MIRROR/LAMP

The odd thing about Abrams' exposition on the late eighteenth century is that the three orientations said to have displaced each other in a chronological sequence – mimetic, pragmatic, and expressive – suddenly reduce to two. Mimetic and pragmatic become conflated implicitly into "neo-classic" and are set against expressive in a binary opposition so that "the radical difference between the characteristic points of view of neo-classic and romantic criticism remains unmistakable."[17] At first, "neo-classic" seems to refer to "pragmatic," that is, Horace to Johnson, but it later becomes clear that the continuity is posited from Plato to Johnson in terms of the mimetic orientation since mirror imagery supposedly predominates in those twelve centuries or so between them.[18] If we were wondering why the reductive distortions were introduced into the history of criticism, what the point was of isolating elements "for convenience" and then arranging them in a chronological sequence, the answer has become clear – in order to set the stage for the notion that there is a radical, epochal break with the past in the late eighteenth century. This is much easier to accomplish if you have fragmented the texts in the first place, and dissociated elements from each other and their contexts. What drives the procedure is the a priori thesis, the notion that, however many continuities exist or however critics may differ within the same chronological period, "one decisive change marks off the criticism in the Age of Wordsworth from that in the Age of Johnson."[19]

This great shift, supposedly, can be traced by a change in the metaphors used to describe art.[20] Mirror, in brief, becomes lamp. Mirror metaphors are said to originate with Plato and to be continuous through Locke and the eighteenth century, while lamp metaphors appear with Plotinus and are prominent in the Cambridge Platonists who influenced Coleridge.[21] However, the isolation of Plotinus and the Cambridge Platonists (actually Neoplatonists, we are told) from the mirror tradition is, on the face of it, as dubious as the previous history that abstracted and isolated critical orientations in order to stage an "evolution."[22] One would have thought, again simply on the face of it, that Plotinus owed something to Plato. We need to go back to the texts in order to see that, in fact, mirror and lamp almost always appear simultaneously and for very good reasons. We need also to take a closer look at Locke, for Abrams, as a Romanticist, appears to have accepted at face value what Coleridge and Blake say of Locke and inquired no further.

Abrams begins his exposition of the history of the mirror metaphor with a citation from the tenth book of Plato's *Republic*, and comments:

> This illustration is not a casual one, for in his writings Plato reverts repeatedly to the analogy of the reflector, either a mirror, or water, or else those less perfect simulacra of things that we call shadows. These he uses to clarify the inter-relations of all the items of the universe: of things, natural or artificial, to their prototypes, or Ideas; and of imitations of things, including those in the arts, to their models in the world of sense.[23]

The mirror metaphor is then said to be "constitutive" of Plato's theory, with the implication that "lamp" or "fire" is constitutive of the expressive orientation, hence the fundamental difference. The mirror analogy tended to exclude or render marginal other aspects of the work and the creative process: "For better or worse, the analogy helped focus interest on the subject matter of a work and its models in reality, to the comparative neglect of the shaping influence of artistic conventions, the inherent requirements of the single work of art, and the individuality of the author." Hence, because of these exclusions, the history of modern criticism "may in some part be told as the search for alternative parallels."[24]

Once again, the error is to isolate an idea in Plato and to lift it out of context. I argue, on the contrary, that the mirror analogy in Plato is in fact related in a constitutive way to the metaphor of fire, and that one cannot understand Plato or the tradition that he inaugurated, stretching in all its variations of emphasis at least through Shelley, unless this interrelation is correctly grasped. The key text is not *The Republic*, but rather *Timaeus*.

The creation myth related to Socrates by Timaeus explains how the Demiurge created first the soul of the world, later Latinized as *anima mundi*, and then the body of the world, or visible nature. The world soul is pictured as an invisible sphere that turns harmoniously according to the rule of logos, that is, reason or proportion, giving us the comforting notion that the universe is ultimately turning according to rational principles. The harmony of the visible cosmos, the recurrence of the seasons and the order of the heavens, is the physical manifestation of the unseen rational soul of things. Human beings were created by the same principles, the relation between them being that of macro- to micro-cosmos. The soul of the individual is a miniature version of the soul of the world, hence it is said to "mirror" it, or to have within it all things *in potentia*. This soul, however, which is said to "mirror" the larger soul, is described by the metaphor of fire, a way of figuring forth its purer essence above the dross of matter.

Thus, the "fire" of the human soul "mirrors" the larger world soul, so that, indeed, as Abrams says, mirror imagery in Plato depicts the interrelations of things on a hierarchy, but this relation is one of fire to fire. Plato appears to have taken these metaphors almost literally, for when the eyelids are closed, Timaeus tells us, they "keep in the internal fire"; and when images appear in a mirror it is because of "the communion of the external and the internal fires."[25]

This basic structure, together with its imagery of fire/mirror, is one of the common denominators of Western epistemology among rationalists, empiricists, and mystics. It is Christianized by the Fathers along with the rest of Greek philosophy and it is a structure common to both Locke and Kant. Let me begin to substantiate this generalization, making certain necessary distinctions along the way. Since we are used to relating "fire" to the imagination as writers like Coleridge and Shelley describe it, we need to remember that "fire" was used originally to describe reason, or nous; and further we must recall that the elevation of imagination occurs only when "reason" becomes associated with what we now call positivism. A very direct remembrance of this ancient usage is found in Wordsworth when he states, toward the end of *The Prelude*, that Imagination

> Is but another name for absolute strength
> And clearest insight, amplitude of mind,
> And reason in her most exalted mood. (1805, XIII.168–70)

Another example of the old sense of nous or "amplitude of mind" is Johnson's reply to Robertson's assertion that "one man had more judgment, another more imagination. – *Johnson*. 'No, sir; it is only, one man has more mind than another.'"[26]

In order to see how these notions were transmitted, we could do worse than focus on the words "ether," and "ethereal." Plato's notion that the soul of man and the world was composed of "fire" was transmitted to Aristotle and the Stoics. Aristotle, however, differentiated between earthly fire, which could not generate life, and heavenly fire or "aether." Aether was thus sometimes called the fifth element. Aether is the active element in all nature, vital heat or spirit, and is the stuff, supposedly, that the stars are made of. For the Stoics the primary element of the universe, the seed of all life, sometimes called the "spermatikos logos" and identified with God, is fire. The human spirit, "pneuma," is a lower form, a mixture of fire and air.[27] The influence of Plato, Aristotle, and the Stoics is quite clear in Cicero who, among other things, translated *Timaeus* into

Latin; this was the version used by both Jerome and Augustine.[28] Throughout Cicero's philosophical writings, he speaks of both God and the soul as fire. In the famous Dream of Scipio passage, he wrote: "each man has been given a soul from those eternal fires called stars and planets."[29]

This philosophical tradition was transmitted massively to the Middle Ages and the Renaissance, but the most important literary source is Virgil. In the sixth book of the *Aeneid*, Anchises explains to Aeneas how the souls of the dead are purged of dross in the underworld:

> No Speck is left, of their habitual Stains;
> But the pure Aether of the Soul remains. (6.1011–12)

A little before this, Anchises had explained:

> Th' Etherial vigour is in all the same,
> And every Soul is fill'd with equal Flame. (6.988–89)

I have cited Dryden's translation of 1697 to demonstrate the continuity in vocabulary, but the philosophical notions would be just as familiar to eighteenth-century readers as the meanings of the words "aether" and "etherial." This is so not only because of their familiarity with Latin texts, but also because Christianity subsumed the pagan philosophical tradition for its own purposes. For instance, the incorporeal gods living in the aether in the outer sphere of the universe in Stoic cosmology were very easily translated into Christian angels. Aquinas provided an authoritative treatment of the angels in his *Summa*. Angels are fiery intelligences who mirror the Divine intelligence: "the intellectual light is perfect in the angel, for he is a pure and most clean *mirror*, as Dionysius says (Div.Nom.iv)."[30]

Aquinas' influence on Hooker and on the seventeenth-century Anglican divines is well documented. Abrams cites Culverwel's famous formulation on reason as "the candle of the Lord."[31] This, for him, is a Plotinian aberration from the supposedly dominant "mirror" tradition, which also, we are told, went underground in the rational eighteenth century but was revived by the "Romantics." What seems to structure this misreading is the need to put Locke in the "mirror" camp. But Locke believed in Christian revelation, a fact that places a limiting condition on his empiricism, and, although he differs in significant ways from the Platonists and the schoolmen, he shares many of their fundamental premises. He also had direct personal contact with Cambridge Platonists like Culverwel and Whichcote.[32] Abrams cites the passage in Locke in which the mind, before it experiences sensation, is likened to a dark room. But he was apparently not aware of the other passage in which Locke speaks of reason, using Culverwel's formulation, as "the candle of the Lord set up by himself in men's minds which it is impossible for the breath or power of man wholly to extinguish" (IV.iii.20).[33] The error here is to assume that, since we have no innate ideas, we likewise have no innate powers; whereas the power of reflection for Locke is very little different from the active powers of reason as they have been described throughout the philosophical tradition, including Culverwel. Burnet fell into this trap, and Locke answered in the margin of Burnet's book in these terms: "I think noe body but this author who ever read my book could doubt that I spoke only of innate *ideas*; for my subject was the understanding, and not of innate *powers*."[34] In this sentence is set up both Locke's difference from, and continuity with, the Western philosophical tradition. Mind, for Locke, is still a light derived from God. Intuitive perception is "like bright sunshine" (IV.ii.2).[35]

I am not arguing, I wish to stress, that there are no significant differences between Locke and Neoplatonism. What I am arguing is that, while their attitudes differ, there are significant shared assumptions, and that we can locate these by noting their use of the traditional, interrelated, metaphors of fire and mirror. It is a fundamental error to say that the "lamp" tradition went underground in the eighteenth century, or from the other direction, that its appearance in the early nineteenth century "has been anticipated by certain English writers of the eighteenth century."[36] For these metaphors do not derive from different traditions, nor do they replace one another in chronological sequence, but are integral parts of traditional Western epistemology. Lockean "reflection," apparently embedding a mirror metaphor, is a case in point. Reflection in Locke is not a passive mirroring; rather it is an active making. When Locke uses the mirror metaphor he refers simply to an undifferentiated registering of sense impressions. In this sense, Locke's distinction between sensation, which is a passive mirroring of an impression, and reflection, which is an active construction of the world, is very similar to Aristotle's distinction in *De Anima* between passive and active reason:

Mind in the passive sense is such because it becomes all things, but mind has another aspect in which it makes all things; this is a kind of positive state like light; for in a sense light makes potential into actual colors. Mind in this sense is inseparable, impassive, and unmixed, since it is essentially an activity; for the agent is always superior to the patient, and the originating cause to matter.[37]

If we turn from philosophers to poets, the continuity is even clearer:

> All are but parts of one stupendous Whole
> Whose body Nature is, and God the soul;
> That changed thro' all, and yet in all the same,
> Great in the earth as in the ethereal frame,
> Warms in the sun, refreshes in the breeze,
> Glows in the stars, and blossoms in the trees;
> Lives thro' all life, extends thro' all extent,
> Spreads undivided, operates unspent;
> Breathes in our soul, informs our mortal part,
> As full, as perfect, in a hair as heart;
> As full, as perfect, in vile man that mourns,
> As the rapt Seraph that adores and burns.

This passage, Pope's *An Essay on Man* (1.267–78), draws upon many of the texts I have already cited. Shelley responded in a letter to Thomas Jefferson Hogg dated 3 January 1811: "I confess I think Pope's 'all are but parts of one tremendous whole' something more than Poetry, it has ever been my favourite theory."[38] From the same tradition, and perhaps even from passages in Pope such as this, it should not be doubted, comes the romantic notion of the "One life, within us and abroad." The depiction of the angel as fire, and of the physical world supported by an "ethereal frame," testify to the longevity of these images. That fire could also mean poetic genius, and that the poet is in some sense like the angel, winged and intellectual, are notions used by Pope in *An Essay on Criticism*:

> O may some spark of your celestial fire
> The last, the meanest of your sons inspire,
> (That on weak wings, from afar, pursues your flights,
> Glows while he reads, but trembles as he writes). (lines 195–98)

If the source of all this fire imagery is ultimately Platonic, then the same source gives us Shelley's use of mirror/fire in the famous passage from *Adonais*: "as each are mirrors of / The fire for which all thirst" (lines 485–86).

MIRROR EQUALS MIMESIS?

Quite aside from the question of the consistent interrelation of the mirror/fire complex in philosophical and poetic texts from antiquity at least up through Shelley's poem of 1820, there is the other issue of whether mimetic/expressive and mirror/fire actually are in any way related, which is Abrams' central assumption. To begin with, "expressive," in Abrams' sense, referring to the poem as emerging out of and expressing emotion, is really a subset of mimesis – what is being represented in this case is emotion. Hence the opposition mimetic/expressive cannot be maintained – it is a false opposition. Second, when we evoke the term "mimesis" it is very misleading to identify the nature of representation as a straight mirroring simply because the mirror metaphor is employed, as in the catch phrase, art is a mirror of nature. Abrams himself is aware of this, and thus classifies mimesis according to its objects, and notes that in many cases, in Johnson, for instance, imitation is precisely not mirror-like, but is highly selective: "If the world be promiscuously described, I cannot see of what use it can be to read the account; or why it may not be as safe to turn the eye immediately upon nature, as upon a mirror which shows all that presents itself without discrimination."[39] All art may be some form of representation, but very few people, it appears, have ever thought that this means some sort of slavish copying of "reality." "Mimesis" for Aristotle, of course, does not mean anything like a "mirror" reproduction of reality since he considers it a more serious fault if the artist neglects artistic coherence than if he paints what doesn't exist. Art should not be mistaken for philosophical realism, but this is precisely the kind of confusion that Abrams' broad use of "mirror" and "lamp" invites, in this case not as descriptive of successive periods but as having conceptual content.

There is another difficulty with trying to maintain an aesthetic of mirroring, or at least trying to describe the early eighteenth century in this way. Abrams tells us at one point that music is "non-mimetic" and that in the late eighteenth century music became a model for the lyric: "music was the first of the arts to be generally regarded as non-mimetic in nature; and in the theory of German writers of the 1790s, music came to be the art most immediately expressive of spirit and emotion."[40] But Addison, in his essays on the pleasures of the imagination, had argued in 1712 that *words* were not mimetic ("iconic" is a better term), or rather that words are the least mimetic compared to statues and painting:

Among the different Kinds of Representation, *Statuary* is the most natural, and shews us something *likest* the Object that is represented . . . *Description* runs yet further from the thing it represents than Painting; for a Picture bears a real Resemblance to its Original, which Letters and Syllables are wholly void of. Colours speak all Languages, but Words are understood only by such a People or Nation.[41]

The central idea, of course, is that words arouse the passions by means of association so that "a Description often gives us more lively Ideas than the Sight of Things themselves." Following Addison, Burke made exactly the same claim, but much expanded, in the final part of his treatise on the Sublime and the Beautiful, "Words": "In reality poetry and rhetoric do not succeed in exact description so well as painting does. Their business is to affect rather by sympathy than by imitation."[42] Therefore, "poetry, taken in its most general sense, cannot with strict propriety be called an act of imitation." Since Addison and Burke are hardly obscure, Abrams need not have gone to Germany for a source to argue that lyric poetry is "expressive." According to Addison and Burke, given the nature of its medium, poetry is partly imitative and partly expressive. To evoke the ancient imagery, we can hold that "mirror" equals "mimesis" only if we understand that it is a question of fire mirroring fire.

Perhaps the clearest statement, for my present purposes, of the view that representation does not, and never did, mean a "realistic" mirroring of external phenomena, as if such a thing could be accomplished in language, comes from a book review by John Richetti:

> The old metaphor of reflection by which literature is said to represent the conditions around it is now generally rejected as a simplistic, static reduction of a complex process whereby literature is not a mirror of meanings but part and parcel of a signifying system for producing meaning, implicated in social-historical events rather than somehow standing apart and recording them.[43]

Richetti's characterization of how the metaphor of reflection was used clearly can not refer to eighteenth-century theorists such as Addison and Burke. What it does refer to, it seems to me, is a way of perceiving history that is now falling out of fashion. The reference is to scholars and their beliefs in their procedures, not to poets. The distinction between scholar and artist, we should note, is quite old. Pope was attacked roughly by Theobald for the errors in his edition of Shakespeare (another commercial venture), and, in retaliation, elevated Theobald to the dubious eminence of king of the dunces. But the author of "Some Remarks on the Tragedy of Hamlet" (1736) prefaced his work by justifying his choice of Theobald's edition over Pope's:

> I would not have Mr. Pope offended at what I say, for I look upon him as the greatest Genius in Poetry that has ever appear'd in England: But the Province of an Editor and a Commentator is quite foreign to that of a Poet. The former endeavours to give us an Author as he is; the latter, by the Correctness and Excellency of his own Genius, is often tempted to give us an Author as he thinks he ought to be.[44]

A more recent statement of the same distinction comes from one of Abrams' teachers at Harvard, John Livingston Lowes: "For some of the greatest poets, partly by virtue of their greatness, have had, like Faust, two natures struggling within them. They have possessed at once the instincts of the scholar and the instincts of the artist, and it is precisely with regard to facts that these instincts perilously clash."[45]

SCHOLARS/CRITICS

I have moved very quickly. I want to step back for perspective. Abrams' book is enormously learned, and that learning remains its permanent contribution. What I question is the paradigm that organizes the erudition. Abrams' construction of intellectual history is deeply informed by the master narrative of Romantic literary history, and hence, introduces identifiable misreadings that have been accepted as useful truths by an astounding number of readers over the past forty years. But I want to go further, and ask, why is it that Romantic literary history was so effective at that moment, and has lasted so long? Just as we may ask, why is it less and less convincing for a younger generation of students and critics? The answer might be given in social terms – women, for instance, exploding romantic myths as their response to white-male literature – but that would be only partially true. It would help explain some of the dynamics of our present moment, but not fully account for that moment then. I think we are on solider ground if we look, as we did with the Wartons, at the professional, institutional situation. Once again, Richetti's statement is useful, for he aligns the "old historicism" with something like what Abrams means by a mirror-like view. What I want to suggest is that mirror/lamp in Abrams actually corresponds to scholar/critic as that debate was being argued in the 1930s, 1940s, and 1950s.

Abrams wrote a first draft of *The Mirror and the Lamp* as a dissertation submitted in 1940. If we look into the professional context of the 1930s and the 1940s we see that this is the moment at which the debate between scholars and critics was at its peak. The terms of the debate are familiar. Scholars are subservient to the text; they edit, emend, discover sources, provide background historical and biographical information. Critics, on the other hand, impatient with scholarly apparatus, are eager to engage the text more directly; they interpret and illuminate.[46] Scholars felt that interpretation was either superfluous or impressionistic; the critic intruded a "personal element."[47] Critics thought that scholars were missing the adventure of art. The tension between the two roles is very clear in a personal memoir such as René Wellek's. Brought up in the old philological tradition, he embraced criticism, and would later argue for the distinction between "intrinsic" and "extrinsic" approaches to a literary work.[48] Simply as an aside, it makes sense that many of the critics of this time also were writers themselves, for criticism was demanding a measure of interpretive or creative freedom. The hiring of Tate and Blackmur at Princeton, Graff observes, was "another case of the unity of interest, in this period, of criticism and creative writing."[49] The shift from philologist-scholar to scholar-critic is the central development of the professional role of the university professor in the first half of the twentieth century. One was a mirror, one was a lamp; mirror became lamp.

The terms of this debate are still with us. Stanley Fish takes the "lamp" side against the self-effacing scholar when he states that criticism actually produces the text:

> No longer is the critic the humble servant of texts whose glories exist independently of anything he might do; it is what he does, within the constraints embedded in the literary institution, that brings texts into being and makes them available for analysis and appreciation. The practice of literary criticism is not something one must apologize for; it is absolutely essential not only to the maintenance, but to the production of the objects of attention.[50]

Martin Mueller echoes the scholar's side of the dialectic when he states that "[f]rom the perspective of other disciplines, literary scholars engage in exegetical activities that are peculiarly unconstrained." They "are extraordinarily ingenious and resourceful, but not necessarily very responsible readers." His focus is Stephen Greenblatt: "Greenblatt reads contexts as if they were metaphysical poems, and his method shares with New Criticism and deconstruction a hermeneutical license that has long been claimed by literary critics and has always been suspect among historians or philosophers."[51]

Harry Levin spoke of the impact of Auerbach's *Mimesis*. There had been "an assumption that the critic's and the scholar's interests were mutually exclusive," wrote Levin, but Auerbach's work proved that one could have both erudition and aesthetic sensitivity.[52] Auerbach's stature exemplified the harmony of scholarly and critical approaches. The same may be said of Abrams' *The Mirror and the Lamp*. It is a masterful blending of scholarly sources put in the service of "lamp," or critical values. Because of its tendency, Arac aligns it with "New Critical ahistoricism."[53] The peculiar achievement of the book, then, is to have united two contexts, the Romantic and the modern institutional. The structure of Romantic literary history not only was superimposed on Abrams' scholarly sources, but was also allegorically encoded in relation to his contemporary moment. Because of the strength of this union it is still very difficult to criticize the book and make any headway. For Abrams provided a parable, and a manifesto, for the modern profession of literary studies. If anyone doubts the efficacy of Abrams' metaphors to work on both levels, literary history and contemporary criticism, and to condense the heterogeneity of history into the simplicity of allegorical correspondence and opposition, they need only read Murray Krieger's thumbnail history of criticism recently published. The opposition between "historicism" and "formalism," or "scholar" and "critic," Krieger presents as beginning with the Tories and Whigs of the eighteenth century. Tory writers are historicist and "imitative," whereas Whigs assert individual "originality."[54] Thus, the Wartons' and Edward Young's construction of Pope, transmitted through the nineteenth century and powerfully again in the mirror/lamp thesis of the mid-twentieth century, determines for Krieger his understanding of the cultural history of the past 200 years: Tory/Whig, Imitation/Originality, Classic/Romantic, Scholar/Critic. This is cultural myth at its most tenacious.

It may strike some as odd, at first, that I should associate Abrams with the New Criticism. For one clichéd story tells us that the New Critics were hostile to Romantic poetry as was the Modernism from which they took their cue. Abrams, however, in a skillful move, simply subsumed Modernism under Romanticism by arguing that these ostensible anti-Romantics were actually using concepts that derived from Coleridge.[55] The effect of this was to identify "criticism" with Romantic values, and this view was powerfully developed by younger critics such as Hartman and Bloom. Hence Romantic discourse became our *episteme*. We are still working our way through the consequences, and past the determinants, of such a world-view. One of the less edifying consequences, it seems to me, at least in the American context, is the isolation of eighteenth-century studies, which in 1984 was characterized as the "least-loved period of study for the Ph.D. in English."[56] For as Culler noted, the distinction between "mirror" and "lamp" was evaluative, "persuading us to prefer Romantic to eighteenth-century poetry by drawing upon the theological notions implicit in the Romantic description of the poet."[57] As I showed in the Introduction, even those critics who no longer accept the "humanist" view of English literature and culture that the generation of Abrams and Wellek promoted, continue to accept, or at least to operate in terms of, a strict period division that implicitly encodes a hierarchical distinction, not between authors, which after all is only natural, but between *centuries*, which seems to me completely untenable. In closing I will focus on the "theological" view of the poet, and by extension, the critic.

In his final section of *The Mirror and the Lamp*, entitled "The Use of Romantic Poetry," Abrams himself drew an analogy between "then" and "now": "The English Romantic Era, which occurred hard upon the French Revolution, amid war and rumors of war, and in the stress of social and political adjustments to the Industrial Revolution, was comparable to our own period between the two World Wars."[58] In citing excerpts from a Harvard committee of 1945 recommending the use of literature as a means of combatting the modern condition, Gerald Graff summarizes: "The answer was that if the *greatest* literature is taught, the fragmentation, discontinuity, and lack of meaning of modern history can be overcome."[59] Literature, as Arnold had foreseen, could be used to fill the place of religion as a means of establishing unity in a culture that saw itself threatened by "modernity." Historical scholarship could be useful as a means toward recovering meaning, but the "universal" values of literary works would be explicitly sought and promoted.

Wordsworth, in such a situation, would be taken up as a secular messiah. Indeed, Wordsworth's whole program in *The Prelude*, described by Abrams and others as a secularization and internalization of traditional paradigms, was a narrative of natural redemption occurring outside the mythological trappings of more orthodox theologies. As Wordsworth told a shocked Crabb Robinson: "I have no need of a Redeemer."[60] Indeed, he was his own; and the implication was, that just like Jesus, through the intercession and mediation of Wordsworth, that is by reading the poetry, one could reach a paradise within in the midst of a fallen world. In his own time, some saw Wordsworth as scandalizing Christianity, but others, like the Oxford Tractarians who embraced him, saw him as spreading it. Aldous Huxley records the religious effect of Wordsworth in his own childhood:

To regard Wordsworth critically, impersonally, is for some of us a rather difficult matter. With the disintegration of the solid orthodoxies Wordsworth became for many intelligent, liberal-minded families the Bible of that sort of pantheism, that dim faith in the existence of a spiritual world, which filled, somewhat inadequately, the place of the older dogmas. Brought up as children in the

Wordsworthian tradition, we were taught to believe that a Sunday walk among the hills was somehow equivalent to church-going: the First Lesson was to be read among the clouds, the Second in the primroses; the birds and the running waters sang hymns, and the whole blue landscape presented a sermon "of moral evil and of good." From this dim religious education we brought away a not very well-informed veneration for the name of Wordsworth, a dutiful conviction about the spirituality of Nature in general, and an extraordinary superstition about mountains in particular.[61]

What was true for Huxley, growing up in the late nineteenth century, remains true for many people a century later. It is still difficult for some to regard Wordsworth "critically, impersonally," because he is wrapped up in complexes of religious feelings; Christological metaphors can still be found in recent criticism, and Romanticism, in some quarters, is still being promoted as substitute theology. "Wordsworth," or that version of Romanticism, is secular religion. In concluding, I want to trace some of the implications of secular religion, especially as it has structured a particular perception of literary history.

If you have a messiah figure analogous to Jesus, then it makes sense, if you think analogically, as many literary critics do, that there must be forerunners. Douglas Bush understood this very clearly: "It has long been the misfortune of the eighteenth-century poets, both good and bad, to be treated not simply as eighteenth-century poets but as either stragglers or forerunners, as neoclassic Pharisees or romantic John the Baptists. Yet such a subject as the mythological tradition compels us to take something like that attitude."[62] Cowper, I suppose, would be playing John the Baptist to Wordsworth's Messiah, while the neoclassicists (was there really such a being?) Dryden and Pope, one supposes, would be playing the Pharisees. If we extend this further, the displacement of the patterns of Christian history and theology into literary history suggests that the distinction classic/romantic is analogous to letter/spirit. Certainly that is Edward Young's claim for "originality" as opposed to an adherence to tradition and the "rules." The poets themselves are responsible for these patterns, and the critics have simply followed their lead.

These patterns, it is important to note, are not simply Christian, but more generally biblical. Trilling's essay, "Wordsworth and the Rabbis," is testimony to how this version of Romanticism blurs the distinction between the Hebrew Bible and the New Testament. And it is worth noting also that the distinction between the letter and the spirit of the law, although applied by Paul to separate the Christian and the Jew, is actually a Hebrew distinction that Jesus, placing himself in the line of the prophets, fully exploited. The prophets continually argued for a figurative interpretation of the law, the law, as Jeremiah said, "written in the heart."

I raise these issues in order to foreground the metaphysical assumptions upon which Romantic literary history, and with it much literary study, is based. For as long as literary study draws upon religious figures and rhetoric for its terms, whether Christian or Jewish, what gets perpetuated is a scapegoat mechanism. The Romantic polemic against precursors, for instance, will be colored by the emotional valences of true religion as opposed to false; and the same rhetoric that infuses the poets' polemic will recur in the language of the critics. One of the best places to see these forces playing themselves out, without the mitigating intervention of sophistication, is in a popular Romantic anthology of the middle of the century.

Ernest Bernbaum, trained at Harvard, gives us in the clearest possible form the lineaments of Romantic academic desire in the first half of the twentieth century. Bernbaum published an anthology of Romantic poetry, and along with it a *Guide Through the Romantic Movement*. The first edition appeared in 1930, and a second updated edition in 1949. Here we have all the essentials. The combined effect of the Romantics, he asserts, "is the most powerful of any of the literary influences that have molded our civilization"; "[f]or better or worse, the modern outlook is chiefly the creation of the Romantics."[63] Somehow, though, the modern outlook also exceeds the Romantics for we need them more than ever now "in a time when the practical, scientific, and material achievements of our country overshadow every other activity."[64] In fact, implying a complete reversal of his first position, it is because not enough attention has been paid to Romantic literature that the twentieth century has fallen into darkness:

The dominating influences of the times were anti-romantic – materialistic, prosaic, scientific, technological, and secular. The world was ruled by the "practical" man, and obsessed by his idols. Religion and philosophy were feeble and confused; the new forces in politics, whether Fascist or Communist, were antidemocratic; poetry whimpered in the darkness; and fiction floundered in sophisticated hopelessness. The inevitable outcome was universal distrust and hatred, the brutalities of genocide, the savagery of biological and atomic warfare, and the paralysis of any confidence in the future of mankind. Everything that the Romantics believed in had been ignored or despised. And the result was the greatest moral failure, and the closest approach to ruin, that civilization had ever experienced. The lesson is indeed obvious. The right way to approach the Romantics today is with the knowledge that those who neglected or derided them have proved false prophets and fatal guides; and that perhaps if we were to understand the grounds of their faith, and were to recover it, we might find a way out of the inferno of evil and fear into which the anti-romantics have misled us.[65]

The term "anti-romantic," of course, has a very wide range of application in Bernbaum's lexicon. It includes "neoclassic" critics who have attacked Romanticism, such as Babbitt, and also New Critics: "The most hostile anti-romantic writers, including the 'Humanists' and the 'New Critics . . .'"[66] Later we are told that the Humanists were "blinded by fear and zeal."[67] In a speculative essay on what kind of modern fiction the Romantics would admire if they were alive today, the evangelical fervor of Bernbaum breaks through once again: "The romantic ideal must be restored – the ideal of the Man of Letters as a Messenger-from-on-High and a Servant and Leader of Mankind, a more enlightened and inspired leader than the dunderheaded politicians, soapy racketeers, and fatuous economists whose greed and fear have brought us to the brink of ruin."[68] If we try to correlate all of these indictments – the claim that genocide, World War II, organized crime, and the New Criticism have brought us to our lamentable condition – is one really supposed to conclude that the world would be a more humane place if only Hitler, Stalin, Al Capone, and Cleanth Brooks had more appreciation for English Romantic poetry?

It is easy to be amused by Bernbaum. But it is too easy merely to dismiss him as irrelevant, for he presents us with a Low Church version of a High Church position: "It has been said by historians of literature that the romantic spirit had two notable manifestations before the Romantic Movement of the early nineteenth century – one in Palestine in the days of Christ, another in England in the days of Shakespeare."[69] There you have it: Jesus, Shakespeare, and the Romantics – literature as modern redemption. This goes to the heart of the difficulty. Is it possible to envisage a humane literary study in our time that does not require the defensive appeal to "the Man of Letters as a Messenger-from-on-High"? My assumption, of course, is that the moment for which these mechanisms were useful is now passing. The cultural imperative to worship literature is coming to seem irrelevant, but the structures that implicitly support such a view are still in place. To come to poetry with a de-idealizing perspective for some is still a kind of heresy rather than a sign of health, as though one could not study poetry carefully and appreciate it unless one subscribed to the values and world-views, many of them outdated, of those who wrote it. The challenge is to conceive a method of viewing literary history "horizontally," that is, without the vertical, metaphysical dimension of a teleological master narrative. I hope this book makes a contribution to that work.

Conclusion, with thoughts on method in literary historiography

This book has put forward the revisionist thesis that Romantic literary history, hence Romantic ideology, is founded on its view of Pope. Since the term "romantic" is so slippery in its positive meanings, I have suggested that what binds together all its various manifestations is the agreement that "romantic" is not "classic," where "classic" is code for "Pope." Or, to bring in another central opposition, it is a question of "feeling" versus "reason," the sublime and the pathetic as the definition of everything that Pope isn't. These polemically effective oppositions have been used to read a tradition that has always been, even in the early eighteenth century, a "heteroglossia" of influences from French, Italian, Spanish (especially *Don Quixote*), Gothic, Classical, and native sources. The result can be seen dramatically by comparing a statement of Madame de Staël's with that of a contemporary graduate student.

Madame de Staël, who is credited with disseminating the German dichotomy classic/romantic (meaning ancient/modern) through her book on Germany in 1810, wrote:

> There are some writings, such as the letters of Abelard, works by Pope, *Werther*, the *Portuguese Letters*, etc., and a unique work, the New Heloise, whose chief merit is the eloquence of emotion. Though their theme may often be moral, what stands out above everything else is the all-powerfulness of the feelings. Such works of fiction are in a class by themselves. In a hundred years we find only one mind, one genius, that can create them.

De Staël, no doubt, has Pope's *Eloisa to Abelard* in mind, but other poems, too, for she says "works by Pope." Lipking cites de Staël for context in his discussion of Donna Julia's letter in *Don Juan*, and comments: "The poet in search of passion must find his way through the Ovidian epistle, and there Pope was master."[1] It is strange to see Pope discussed this way, and put in the company of Rousseau in 1810, for our training tells us that Wordsworth should be mentioned in connection with Rousseau and powerful emotion, and that Pope has nothing to offer in that way. But, within the last few years, Barbara Packer distributed a questionnaire at UCLA asking people to cite lines of poetry that had given them intense pleasure: "a graduate student told me that she really wasn't a fan of Alexander Pope but quoted several couplets from 'Eloisa to Abelard' because they had given her shivers and convinced her that emotion could, after all, survive in heroic couplets."[2] This student is slightly apologetic; she is "not really a fan" of Pope. And she is surprised; how could emotion and couplets go together? Nonetheless, the actual experience of the poetry is so strong that she memorizes it.

This book has been about the historical and epistemological gap that has opened up between the time of Madame de Staël and the present, and thus it began with the dissociation of "Eloisa" from Pope by Thomas Warton, and with Joseph Warton naming Pope "the poet of reason." The line from there, as I have shown, to mirror and lamp, and to the introductory course in "Romanticism" is fairly direct. It would be a mistake, in my view, to respond to de Staël by considering Pope a "romantic" after all, for that is precisely the mechanism of retrospective assimilation that a teleological perspective puts into operation, and which it has been the task of this book to analyze and challenge.

Romanticism's "Pope," I want to speculate, refers to something within "Romanticism" itself. The dichotomies it establishes are symptoms of a split within the subject, here understood as expressing itself as cultural discourse. The opposition classic/romantic is a "Romantic" construction, and tells us something about the synchrony of Romanticism as a concept, not about the diachrony that it purports to describe. I have tried to describe how this particular cultural fiction came into being, and to sketch key moments in its history. Thus my work complements other ongoing investigations that seek to understand what Romanticism is and where it came from. The synchronic quality of Romantic literary history is best described by reference to what Thomas Vogler has called "conceptual history." Examples are drawn from Barthes (writerly/readerly), Schiller (naive/sentimental), and Nietzsche (Dionysian/Apollonian). Another example would be Arnold's hebraic/hellenic, which he thought the key to the understanding of culture. The fault, Vogler explains, is in "historicizing a binary opposition that is itself conceptual and synchronic rather than historical."[3] But as the examples show, although bad history, these stark oppositions, mirror/lamp another instance, have tremendously seductive narrative power and the stamina to outlast any falsification. In fact, some of our greatest names are identified with them. The reason this is so, it seems to me, is that these narratives do not necessarily refer to history at all. Rather, they externalize and allegorize internal conflicts, hence are often much more vivid and interesting than the pedestrian objections that an unmannered pedant might insist on. The pertinent example of this is the way psychological faculties are projected as history in the supposed replacement of "Reason" by "Imagination." These fictions elicit assent and recognition even though they may have no verifiable external referent, or, alternatively, because they are built on half-truths.

My thesis that the element "Pope" in Romantic literary history is a symptom of a repression of the historical Pope, a body of texts that might admit of alternative constructions, is based on the evidence presented throughout the book. The methods employed in arriving at that thesis derive from previous scholarship as cited in the notes, but more broadly from Derrida and deconstruction generally, from Foucault's work on discursive formations, from the new-historical and cultural-materialist drive to historicize post-structuralist theories, from feminist literary criticism, from psychoanalysis, particularly as used by Harold Bloom, from the traditional understanding of "scholarship" as research into primary texts, and of "reading" as the imperative to pay close attention to the details of texts. With the exception of Bloom, this is fairly standard equipment after decades of theoretical ferment and debate. Although Marxists such as Jameson, and Romantic critics such as Alan Liu and Mary Jacobus, draw upon psychoanalysis in various ways, the Bloomian reading of literary history as oedipal struggle and swerve has not really been adopted widely by critics with historical interests even though he defines his project as "diachronic rhetoric."[4] Since I have used Bloom's theory in this study I want to reflect on why it is useful, and what its relation to other methods might be.

Let me say, first of all, that I take "theory" to be provisional. At best, theory does indeed lead to innovative research. At worst, theory is a totally separate discourse with internal pressures of its own, which, so far from being a discipline of self-consciousness, a mode of wariness in the face of untenable assertions and ideological reflexes, becomes that very thing it sets up to combat. I do not consider theory another religion that must be defended at all costs against heretics and infidels. I understand it rather as providing tools and frameworks for analysis that actually lead one to better understandings, hence my use of the word "method" in the title of this section. Implicit in this view is an attitude toward the material under study. A game whose rules are given in advance, whose beginning, middle, and end, are defined with clarity, and which takes place within a bracketed space and time, admits of total theorization. History, culture, and literature do not. Theory then is a guide in making sense of historical particulars. It is never complete, but it is the best we can do.

What follows from this is that no one theory can claim a total view of the field. In actual practice, everyone must draw on several methods. The crucial question then becomes, what is the *relation* of theories to each other? Jameson addresses this issue under the rubric of "transcoding." Given the proliferation of theoretical codes we enter a new situation: "It will, in other words, today be less a question of finding a single system of truth to convert to, than it will of speaking the various theoretical codes experimentally."[5] Jameson is honest enough to recognize that "Marxism must also take its chances" in such a situation, but he is more sanguine than I that historical materialism really is the baseline to which we must always return, rather than an important contributing factor to cultural analysis. Franco Moretti addresses the relation of methods to each other by positing the notion of a "hierarchy of different historical factors." Conditions themselves orient us empirically toward the decision of which factors must be given more weight than others:

> In an essentially agrarian society, climatic changes will have a far greater importance than in a basically industrial one. If the majority of the population is illiterate, the written culture will oscillate between playing a wholly negligible part and having an overwhelming and traumatic function (as the printing of the Bible demonstrated). If, on the other hand, everyone is able to read, the written culture is unlikely to turn up such extreme effects, but in compensation it will become the regular and intimate accompaniment to every daily activity.
>
> As historical periods change, then, the weight of the various institutions, their function, their position in the social structure change too. When, therefore, the historian of literary forms begins to look for those extra-literary phenomena which help him (whether he knows it or not) orient and control his research, the only rule he can set himself is to assess *each instance* carefully.[6]

I applaud the emphasis on empirical procedure, but the whole question of "transcoding," or of establishing some sort of hierarchy of particulars highlights the fact, which both Jameson and Moretti are aware of, that our methods impose their own frames.

Let us take this a little further. Many years ago R. S. Crane urged scholarship to proceed empirically, cautious of the "high priori road." Crane was aware that the scholar must always make a selection of data, and that this selection implies a system of values, but the appeal had always to be made to evidence that other scholars could verify.[7] Since then we have become even more aware of the extent to which empirical evidence is theory-dependent. Yet, Siegfried Schmidt, in a paper on the constructedness of literary history, still calls for a radically empirical method of proceeding. The difference between Crane's time and ours is that Schmidt treats the models themselves as empirical data to be accounted for.[8] But once we have done this we are led to reflect, as above, on the relation of models to each other. The next step, it seems to me, is one implied by Moretti, although it is not a particularly fashionable one, for at least since the opening pages of Saussure it has been taken as a given that the object of study is defined by the frame you apply to it. This is true but in a limited way.[9] The objects also offer some resistance to our ways of theorizing them. What I suggest is that we think of this problem in terms of *scale*.

The particular frame one applies, I want to argue, implies a particular scope or scale. Moreover, the results one obtains are dependent on the scale one employs. The argument for the scale-dependency of results is demonstrated by Mandelbrot. The circumference of the coast of England, his example, yields a different measurement depending on whether one measures it in miles, or in feet, or in inches.[10] As true as this is, the example also implies, not necessarily that some scales are used for different purposes and that scientifically they are all equal, but that the object itself helps orient us to the proper scale. If one wants to know the circumference of England, one will most likely not measure it in feet or inches. Alternatively, if one wants to measure the size of a house, one will most likely not measure it in square miles. The same holds for cultural artifacts. Rhetorical, psychoanalytical, and socio-historical explanations have significant areas of overlap, but all work on different scales, and seem to me radically incompatible as modes of knowledge only if each one simultaneously claims a total explanation of the field.

Shklovsky, expositing the "literariness" of plot over story in *Tristram Shandy*, ended by exclaiming that *Shandy* was "the most typical novel in the world." Replying to this, Lacan exclaimed that it was "the most analytical novel in the world."[11] A Marxist critic could easily claim that *Shandy* is the most bourgeois novel in the world, and she or he would certainly have a point. In theory, at least, these claims are not mutually exclusive, but if coordinated in practice they would modify each other according to the particular case. What occurs too often, however, is that the reading of a text is flattened out by the application of one exclusive method and opposed polemically to another reading that flattens out the text by using a different method. The opposition between "structure" and "agency" is another case in point. Traditional critics argue for the free will of the individual agent. Post-structuralists argue that individuals are determined by large-scale structural conditions of which they are usually unaware, such as language, gender, class, and nation. These explanations need not clash if we understand them to relate to different scales.[12] When set in opposition, however, they simply argue past one another from different premises and using different measures.

So where do I place Bloom? Let me approach this indirectly by looking at the anomalous place of "influence" generally under the paradigm of "criticism" that came into ascendency in the 1950s. One of the central issues in the theory of literary history is the distinction between "extrinsic" and "intrinsic" approaches. For the Formalists this distinction defines what is specifically "literary" and what "extra-literary." In the Anglo-American debate, the intrinsic/extrinsic distinction related to the different activities of the critic on the one hand, who interprets and evaluates, and the scholar on the other, who provides historical references in explanatory footnotes, identifies sources, and in general thinks that interpretation is the product of arrogant and unlicensed speculation. It is the difference, then, between criticism and history, a debate that in the 1950s was settled decisively in favor of the critic. More recently, whether in the New Historicism or in the overtly political readings that have gathered strength since the early 1980s, criticism has redefined its goals and attempted to recover the "extrinsic." Thus, placing in perspective the recent history of literary history, Lee Patterson observes that "the mainstream of literary studies over the last hundred years or so has tended to move first from the extrinsic to the intrinsic and then back again."[13]

In the preliminary stage of analysis there remains good reason for saying that a letter by the author or an advertisement in a contemporary gazette is "external" to the poem or novel under discussion. Post-structuralism, however, challenged any easy differentiation between inside and out in a way that cannot be ignored. We are now more acutely aware of the degree to which "history" itself is mediated through texts. Hence the relation of a poem to history can be as intertextual as its relation to a precursor poem. Ideology, John Frow has argued, is "semiotic."[14] When the "extrinsic" returns, therefore, it comes to disrupt the old distinctions and to claim that history is not external, it is "in" the text.

In retrospect this was the inevitable response to a method that had developed its technology of reading by operating a series of exclusions, stated as fallacies of method. For example, the genetic fallacy is the error of reducing a work to its sources; a subset of this, the intentional fallacy, is the error of referring a work to the psychology of its author (Shakespeare was depressed when he wrote *Hamlet*), or to stated authorial intentions rather than ones inferable from the work. William Wimsatt sums up these objections succinctly when he says that "the author himself and his inspirations can be related to the produced poem only somewhat dubiously and irrelevantly."[15] Finally, the affective fallacy is the error of evaluating a work according to whether it raises the hairs on one's neck, or makes one weep. To the extent that this ascesis of method was directed against naive and confused forms of reading it was useful and necessary. But it was achieved at the cost of severing the work from its historical milieu, the mind of the author, and the sensibilities of its audience. History, psychology, and reception were bound to return at a higher level of reflection and return they did.

We may ask, how is it, specifically, that history is "in" the text? The short answer is that this is so because the text constitutes itself in history. It may have its own particularity as a structure, but it is not separate, neutral, or autonomous with respect to the language it employs or the contexts within which it is, by necessity, situated. Morever, the last thing one would claim a text is free of is its reception, which is capricious and unpredictable. Authors appeal to posterity, but none of them knows what it looks like. There is a sense, it is true, in which a text produces its readers, and by that process becomes a historical agent. But this fact only reinforces the argument for the historical embeddedness of literature. History, in the broadest sense, is the primary condition of its signification. Thus, context is not outside the text, but part of its internalized code. The intricacies of meaning construction in the reading process depend on recognizing codes often not given explicitly in the text itself, but simply presupposed. Without knowledge of these contexts of signification, reading proceeds in a vacuum, deluding itself as it goes. A graphic illustration of what I mean is the "Reveal Codes" facility in word processing software. By pressing a key, the invisible, yet nonetheless present, commands that format the text appear on the screen. In the absence of such magical aids to reading texts, the interpretative process requires patient reconstruction of implicit, yet powerfully determining forces that are as likely to be social as they are literary. (This remains the case especially when we recognize that, because contexts are multiple and varied, reading is not simply a de-coding.)

An example is in order. In an essay on the relationship between history and criticism, Wimsatt allowed that in some cases history entered the text as part of its significance. He drew the distinction between history as "antecedent," and thus external to the work, and history as "lexicography," or meaning.[16] His example is the dependency of writers in the seventeenth and eighteenth centuries on patronage. This social relation "created opportunities for a certain kind of servility – in prefaces and dedications," a servility that could in certain instances generate "a special kind of irony," as in Dryden's debate with Sir Robert Howard about rhyme or Pope's *Epistle to Augustus*: "Here we have a social relation which becomes part of the mind and expression of authors in their work. In such cases, and they are many, historical causes enter in a pronounced way into the very meaning of literary works."[17]

A measure of the difference between Wimsatt and current historical sensibility is that we now assume the social relation to be always present, not just in special cases however numerous. We do not need to be convinced that the protocols for reading the rhetoric of Dryden and Pope, or of Charlotte Smith and Byron, are as social and political as they are literary. In fact, we may have gone too far in efforts to compensate for the oversights of aesthetic formalism. Pope's *Epistle to Augustus*, just mentioned, is an apt text in this regard because any reading of it, it seems to me, must take into account the *intersection* of political and literary reference. Pope equates Horace's Augustus with George II – any reading that chooses one context over another will not sufficiently respect the juxtaposition that allows the irony of the poem to emerge. This is a fairly obvious case, but the same principle holds in cases where either the literary or the political contexts, or both, are more submerged. My argument about Romanticism and Pope tries to demonstrate the extent to which Pope is a submerged context for the late eighteenth and early nineteenth centuries.

I make this point because it serves to introduce the problem of influence, in discussing which I refer primarily to Harold Bloom's theory of "the anxiety of influence." Under the new historical paradigm influence suffers a double handicap. It works with intertextual relations, hence smacks of formalism, and it employs the interpretative concepts of psychoanalysis, hence opens itself to charges of a retrograde interest in individual subjectivity at a moment when the subject has been de-centered and the focus of significance has become larger-scale cultural and political forces. In fact, Bloom is in general something of an anomaly, for influence, which is not synonymous with intertext, was never a great favorite of formalist method either. Jakobson and Tynjanov were suspicious of it. For the new critics, similarly, influence study is associated either with source study or with the subjectivism of author psychology, neither directly relevant to the work as a public structure. Bloom's theory directly challenges Wimsatt's intentional fallacy by returning the mind of the author to the text, much as Stanley Fish's "affective stylistics" challenged the affective fallacy by putting the reading process back into the text. But whereas Fish's initiative, together with the one made by Jauss at roughly the same time, led to more widespread focus on historical reception, which in Jauss's view was a way of bridging the gap between formalist and historical approaches, Bloom's theory, which is another version of reception, has by and large not been followed up with the return to history. For while the new historicism recuperates the antiquarian source study of the old historical scholars – what Greenblatt refers to lovingly as "the elephant's graveyard" – it remains wary of, when not hostile to, psychoanalysis.

Actually, however, the same logic that opens the text to history (or rather opens one's eyes to what is already there) extends to psychological analysis as well. There seems to me no reason why psychology should not become part of historical poetics. Subjectivity is "in" the text, because the subject, like the text, is produced in history. If a text is constituted from within cultural and historical forces, so too is the psyche constituted in language and in society. The psychological is often only the social and historical written small. Therefore, if literary and socio-historical structures intersect in a text, so also do psychological ones. We need not make any appeal to what we have no knowledge of as in the intentional fallacy. Rather, we hypothesize certain psychic dynamics structuring the text, and build evidence toward an argument as in any interpretation. Let me take up some of the objections.

Howard Weinbrot, in a very informative essay on Collins, falls below the mark in my view by calling the anxiety of influence theory a "well-marinated fantasy": "According to this scheme, all English poetry declines after the intimidating greatness of John Milton. Subsequent poets try to do what Milton has done, at the last moment are made fearful and anxious by such fruitless competition, and swerve from their better's purpose."[18] Weinbrot has not distinguished the anxiety of influence as a phenomenon from the literary-historical narrative in which it is embedded. These are two distinct questions. Much of my book has questioned the central role of Milton in Romantic literary history, not to deny his importance but to balance it by calling our attention to Pope. If we separate out this issue from the psychology that Bloom proposes, however, and consider if that has any validity, we may fairly question

Weinbrot first about what view he would supplant this one with. In an article on emulation, Weinbrot puts forward the thesis that Renaissance emulation was hostile, envious, and satanic, whereas, under the influence of Longinus's treatise, emulation in the later seventeenth and early eighteenth centuries becomes a friendly and productive rivalry. Thus when a poet challenged a precursor, "he did so not out of envy but admiration; not with fear of failure but hope of success shared by competitors who knew that, whatever the outcome, such contest worked the good of men."[19] I think Weinbrot unnecessarily idealizes male rivalry and thus misses the extent to which envy and admiration, to use his terms, can coexist. There need not be a choice between the two; Freudian ambivalence describes this emotional situation quite well.

Jonathan Culler grants that poems are intertextual constructs, but he objects to analysts who

> will be tempted to personalize the intertextual and reduce it to a specular struggle between a poet and a single great precursor, in whom he sees himself. This reduction can generate powerful readings but must appeal to a totalizing notion of the self which is irreparably subverted by aspects of language such readings must neglect: the uncertain status of citation and allusion, whose interpretation can never be limited by an authorial project, and the uncanny displacements of figural logic from one text to another.[20]

At the beginning of Chapter 3, working from an analysis of the sublime made by Neil Hertz, I argued that the reduction of a plurality of sources and influences to an oedipal encounter between a poet and a precursor with whom the poet has identified is not necessarily a reduction performed by the critic, but is actually part of the oedipal mechanism itself. In the case of reactions to Pope, an entire discourse was produced whose reductiveness can be analyzed from many angles. If Joseph Warton, or Cowper, or Wordsworth focus their hostility on Pope and offer us an ambivalent and reductive construction of Pope, that does not mean that we, as critics, take this view to be the final word on Warton, Cowper, Wordsworth, or, for that matter, Pope. It does not follow, moreover, that to analyze this construction means that we appeal to "a totalizing notion of the self." On the contrary, a constant implication of my argument has been that the presence of Pope in the text of these poets suggests self-division of the most fundamental kind. Nor, to pick up another thread, does a belief in the artistic consciousness and agency of the artist preclude a belief that the artist is simultaneously determined in many unconscious ways. Agency merely operates dialogically within and upon conditions already established. As for the uncertain status of allusion, I have not tried to speculate whether a particular echoing of Pope is conscious or not. That I have no way of knowing. What is patent, however, are the contradictions, emotional and doctrinal, that striate the texts, and that suggest to interpretation that a repression is at work.

The status of the trope of "repression" is a sticky issue. Mark Edmundson has objected to its use because it admits of no reply: "Once someone makes central use of the category of repression no real critical conversation is possible. What one faces then is a cultural politics by fiat."[21] In another article, Edmundson argues that the appeal to a "latent" cause for which there is no direct evidence characterizes the professional guild of criticism in its separation from common discourse, and in its will to power over the text.[22] Latent meanings are invisible to the layman, but affirmed by those in the know. I agree with Edmundson that poetry has its own generative power and is not to be contained, packaged, and summed up by critical theories. I also agree that the language of criticism should be as clear as possible. But beyond those practical proposals his argument cannot be sustained, for his real target is more a certain attitude and a certain style. All meaning is to some extent latent and must be produced by interpretation. This is as true of ordinary linguistic situations as it is of high-powered, specialist, literary interpretation. Irony, by one definition, says one thing but means another, and, because it is notoriously evasive in this way, critics continue to debate whether a passage in a given text is ironic or not, and if it is, in what way. This situation is built into the nature of signs as mediators between speakers and between writers and readers. Therefore, repressed or latent meanings are not different in kind from other instances of the general indirection of language. The question is really whether the evidence justifies us in making that particular hypothesis. And here I would have to agree that I have seen cases where a certain theoretical frame has been simply imposed on material without sufficient justification. Freud observed that "the case of unsuccessful repression will have more claim on our interest than that of repression which is eventually successful; the latter will for the most part elude our study."[23] For this reason, among others equally cogent, I began with the Wartons, for there the repression is not successful and leaves many traces for the interpreter.

A remark by Jameson leads us back to the issue of scale:

First, we must try to rid ourselves of the habit of thinking about our (aesthetic) relationship to culturally or temporally distant artifacts as being a relationship between individual subjects (as in my *personal* reading of an *individual* text written by a biographical individual named Spenser or Juvenal. . .). It is not a question of dismissing the role of individual subjects in the reading process, but rather of grasping this obvious and concrete individual relationship as being itself a mediation for a nonindividual and more collective process: the confrontation of two distinct social forms or modes of production. We must try to accustom ourselves to a perspective in which every act of reading, every interpretative practice, is grasped as the privileged vehicle through which two distinct modes of production confront and interrogate each other. Our individual reading thus becomes an allegorical figure for this essentially collective confrontation of two social forms.[24]

There is much to agree with here. To save time, what I object to is not the emphasis on collective significance, for I have been arguing for the persistence of a collective Romantic paradigm, but the too-easy transition from the individual to the collective. If we measure every reading in terms of the social forces accumulated massively behind the individual reader and the text, first, we have no way of measuring more subtle shifts and changes taking place on a smaller scale, and, second, we are left without a guide for making distinctions for encounters that take place *within* the same mode of production.

What I have argued, in fact, is that many of the poets who follow Pope are, in relation to the changes occurring in the larger culture, in precisely the same situation that he was. Robert Folkenflik traces many eighteenth-century examples, including Pope and Johnson, and concludes that "a number of the conceptions we have – of the nature of the poet, of his independence from power and society, and of his status as spokesman for his culture – took shape before the arrival of the Romantics and the Moderns."[25] The crucial difference on this level of determination are the possibilities for differentiation given in the opposition of urban to country and in the discernible shift, in the 1740s, in the rhetoric of civic virtue from public duty to private consciousness.[26] However, rather than affirm the sorts of continuity that existed between themselves and Pope, and in Edward Young's case in the same generation as Pope, the Wartons and those that follow them assert not only difference but at times contempt. They borrow from Pope while arguing he is not a poet. Here is where the notion of an anxiety of influence makes perfect sense, for it is both a way of discussing the competitive relations between texts that are intimately related, and a way of theorizing elements of those relations that contemporaries noticed themselves. I have adduced many examples, but I will turn again to Byron, whose language is violent and colorful, but who covers all the bases. Byron writes to Murray to complain of those "who add insult to their Parricide – by sucking the blood of the parent of English *real* poetry – poetry without a fault – and then spurning the bosom which fed them."[27]

I will end by saying that although I have focused on Pope's influence and argued its centrality to the Romantic paradigm, I by no means think that this explains all there is to explain. I have suggested, rather, that the relation to Pope is an important negative condition that need not account for every positive manifestation of "Romanticism." For that reason I have not surveyed Pope's impact on every poet, for all writers need not have been affected by Pope equally, or even at all. Shelley is a good example. Shelley responded to a letter from Byron on the Pope controversy by stating he was "neuter" on this subject, and I have no reason to disbelieve him. What I have studied is the genesis and transmission of a historiographical narrative that has shaped a normative understanding of English literary history, that constitutes thereby a normative version of periodization, and to this day authorizes the foundational distinction between "classic" and "romantic."

Notes

INTRODUCTION

1. James Chandler, "The Pope Controversy: Romantic Poetics and the English Canon," *Critical Inquiry* 10 (1984): 481.
2. J. G. A. Pocock, "Cambridge Paradigms and Scotch Philosophers: A Study of the Relations Between the Civic Humanist and the Civil Jurisprudential Interpretation of Eighteenth-Century Social Thought," in *Wealth and Virtue: The Shaping of Political Economy in the Scottish Enlightenment*, eds. Istvan Hont and Michael Ignatieff (Cambridge University Press, 1983), p. 246.
3. Clifford Siskin, *The Historicity of Romantic Discourse* (Oxford University Press, 1988), p. 5.
4. Alan Liu, "The Power of Formalism: The New Historicism," *ELH* 56 (1989): 739.
5. Jonathan Bate, *Romantic Ecology: Wordsworth and the Environmental Tradition* (London: Routledge, 1991), p. 49.
6. This couplet from *Epistle II.ii*, lines 67–8, is cited by Ian A. Bell, "'Not Lucre's Madman': Pope, Money, and Independence," in *Alexander Pope: Essays for the Tercentenary*, ed. Colin Nicholson (Aberdeen University Press, 1988), p. 63. For further evidence that financial independence was Pope's motive, see John Paul Russo, *Alexander Pope: Tradition and Identity* (Cambridge, Mass.: Harvard University Press, 1972), pp. 83ff.
7. *Beyond Romanticism: New Approaches to Texts and Contexts, 1780–1832*, eds. Stephen Copley and John Whale (London: Routledge, 1992), p. 1.
8. Lawrence Lipking, "Inventing the Eighteenth Centuries: A Long View," in *The Profession of Eighteenth-Century Literature: Reflections on an Institution*, ed. Leopold Damrosch (Madison: University of Wisconsin Press, 1992), p. 8.
9. Paul De Man, "Autobiography as De-Facement," in *The Rhetoric of Romanticism* (New York: Columbia University Press, 1984), p. 79. See also Sanford Budick's reading of *Essays on Epitaphs* in "Chiasmus and the Making of Literary Tradition: The Case of Wordsworth and 'The Days of Dryden and Pope.'" *ELH* 60 (1993): 961–88.
10. In 1842 Wordsworth wrote of Burns and Cowper: "It gives me pleasure, venial I trust, to acknowledge at this late date my obligations to these two great authors, whose writings in conjunction with Percy's *Reliques*, power-

fully counteracted the mischievous influence of Darwin's dazzling manner, the extravagance of the earlier dramas of Schiller, and that of other German writers upon my taste and natural tendencies." *The Poetical Works of William Wordsworth*, eds. Ernest de Selincourt and Helen Darbishire, 2nd ed., 5 vols. (Oxford: Clarendon Press, 1940–49), III.442.

11. Stephen M. Parrish, "Wordsworth as Satirist of His Age," in *The Age of William Wordsworth: Critical Essays on the Romantic Tradition*, eds. Kenneth R. Johnston and Gene W. Ruoff (New Brunswick: Rutgers University Press, 1987), p. 37. It is worth noting that a sympathetic friend of Wordsworth's, Henry Crabb Robinson, regretted his publishing this Essay because he foresaw a negative reception: "it will afford a triumph to his enemies. He betrays resentment and that he has suffered pain. His reproaches of the bad taste of the times will be ascribed to merely personal feelings, and to disappointment." *Henry Crabb Robinson on Books and Their Writers*, ed. Edith J. Morley, 3 vols. (London: J. M. Dent, 1938), 1.165.

12. J. G. A. Pocock, "The Varieties of Whiggism from Exclusion to Reform: A History of Ideology and Discourse," in *Virtue, Commerce, and History: Essays on Political Thought and History, Chiefly in the Eighteenth Century* (Cambridge University Press, 1985), p. 242. This ninety-five-page essay, roughly a third of the volume, is actually a monograph that takes us from the late seventeenth century up through Macaulay and the Reform Bill.

13. My language here draws upon Gene Ruoff's tribute to Karl Kroeber when he notes the similarities between Kroeber and new-historical work, but suggests that the difference is "attitudinal," meaning "Romanticism" for Kroeber is unproblematically an honorific term: "Kroeber is caught between two modes of Romantic criticism. His work is a celebration of the Romantic achievement. Attitudinally, then, it is in keeping with the older theological/organicist/formalist strain of Romantic studies that finds its apotheosis in *Natural Supernaturalism*." See Ruoff, "Romanticism with a Difference: The Recent Criticism of Karl Kroeber," *Boundary 2* 18 (1991): 233.

14. Stephen Greenblatt, "Introduction," in *Learning to Curse: Essays in Early Modern Culture* (London and New York: Routledge, 1990), p. 2.

15. Jonathan Arac, *Critical Genealogies: Historical Situations for Postmodern Literary Studies* (New York: Columbia University Press, 1987), p. 26. The next sentence reads: "Arnold, Eliot, and Leavis subsequently accepted this call."

16. For this observation, see Pocock, "The Political Economy of Burke's Analysis of the French Revolution," in *Virtue, Commerce, and History*, p. 210; and especially "The Varieties of Whiggism," p. 291.

17. Peter Manning, *Reading Romantics: Texts and Contexts* (Oxford University Press, 1990), p. 261. Compare Ronald Paulson's observation on Scott: "He displaces the experience of the French Revolution back to the English revolution/civil war of the seventeenth century." *Representations of Revolution, 1789–1820* (New Haven: Yale University Press, 1983), p. 252, n. 1.

18. Pocock, "The Varieties of Whiggism," in *Virtue, Commerce, and History*, p. 292.

19. Pocock, "The Mobility of Property and the Rise of Eighteenth-Century Sociology," in *Virtue, Commerce, and History*, pp. 114–15.
20. Charles Burney, Review of *Lyrical Ballads*, *The Monthly Review* 29 (May–August 1799): 209.
21. Pocock, "The Mobility of Property," in *Virtue, Commerce, and History*, p. 115.
22. David Simpson, *Wordsworth's Historical Imagination: The Poetry of Displacement* (New York: Methuen, 1987), p. 65.
23. Raymond Williams, *The Country and the City* (Oxford University Press, 1973), pp. 58ff, 127ff.
24. See especially Peter Manning's remarkable essay on Lonsdale's exploitation of the Convent of St. Bees and Wordsworth's praise of him as its benefactor. "Wordsworth at St. Bees: Scandals, Sisterhoods, and Wordsworth's Later Poetry," in *Reading Romantics*, pp. 273–99.
25. Raymond Williams, *The Country and the City*, p. 79.
26. Leopold Damrosch, Jr., *The Imaginative World of Alexander Pope* (Berkeley and Los Angeles: University of California Press, 1987), p. 127, but see the entire discussion, pp. 120–30. On Pope's affinities with those he attacks, see also Dustin Griffin, *Alexander Pope: The Poet in the Poems* (Princeton University Press, 1978), and Fredric V. Bogel, "Dulness Unbound: Rhetoric and Pope's Dunciad," *PMLA* 97 (October 1982): 844–55.
27. See, for example: Jerome J. McGann, *The Romantic Ideology: A Critical Investigation* (University of Chicago Press, 1983), and his more recent reflections in "Rethinking Romanticism," *ELH* 59 (1992): 735–54; Marilyn Butler, *Romantics, Rebels and Reactionaries* (Oxford University Press, 1981); Frances Ferguson, "On the Number of Romanticisms," *ELH* 58 (1991): 471–98; Mark Parker, "Measure and Countermeasure: the Lovejoy–Wellek Debate and Romantic Periodization," in *Theoretical Issues in Literary History*, ed. David Perkins (Cambridge, Mass.: Harvard University Press, 1991), pp. 227–47.
28. Arthur O. Lovejoy, "On the Discrimination of Romanticisms," *PMLA* 39 (1924): 235–36.
29. René Wellek, "The Concept of Romanticism in Literary History," in *Concepts of Criticism* (New Haven: Yale University Press, 1963), pp. 129, 161; the essay is reprinted from *Comparative Literature* 1 (1949): 1–23, 147–72.
30. McGann, "Rethinking Romanticism," 735.
31. René Wellek, "The Concept of Romanticism," in *Concepts of Criticism*, p. 129. Of course, scholars accepted the implicit values of a canon even though they did not dabble in overt interpretations. The debate between critics and scholars in the 1930s and 1940s has been widely written about. See, for example, Gerald Graff, *Professing Literature: An Institutional History* (University of Chicago Press, 1987), and Vincent B. Leitch, *American Literary Criticism from the Thirties to the Eighties* (New York: Columbia University Press, 1988).
32. Mark Parker, "Measure and Countermeasure," p. 239. Compare Hartman's statement in the early 1970s: "The debate is a twenty-year stand-

off." "On the Theory of Romanticism," in *The Fate of Reading and Other Essays* (University of Chicago Press, 1975), p. 277.
33. McGann, "Rethinking Romanticism," 738–39.
34. A representative collection of essays is assembled in *Romanticism and Feminism*, ed. Anne K. Mellor (Bloomington: Indiana University Press, 1988). For a brief overview, see Mellor's introduction, "On Romanticism and Feminism."
35. Fredric Jameson, *The Political Unconscious: Narrative as a Socially Symbolic Act* (Ithaca: Cornell University Press, 1981), p. 28.
36. Thomas A. Vogler, "Romanticism and Literary Periods: The Future of the Past," *New German Critique* 38 (1986): 131–60; Jon Klancher, "Romantic Criticism and the Meaning of the French Revolution," *Studies in Romanticism* 28 (1988): 463–91; David Perkins, "The Construction of English Romantic Poetry as a Literary Classification," in *Is Literary History Possible?* (Baltimore: Johns Hopkins University Press, 1992), pp. 85–119. See also McGann's description, in "Rethinking Romanticism," of his selections for his new Oxford anthology as a way of breaking down the received narrative.
37. See David Perkins on the second half of the nineteenth century: "The 'romantic ideology' was formed at this time and not in the romantic period itself." *Is Literary History Possible?*, p. 104.
38. René Wellek, *Concepts of Criticism*, p. 152 ; also see Wellek's fuller account of Thomas Warton in *The Rise of English Literary History* (Chapel Hill: University of North Carolina Press, 1941).
39. Harold Bloom, *A Map of Misreading* (New York: Oxford University Press, 1975), p. 35.
40. Lawrence Lipking, *The Ordering of the Arts in Eighteenth-Century England* (Princeton University Press, 1970), pp. 338, 331.
41. Harold Bloom, *The Ringers in the Tower: Studies in Romantic Tradition* (University of Chicago Press, 1971), p. 15.
42. René Wellek, "English Literary Historiography during the Nineteenth Century," in *Discriminations* (New Haven: Yale University Press, 1970), p. 145.
43. Howard Felperin, "Romance and Romanticism," *Critical Inquiry* 6 (1980): 706.
44. *From the Dawn of the Romantic Movement to the World War*, vol. II, *The Literature of England: An Anthology and a History*, eds. George B. Woods, *et al.* (New York: Scott, Foresman & Co., 1941), p. 2.
45. Perkins, *Is Literary History Possible?*, p. 65.
46. *Ibid.*, p. 118; Annabel Patterson, *Pastoral and Ideology: Virgil to Valéry* (Berkeley and Los Angeles: University of California Press, 1987), p. 9.
47. McGann, "Rethinking Romanticism," 740.

1. THE EIGHTEENTH-CENTURY CONSTRUCTION OF ROMANTICISM

1. Francis Jeffrey, Review of William Hayley's *Life of Cowper*, *Edinburgh Review* (April 1803), in *Contributions to the Edinburgh Review*, 4 vols. (London, 1844),

1.411. Jeffrey's "this-will-never-do" review of *The Excursion* is the infamous and standard example of the forces Wordsworth had to overcome in order to obtain recognition.
2. Marlon Ross, *The Contours of Masculine Desire: Romanticism and the Rise of Women's Poetry* (Oxford University Press, 1989), p. 54.
3. Lord Byron, *Selected Prose*, ed. Peter Gunn (Harmondsworth: Penguin, 1972), p. 406.
4. See in particular Henry Knight Miller, "The 'Whig Interpretation' of Literary History," *Eighteenth-Century Studies* 6 (Fall 1972): 60–84, esp. 78. Marshall Brown defends the notion of teleology in *Preromanticism* (Stanford University Press, 1991).
5. Ernest Bernbaum, *Guide Through the Romantic Movement*, 2nd ed. (New York: The Ronald Press, 1949), pp. 6–7.
6. Edith Morley, "Joseph Warton: A Comparison of His *Essay on the Genius and Writings of Pope* with His Edition of Pope's *Works*," in *Essays and Studies* 9, ed. W. P. Ker (Oxford University Press, 1924), p. 102.
7. See Chalmers' "Life of Cowper" in *The Works of the English Poets from Chaucer to Cowper*, ed. Alexander Chalmers, 21 vols. (London, 1810), XVII.602. For Jeffrey, see his review of John Ford, August 1811, in *Contributions*, II.294. Coleridge's comment appears in *Biographia Literaria*, eds. W. J. Bate and James Engell, 2 vols. (Princeton University Press, 1983), I.54. For Christopher North, see John Wilson, *et al.*, *Noctes Ambrosianae*, 5 vols. (New York, 1854), V.27.
8. The anonymous reviewer of *The Prelude* is Whitwell Elwin, *Quarterly Review* (December 1852): 233. For more information, see Thomas C. Richardson, "Lockhart and Elwin on Wordsworth," *Wordsworth Circle* 20 (Summer 1989): 156.
9. See Oliver Ferguson, "Warton and Keats: Two Views of Melancholy," *Keats–Shelley Journal* 18 (1969): 12–15; and Nathaniel Teich, "A Comparative Approach to Periodization: Forms of Self-Consciousness in Warton's 'The Pleasures of Melancholy and Keats's 'Ode on Melancholy,'" in *Proceedings of the Xth Congress of the International Comparative Literature Association*, vol. 1: *General Problems of Literary History*, ed. Douwe Fokkema (New York: Garland, 1982): pp. 158–63. In relation to Teich, I would only suggest that it may be more useful to compare "forms of self-consciousness" in two major poets, rather than pitting a major one against a minor one, especially in this case since Warton's poem was raw material for Keats.

    The best overview of both Wartons, and the place to begin, is Lawrence Lipking's *The Ordering of the Arts in Eighteenth-Century England* (Princeton University Press, 1970). For a selection of scholarship, see John A. Vance, *Joseph and Thomas Warton: An Annotated Bibliography* (New York: Garland, 1983).
10. Although written in 1745, the poem was first published in 1747; a revised version was printed by Dodsley in 1755. The first edition is reprinted in *Eighteenth Century Poetry and Prose*, eds. Bredvold, McKillop, and Whitney

(New York: The Ronald Press, 1939), pp. 565–70. I quote from this anthology except where I indicate the 2nd edition, which I cite from *A Collection of Poems, in Six Volumes, by Several Hands, with Notes*, ed. Robert Dodsley (London, 1782), IV.224–35.
11. My text for "Eloisa" and "The Unfortunate Lady" is *Twickenham Edition: The Poems of Alexander Pope*, eds. John Butt, *et al.*, 11 vols. (London: Methuen, 1939–69). However, I have modernized some of the spellings.
12. Sigmund Freud, "Repression" (1915), in *General Psychological Theory: Papers on Metapsychology*, ed. Philip Rieff (New York: Collier, 1963), p. 108.
13. Patrocinio Schweickart, "Reading Ourselves: Toward a Feminist Theory of Reading," in *Contemporary Literary Criticism: Literary and Cultural Studies*, eds. Robert Con Davis and Ronald Schleifer, 2nd ed. (New York and London: Longman, 1989), p. 126.
14. Gillian Beer, "'Our unnatural no-voice': The Heroic Epistle, Pope, and Women's Gothic," in *Modern Essays on Eighteenth-Century Literature*, ed. Leopold Damrosch, Jr. (Oxford University Press, 1988), p. 411. See also Rachel Trickett, "The *Heroides* and the English Augustans," in *Ovid Renewed: Ovidian Influences on Literature and Art from the Middle Ages to the Twentieth Century*, ed. Charles Martindale (Cambridge University Press, 1988). For an excellent scholarly study of Pope's reception, see Claudia N. Thomas, *Alexander Pope and His Eighteenth-Century Women Readers* (Carbondale and Edwardsville: Southern Illinois University Press, 1994).
15. John Milton, *Poems upon Several Occasions*, ed. Thomas Warton (London, 1785), p. xi.
16. Warton introduces the anecdote by saying, "My brother remembers to have heard my father say." Milton, *Poems*, pp. viii-ix.
17. *Ibid.*, p. 186.
18. Arthur Scouten, "The Warton Forgeries and the Concept of Preromanticism in English Literature," *Etudes Anglaises* 40 (1987): 438.
19. Wordsworth, "Essay, Supplementary to the Preface," in *The Prose Works of William Wordsworth*, eds. W. J. B. Owen and Jane Worthington Smyser, 3 vols. (Oxford: Clarendon Press, 1974), III.70.
20. Edmund Gosse, "Two Pioneers of Romanticism: Joseph and Thomas Warton," *Proceedings of the British Academy* 7 (1915–16), 158.
21. *Romanticism Reconsidered*, ed. Northrop Frye, English Institute Essays (New York: Columbia University Press, 1963), pp. v-vi.
22. Thomas Warton the Elder, *Poems on Several Occasions* (New York: The Facsimile Text Society, 1930), p. 180.
23. David Fairer, "The Poems of Thomas Warton the Elder?" *Review of English Studies* 26 (1975): 287–300, 395–406; "The Poems of Thomas Warton the Elder? – A Postscript," *Review of English Studies* 29 (1978): 61–5; Christina Le Prevost, "More Unacknowledged Verse by Joseph Warton," *Review of English Studies* 37 (1986): 314–47.
24. Joseph Warton, *Odes on Various Subjects*, ed. Joan Pittock (Delmar, N.Y.: Scholars' Facsimiles & Reprints, 1977), p. 4.

25. John Sitter's account of mid-century poetry calls attention to the importance of the conversion experience. See *Literary Loneliness in Mid-Eighteenth-Century England* (Ithaca and London: Cornell University Press, 1982), pp. 104–53.
26. Le Prevost, "More Unacknowledged Verse," 320.
27. Ibid., 327.
28. Joseph Warton, *An Essay on the Writings and Genius of Pope* (London, 1756), pp. iii-iv. For information about the genesis, publication, reception, and the many revisions from edition to edition, including the title, see William D. MacClintock, *Joseph Warton's Essay on Pope* (New York: Russell & Russell, 1933).
29. Warton, *Essay on Pope*, p. x. In the second edition the last sentence becomes: "What is there transcendently sublime or pathetic in Pope?" See MacClintock, *Warton's Essay*, p. 56.
30. Owen Ruffhead, *The Life of Alexander Pope, Esq. compiled from Original Manuscripts; with a Critical Essay on his Writings and Genius* (London, 1769), p. 445.
31. The lists vary from edition to edition. For a detailed comparison, see MacClintock, *Warton's Essay*, p. 58.
32. Warton, *Essay on Pope*, 2 vols. (1782), II.410–411. Volume II was published twenty-six years after volume I, giving rise to much speculation over the causes of the delay. See Joan Pittock, "Joseph Warton and His Second Volume of the Essay on Pope," *Review of English Studies* 18 (1967): 264–73.
33. Warton, *Essay on Pope* (1756), p. 318.
34. Warton, *Essay on Pope* (1782), II.77.
35. Warton, *Essay on Pope* (1756), p. 229.
36. Paul F. Leedy, "Genres Criticism and the Significance of Warton's Essay on Pope," *Journal of English and Germanic Philology* 45 (1946): 144.
37. Samuel Johnson, Review of Ruffhead, reprinted in *Pope: the Critical Heritage*, ed. John Barnard (London and Boston: Routledge & Kegan Paul, 1973), p. 464.
38. Campbell speaks of "the popularity with which it continues to be read," but concludes that "while much ingenuity and many truths are scattered over the Essay, it is impossible to admire it as an entire theory, solid and consistent in all its parts." *Specimens of the British Poets, with biographical and critical notes, and An Essay on English Poetry*, 7 vols. (London, 1819), VII.324–25.
39. Ruffhead, *Life of Alexander Pope*, p. 443.
40. Rev. John Wooll, *Biographical Memoirs of . . . Joseph Warton* (London, 1806), p. 74; cited in Leedy, "Genres Criticism," 145, n. 26.
41. Joan Pittock, *The Ascendency of Taste: The Achievement of Joseph and Thomas Warton* (London: Routledge & Kegan Paul, 1973), p. 128.
42. *Memoirs of the Life and Writings of Alexander Pope* (London, 1745), II.48; cited in Leedy, "Genres Criticism," 141.
43. Samuel Johnson, "The Life of Pope," in *Lives of the English Poets*, ed. G. B. Hill, 3 vols. (Oxford: Clarendon Press, 1905), III.220ff.

44. James Boswell, *London Journal, 1762–1763*, ed. Frederick A. Pottle (New York: McGraw-Hill, 1950), p. 115.
45. Martin Price, *To the Palace of Wisdom: Studies in Order and Energy from Dryden to Blake* (Garden City: Doubleday, 1965), p. 347. See also Daniel W. Odell, "Young's *Night Thoughts* as Answer to Pope's *Essay on Man*," *Studies in English Literature* 12 (Summer 1972): 481–501.
46. Coleridge, *Marginalia: Abbt to Byfield*, ed. George Whalley (Princeton University Press, 1980), p. 51. *Essays of George Eliot*, ed. Thomas Pinney (New York: Columbia University Press, 1941), p. 337.
47. Johnson, *Lives of the Poets*, III.219.
48. Much of the detail about Young's career I take from Isabel St. John Bliss, *Edward Young* (New York: Twayne, 1969).
49. *Ibid.*, p. 93.
50. George Sherburn, *The Early Career of Alexander Pope* (Oxford: Clarendon Press, 1934), pp. 139–45; see also Young's letters to Pope and Tickell, *The Correspondence of Edward Young*, ed. Henry Pettit (Oxford: Clarendon Press, 1971), pp. 3–6.
51. *Eighteenth-Century English Literature*, eds. Geoffrey Tillotson, *et al.* (New York: Harcourt Brace Jovanovitch, 1969), p. 804.
52. *The Works of the English Poets from Chaucer to Cowper*, ed. Alexander Chalmers, 21 vols. (London, 1810), XIII.513.
53. Edward Young, *Night Thoughts*, ed. Stephen Cornford (Cambridge University Press, 1989), p. 48.
54. Warton, *Essay on Pope*, (1782), II.220; Joseph Spence, *Observations, Anecdotes, and Characters of Books and Men, Collected from Conversation*, ed. James M. Osborn, 2 vols. (Oxford: Clarendon Press, 1966), 1.83; Ruffhead, *Life of Alexander Pope*, p. 291; Pope to Gay, 4 May, 1714, *The Correspondence of Alexander Pope*, ed. George Sherburn, 5 vols. (Oxford: Clarendon Press, 1956), I.223.
55. Johnson, *Lives of the Poets*, III.383.
56. *Ibid.*, III.386. This seems to have been a widespread opinion. Goldsmith may be the source for he said something similar, comparing Young's old age and young style, in his review for *The Critical Review* 7 (June 1959): 48; Bliss quotes Young's friend, Mrs. Delany, to the same purpose (*Edward Young*, p. 147).
57. Edward Young, *Conjectures on Original Composition*, ed. Edith J. Morley (London: Longmans, Green & Co.; Manchester University Press, 1918), pp. xvii, xii.
58. In what follows I am indebted to Joel Weinsheimer's shrewd deconstruction of Young's thesis in "Conjectures on Unoriginal Composition," *The Eighteenth Century: Theory and Interpretation* 22 (1981): 58–73.
59. Edward Young, *Conjectures on Original Composition* (1759) (Leeds: The Scolar Press, 1966), pp. 9, 10. Subsequent references to Young's *Conjectures* are to this edition.
60. *Ibid.*, p. 28.

61. William K. Wimsatt, "Imitation as Freedom – 1717–1798," *New Literary History* 2 (Winter 1970): 215–36.
62. Pope, *Correspondence*, 1.19–20.
63. Geoffrey Hartman, "Romantic Poetry and the Genius Loci," in *Beyond Formalism* (New Haven and London: Yale University Press, 1970), pp. 311–36.
64. Young, *Conjectures*, p. 15.
65. *Ibid.*, p. 57.
66. *Ibid.*, p. 59.
67. *Ibid.*, pp. 54, 55.
68. *Ibid.*, pp. 67–8.
69. James Boswell, *Life of Johnson*, ed. G. B. Hill, rev. L. F. Powell, 6 vols. (Oxford: Clarendon Press, 1934), II.126.
70. Young, *Conjectures*, pp. 31, 52–3, 5.
71. Sir Walter Scott, *The Life of John Dryden*, ed. Bernard Kreissman (Lincoln: University of Nebraska Press, 1963), p. 405.
72. Horace Walpole to William Mason, 25 June 1782, *Eighteenth-Century English Literature*, eds. Tillotson, et al., p. 1198.
73. Warton, *Essay on Pope* (1756), p. 203.
74. Sitter, *Literary Loneliness*, pp. 84, 108.
75. Freud, "Repression," p. 104.
76. Sitter, *Literary Loneliness*, p. 125.
77. William Dowling, "Ideology and the Flight from History in Eighteenth-Century Poetry," in *The Profession of Eighteenth-Century Literature: Reflections on an Institution*, ed. Leo Damrosch (Madison: University of Wisconsin Press, 1992), p. 146.
78. Douglas Lane Patey, "The Eighteenth Century Invents the Canon," *Modern Language Studies* 18 (Winter 1988): 17–37. See also the continuation of this thesis in "'Aesthetics' and the Rise of the Lyric in the Eighteenth Century," *Studies in English Literature* 33 (1993): 587–609.
79. John Barrell and Harriet Guest, "On the Use of Contradiction: Economics and Morality in the Eighteenth-Century Long Poem," in *The New Eighteenth Century: Theory, Politics, English Literature*, eds. Felicity Nussbaum and Laura Brown (New York and London: Methuen, 1987), p. 141.
80. Peter Burger, "The Problem of Aesthetic Value," in *Literary Theory Today*, eds. Peter Collier and Helga Geyer-Ryan (Cambridge: Polity Press, 1990), pp. 28–29. Martha Woodmansee, "Toward a History of Modern Criticism: The Emergence of a Paradigm," in *Proceedings of the Xth Congress of the International Comparative Literature Association*, vol. 1: *General Problems of Literary History*, ed. Douwe Fokkema (New York and London: Garland, 1985), p. 179. John Barrell, *English Literature in History, 1730–1780: An Equal, Wide Survey* (London: Hutchinson, 1983).
81. Peter Stallybrass and Allon White, "The Grotesque Body and the Smithfield Muse: Authorship in the Eighteenth Century," in *The Politics and Poetics of Transgression* (Ithaca: Cornell University Press, 1986), p. 120.

82. Marilyn Butler, "Romanticism in England," in *Romanticism in National Context*, eds. Roy Porter and Mikulas Teich (New York: Cambridge University Press, 1988), pp. 41f.
83. See *Pope Versus Dryden: A Controversy in letters to* The Gentleman's Magazine, *1789–1791*, ed. Gretchen M. Foster (University of Victoria Press, 1989).
84. Upali Amarasinghe, *Dryden and Pope in the Early Nineteenth Century: A Study of Changing Literary Taste, 1800–1830* (Cambridge University Press, 1962), pp. 11, 170. See also W. J. Bate, *The Stylistic Development of Keats* (Cambridge, Mass.: Harvard University Press, 1945), p. 86.
85. David Fairer, "Oxford and the Literary World," in *The History of the University of Oxford*, vol. v: *The Eighteenth Century*, eds. L. S. Sutherland and L. G. Mitchell (Oxford: Clarendon Press, 1986), p. 784.
86. Milton, *Poems*, p. 95, my emphasis.
87. Cited in Fairer, "Oxford and the Literary World," p. 791. Fairer's paraphrase of a key theme in "The Triumph of Isis" no doubt refers to the following lines: "Scorning and scorn'd by courts, youn Muse's bower / Still nor enjoys, nor seeks, the smile of power" (lines 62–3).
88. Brian Gardner, *The Public Schools: An Historical Survey* (London: Hamish Hamilton, 1973), pp. 21–2. Gardner describes the Wykehamist type as "a reticent sort of person with a respect for scholarship." Famous Wykehamists include Matthew Arnold (briefly) and in our century William Empson.
89. G. E. Aylmer, "Seventeenth-Century Wykehamists," in *Winchester College: Sixth Centenary Essays*, ed. Roger Custance (Oxford University Press, 1982), p. 286.
90. Bliss, *Edward Young*, p. 18.
91. I have pieced together this information from a variety of sources, most prominently the *Dictionary of National Biography*.
92. Ronald Paulson, *Breaking and Remaking: Aesthetic Practice in England, 1700–1820* (New Brunswick and London: Rutgers University Press, 1989), p. 83. Robert Folkenflik, "The Artist as Hero in the Eighteenth Century," *Yearbook of English Studies* 12 (1982): 94, n. 9. The relation between satire and elegy is addressed by Michael Cooke in *Acts of Inclusion* (New Haven: Yale University Press, 1979) and Herbert Lindenberger in *The History in Literature* (New York: Columbia University Press, 1990).
93. Fairer, "Oxford and the Literary World," p. 779.
94. William Cowper to Samuel Rose, 2 February 1790, *The Letters and Prose Writings of William Cowper*, eds. James King and Charles Ryskamp, 5 vols. (Oxford: Clarendon Press, 1979–86), III.342.
95. *The Works of William Cowper*, ed. Robert Southey, 15 vols. (London, 1835–37), II.164.
96. Martin Priestman, *Cowper's Task: Structure and Style* (Cambridge University Press, 1983), pp. 7, 24.
97. Johnson, "The Life of Milton," in *Lives of the Poets*, I.193. For Pope's similar opinion, see George Sherburn, *The Early Career of Alexander Pope*, p. 192.
98. Humphrey House, *Coleridge* (London: Rupert Hart-Davis, 1969), p. 73.

99. See Byron's epigram on "Bowles and Campbell": "Why, how now, Billy Bowles? / Sure the priest is maudlin!" (lines 5–6); cf. "English Bards": "The maudlin prince of mournful sonneteers"; *Byron: Poetical Works*, ed. Frederick Page, corrected by John Jump (Oxford University Press, 1970), pp. 108, 117. Warton had claimed that modern poetry was written "from and to the head rather than the heart" (*Essay on Pope* [1756], p. 204), conveniently forgetting his remarks about the pathetic in *Eloisa* and the *Elegy to an Unfortunate Lady*.
100. Lord Byron, *Selected Prose*, p. 420.
101. Chandler raises the issue in two places, showing that he had considered the possibility before rejecting it. His most direct statement comes when he says that he does not "propose to argue the extreme case that the principles of Romantic poetics can be explained solely as an ad hoc contrivance to justify the ouster of Pope." James Chandler, "The Pope Controversy: Romantic Poetics and the English Canon," *Critical Inquiry* 10 (1984): 498.
102. Henry Crabb Robinson's diary entry for 24 May 1812 reads: "We talked of Lord Byron. Wordsworth allowed him power, but denied his style to be English." *Henry Crabb Robinson on Books and Their Writers*, ed. Edith J. Morley, 3 vols. (London: Dent, 1938), 1.85. Based on the same criteria, a character in an imaginary conversation in *Blackwood's Magazine* could arrive at the opposite conclusion: ". . . what poet of this age, with the exception, perhaps, of Byron, can be justly said, when put into close comparison with Pope, to have written the English language at all?" *Noctes Ambrosianae*, John Wilson, *et al.*, 5 vols. (New York, 1854), II.64.
103. For an excellent survey, see Oscar Maurer, Jr., "Pope and the Victorians," in *Studies in English, 1944* (Austin: University of Texas Press, 1945): 211–38.
104. Leigh Hunt, *Examiner* (1817), in *Romantic Critical Essays*, ed. David Bromwich (Cambridge University Press, 1987), p. 127.
105. Walter Bagehot, "William Cowper," in *Literary Studies*, ed. Ernest Rhys, Everyman's Library, 2 vols. (London: Dent; New York: Dutton, n.d.), 1.256.
106. *The Poems of Gray, Collins, and Goldsmith*, ed. Roger Lonsdale (London: Longman, 1969), pp. 154–55.
107. My last words are adapted from Andrew Elfenbein, "Cowper's *Task* and the Anxiety of Femininity," *Eighteenth-Century Life* 13 (1989): 1. In reference to Collins, Paul Fry is the only critic I know who thinks that Waller in Collins' "Poetical Character" is not so easily dismissed. He arrives at this conclusion, not by way of a broader contextualization as I have done, but by reading the poem carefully. Fry notices that "Waller's myrtle" is an erotic emblem, and that so is the "cest" that is the emblem of poetic power. See *The Poet's Calling in the English Ode* (New Haven: Yale University Press, 1980), pp. 112f.

2. REFINEMENT, ROMANTICISM, FRANCIS JEFFREY

1. Most recently, Dustin Griffin challenges Bloom's claim that Milton inhibits poets who follow him in the eighteenth century, in *Regaining Paradise: Milton*

and the Eighteenth Century (Cambridge University Press, 1986). Griffin himself is challenged at certain points by a book that has just appeared: Lucy Newlyn, Paradise Lost *and the Romantic Reader* (Oxford, Clarendon Press, 1993). I regret not having been able to address Newlyn's thesis.
2. Milton, *Poems upon Several Occasions*, ed. Thomas Warton (London, 1785), p. xi, my emphasis.
3. Herbert Lindenberger, *The History in Literature: On Value, Genre, Institutions* (New York: Columbia University Press, 1990), pp. 66–7.
4. See Warton on *Dunciad* IV: "Some of his most splendid and striking lines are indeed here to be found; but I must beg leave to insist that they want *propriety* and *decorum*"; *An Essay on the Genius and Writings of Pope*, 2 vols. (London, 1782), II.375.
5. "The trouble at the core of Milton is also Pope's, whose whole relation to Milton was very unlike his relation to Dryden. Whatever the force of the poetic past was to Pope, that part of it he felt emanating from Milton was beyond refinement. 'Darkness visible,' the Miltonic legacy after all, returned as the inevitable trope for Pope's sense of what lay always beyond the possibilities of the Enlightenment." *Modern Critical Views: Alexander Pope*, ed. Harold Bloom (New York: Chelsea House, 1986), p. 8.
6. Howard Erskine-Hill, *The Augustan Idea in English Literature* (London: Edward Arnold, 1983), pp. 244–45.
7. William Hazlitt, *Conversations of James Northcote, Esq., R.A.* (London, 1830), p. 150.
8. W. J. Bate, *The Burden of the Past and the English Poet* (Cambridge, Mass.: Belknap Press, 1970), pp. 54–6.
9. Joseph Warton, *An Essay on the Writings and Genius of Pope* (London, 1756), p. 204.
10. Francis Jeffrey, *Contributions to the Edinburgh Review*, 4 vols. (London, 1844), I.411.
11. Cited in Bate, *Burden of the Past*, p. 81.
12. Discussing Bate, Patey observed: "Bate himself is a Wartonian, in his interpretation of the Restoration, his careful separation of 'art' from 'ideas', and – like Warton's other modern epigoni – his valuing of the eighteenth century mainly for having ended in Romanticism." Douglas Lane Patey, "The Eighteenth Century Invents the Canon," *Modern Language Studies*, 18 (Winter 1988): 28. It is perhaps only fair to add that Bate is one of the very few critics with a primarily "romantic" orientation who has taken the eighteenth century seriously and produced landmark works in the field.
13. Cited in Upali Amarasinghe, *Dryden and Pope in the Early Nineteenth Century: A Study of Changing Literary Taste, 1800–1830* (Cambridge University Press, 1962), p. 88.
14. James Engell, *Forming the Critical Mind: Dryden to Coleridge* (Cambridge, Mass.: Harvard University Press, 1989), pp. 68, 63. Engell's chapter "The Paradox of Refinement: Progress and Decline in Literature," pp. 44–75, provides a wealth of citations for the eighteenth century's concern with this issue.

15. Returning to Lamb's after the play, they found Hazlitt and Coleridge: "A half-hour's chat." *Henry Crabb Robinson on Books and Their Writers*, ed. Edith J. Morley, 3 vols. (London: J. M. Dent, 1938), I.28.
16. Isaac D'Israeli, Review of Spence's *Ancedotes of Pope* and Bowles's *Invariable Principles of Poetry*, *Quarterly Review* 23 (July 1820): 431.
17. *Essays of George Eliot*, ed. Thomas Pinney (New York: Columbia University Press, 1941), p. 362.
18. John Henry Newman, *The Idea of a University*, ed. Martin J. Svaglic (New York and Toronto: Rhinehart, 1960), p. 234.
19. *The Correspondence of Henry Crabb Robinson with the Wordsworth Circle (1808–1866)*, ed. Edith J. Morley, 2 vols. (Oxford: Clarendon Press, 1927), I.514. Quillinan was a Catholic. In a later letter to Robinson after Wordsworth's death, Quillinan recalls how he used to "laud Pope to the skies" to Wordsworth, who would reply sarcastically that he had "a Catholic taste" (II.779).
20. *Ibid.*, I.518; this passage is cited in Amarasinghe, *Dryden and Pope*, p. 195. Amarasinghe also records Robinson's account of reading *Dunciad* IV, *Arbuthnot*, etc., to Mr. Monkhouse on the evening of 11 September 1837: "I relished this as I did forty years ago."
21. John Wilson, et al., *Noctes Ambrosianae*, 5 vols. (New York, 1854), II.64.
22. *A Complete Edition of the Poets of Great Britain*, ed. Robert Anderson, 14 vols. (London and Edinburgh, 1795), VIII.*xv*.
23. *The Wit and Wisdom of Sydney Smith* (London, 1860), p. 291.
24. William Hazlitt, "On the Periodical Press," in *Collected Works of William Hazlitt*, eds. A. R. Waller and Arnold Glover, 12 vols. (London: Dent, 1904), X.204.
25. Hazlitt, *Conversations of Northcote*, pp. 198, 10.
26. *Select British Poets, or New Elegant Extracts from Chaucer to the Present Time, with Critical Remarks by William Hazlitt* (London, 1824), p. ix.
27. "Pope," in *Hazlitt on English Literature*, ed. Jacob Zeitlin (New York: Oxford University Press, 1913), p. 132.
28. Byron to John Murray, 12 April, 1818, *Byron's Letters and Journals*, ed. Leslie A. Marchand, 8 vols. (London: John Murray, 1973–79), VI.31.
29. Amarasinghe, *Dryden and Pope*, pp. 65ff.
30. Sheldon Halpern, *Sydney Smith* (New York: Twayne, 1966), pp. 32–3.
31. Marilyn Butler, *Romantics, Rebels and Reactionaries* (Oxford University Press, 1981), p. 61. See also Bate, *Burden of the Past*, pp. 99–103. David Bromwich offers a richly detailed view of Jeffrey on Byron, Keats, and Shelley in "Romantic Poetry and the *Edinburgh* Ordinances," *Yearbook of English Studies* 16 (1986): 1–16. For an excellent introduction to Jeffrey, see Amarasinghe, "The Edinburgh Review," in *Dryden and Pope*, pp. 63–92. I differ from Amarasinghe in one crucial point. He sees Jeffrey gradually coming to an appreciation of the Elizabethans until he is finally converted around 1810; before that time he is supposedly committed to the Augustans. Evidence shows, however, that, quite independently of any attitude to the

Elizabethans, Jeffrey had already rejected the Augustans in favor of Cowper by 1803 if not before.
32. Halpern, *Sydney Smith*, p. 136.
33. Lindenberger, *The History in Literature*, p. 28.
34. René Wellek, *A History of Modern Criticism*, vol. 2: *The Romantic Age* (New Haven: Yale University Press, 1955), pp. 110–20; for "moderate romanticism," see p. 119.
35. Ian Jack, *English Literature 1815–1832*, Oxford History of English Literature, vol. x (Oxford: Clarendon Press, 1963), pp. 324–29, 8ff.
36. Bate, *Burden of the Past*, p. 99.
37. Jeffrey, *Contributions*, I.158.
38. *Ibid.*, I.161, 166.
39. *Ibid.*, III.102. The connection between Romanticism and the Elizabethan revival has been widely noted. Stuart Curran is the most recent critic to comment on the phenomenon in "The Second Renaissance," in *Poetic Form and British Romanticism* (Oxford University Press, 1986), pp. 14–28.
40. Jeffrey, *Contributions*, I.125. For more examples, consult Pat Rogers, "North and South," *Eighteenth-Century Life* 12 (1988): 45–75.
41. Jeffrey, *Contributions*, II.284–85.
42. *Ibid.*, I.161.
43. *Ibid.*, I.163–64.
44. *Ibid.*, II.288.
45. *Ibid.*, II.292.
46. *Ibid.*, I.163.
47. *A Select Collection of Old Plays*, ed. Robert Dodsley, corrected by Isaac Reed, 12 vols. (London, 1780), I.xii. Dodsley tells us in his Preface that he collected the plays both to preserve them and to show the gradual improvement of the national taste.
48. *Collected Works of Oliver Goldsmith*, ed. Arthur Friedman, 5 vols. (Oxford: Clarendon Press, 1966), I.118. Thomas Warton opened his *History of English Poetry* with a similar observation: "In an age advanced to the highest degree of refinement, that species of curiosity commences, which is busied in contemplating the progress of social life, in displaying the gradations of science, and tracing the transitions from barbarism to civility." "Authors's Preface," *History of English Poetry from the Twelfth to the Close of the Sixteenth Century* (1774–1781), ed. W. Carew Hazlitt (1871), 4 vols. (New York: Haskell House, 1970), I.3.
49. W. K. Wimsatt and Cleanth Brooks, *Literary Criticism: A Short History* (New York: Knopf, 1957), p. 369.
50. Jeffrey, *Contributions*, II.460.
51. *Ibid.*, II.461.
52. Joseph Trapp, *Lectures on Poetry* (London, 1742), p. 57.
53. Joseph Warton, "A Dissertation on the Nature and Conduct of the Aeneid," in *The Works of Virgil in English Verse*, ed. Joseph Warton, 4 vols. (London, 1753), II.17–18.
54. *Ibid.*, II.13.

55. Samuel Johnson, "Life of Pope," in *Lives of the English Poets*, ed. G. B. Hill, 3 vols. (Oxford: Clarendon Press, 1905), III.239.
56. Anna Seward, *Gentleman's Magazine* 59 (June 1789), in Gretchen M. Foster, ed., *Pope Versus Dryden: A Controversy in Letters to* The Gentleman's Magazine, *1789–1791* (University of Victoria Press, 1989), p. 54.
57. Warton, *Essay on Pope* (1782), II.208; Johnson, *Lives of the Poets*, III.216–17.
58. Jeffrey, *Contributions*, 1.164, my emphasis.
59. Wordsworth to Dyce, 10 May 1830, *The Letters of William and Dorothy Wordsworth*, 2nd ed., 6 vols., ed. Ernest de Selincourt, rev. A. G. Hill (Oxford: Clarendon Press, 1979), v.260.
60. Henry Crabb Robinson's diary, 3 January 1839, in *On Books and Their Writers*, II.562.
61. "Essay, Supplementary to the Preface," in *The Prose Works of William Wordsworth*, eds. W. J. B. Owen and Jane Worthington Smyser, 3 vols. (Oxford: Clarendon Press, 1974), III.80, my emphasis.
62. "Appendix on Poetic Diction," cited in Donald Davie, *The Purity of Diction in English Verse* (Oxford University Press, 1953), p. 19. Davie links Wordsworth's notion of "chastity" to Goldsmith's, namely propriety in the management of metaphor.
63. Preface, *Lyrical Ballads*, ed. W. J. B. Owen (Oxford University Press, 1969), p. 169, my emphasis.
64. Coleridge, *Biographia Literaria*, eds. W. J. Bate and James Engell, 2 vols. (Princeton University Press, 1983), II.142. In the passage Coleridge alludes to (II, chapter 16), he deliberately reverses the received notions of literary development, finding more "art" and purer diction in the earlier writers, but less interesting matter, whereas the present writers excel in matter but lack art; like Jeffrey, however, the ideal is a union of both. Coleridge cites Pope's Homer together with Darwin's "The Temple of Nature" as examples of vicious style. Darwin must be read in order to gauge the true perversity of the comparison.
65. Coleridge, *Biographia Literaria*, II.18. For a critique of the body–soul trope, but in Wordsworth's incarnation theory of language, see Paul De Man, "Autobiography as De-Facement," in *The Rhetoric of Romanticism* (New York: Columbia University Press, 1984), pp. 79–80.
66. Cited by the editors in a note, *Biographia Literaria*, II.18.
67. David Hume, "Of the Standard of Taste," in *Of the Standard of Taste and Other Essays*, ed. John W. Lenz (Indianapolis: Bobbs-Merrill, 1965), p. 21. The context is the example of a man who is shocked by foreign or ancient manners thus leaving no allowance for his own prejudices.
68. Warton, *Essay on Pope* (1782), II.175.
69. D'Israeli, *Quarterly Review* 23 (July 1820): 431.
70. *The Letters and Prose Writings of William Cowper*, eds. James King and Charles Ryskamp, 5 vols. (Oxford: Clarendon Press, 1979–86), I.433.
71. *Ibid.*, I.434. The charge that Pope sacrificed sense to sound was made recurrently, perhaps most influentially by Spence in *An Essay on Pope's Odyssey* (London, 1727).

72. Thomas Campbell, *Specimens of the British Poets*, 7 vols. (London, 1819), I.260–61.
73. Gilbert Wakefield, *Observations on Pope* (London, 1796), pp. vii-viii. This volume gathers together Wakefield's notes for an edition of Pope that was never undertaken because the publishers commissioned Joseph Warton instead.
74. Foster, *Pope Versus Dryden*, p. 89.
75. Ibid., p. 105.
76. Jeffrey, *Contributions*, II.294.
77. Ibid., II.294–95.
78. Ibid., I.165.
79. Ibid., II.285–86.
80. Ibid., II.287.
81. Ibid., II.291.
82. Ibid., II.390, my emphasis.
83. Ibid., II.390–91.
84. Ibid., II.392.
85. Ibid., II.384.
86. D'Israeli, *Quarterly Review* 23 (July 1820): 434.
87. Susan Staves, "Pope's Refinement," *The Eighteenth Century: Theory and Interpretation* 29 (1988): pp. 146, 151, 153.
88. Sydney Smith, *Selected Writings of Sydney Smith*, ed. W. H. Auden (London: Faber and Faber, 1957), pp. 316–17.
89. John Barrell, *English Literature in History, 1730–1780: An Equal, Wide Survey* (London: Hutchinson, 1983), pp. 121, 125. Robert Markley challenges the factual basis of a late seventeenth- and early eighteenth-century sense of improvement and refinement that I have been expositing as part of the age's self-representation in "The Rise of Nothing: Revisionist Historiography and the Narrative Structure of Eighteenth-Century Studies," *Genre* 23 (1990): 77–101.
90. M. H. Abrams, "The Romantic Period," *The Norton Anthology of English Literature*, vol. II (New York: Norton, 1974), p. 5.
91. Marilyn Butler, *Romantics, Rebels and Reactionaries*, pp. 100ff.
92. "The Literary Restoration, 1790–1830," *Cornhill Magazine* 46 (September 1882): 320.
93. Joan Richardson, *Wallace Stevens: The Early Years, 1879–1923* (New York: William Morrow, 1986), p. 65. The ambivalence associated with modern refinement similarly does not go away. See especially Geoffrey Hartman, *Criticism in the Wilderness: The Study of Literature Today* (New Haven: Yale University Press, 1980), where the meditation on refinement or purity of style demonstrates its contemporary force.

3. WORDSWORTH'S POPE

1. Neil Hertz, "The Notion of Blockage in the Literature of the Sublime," in *The End of the Line: Essays on Psychoanalysis and the Sublime* (New York: Columbia University Press, 1985), p. 53.

2. Stuart Curran, *Poetic Form and British Romanticism* (Oxford University Press, 1986), p. 92.
3. *The Prose Works of William Wordsworth*, eds. W. J. B. Owen and Jane Worthington Smyser, 3 vols. (Oxford: Clarendon Press, 1974), III.372.
4. Stephen Gill, *William Wordsworth: A Life* (Oxford: Clarendon Press, 1989), p. 29.
5. Paul D. Sheats, *The Making of Wordsworth's Poetry, 1785–1798* (Cambridge, Mass.: Harvard University Press, 1973), p. 261, n.2.
6. Sheats, *The Making of Wordsworth's Poetry*; Edwin Stein, *Wordsworth's Art of Allusion* (University Park: Pennsylvania State University Press, 1988); Bruce Graver, "Wordsworth's Georgic Beginnings," *Texas Studies in Literature and Language* 33 (1991): 137–59.
7. The discontinuity between these early poems and the mature ballads and blank verse was noticed in 1815 by Crabb Robinson: "I read some of Wordsworth's poems, particularly the extracts from his first published works, which are in so different a style from his subsequent works as not to be recognized as his; and I could not relish them though they appear to be full of those elaborately fine descriptions which have given reputation to other and inferior poets." 7 May 1815, *On Books and Their Writers*, ed. Edith J. Morley, 3 vols. (London: J. M. Dent, 1938), 1.165.
8. Stuart Curran, "Wordsworth and the Forms of Poetry," in *The Age of William Wordsworth: Critical Essays on the Romantic Tradition*, eds. Kenneth R. Johnston and Gene W. Ruoff (New Brunswick: Rutgers University Press, 1987), p. 117.
9. Wordsworth, *Prose Works*, II.75.
10. *Ibid.*, II.84.
11. Wordsworth to Walter Scott, 18 January 1808, *The Letters of William and Dorothy Wordsworth*, 2nd ed., 6 vols., ed. Ernest de Selincourt, rev. Mary Moorman (Oxford: Clarendon Press, 1969), II.191.
12. Wordsworth, *Prose Works*, III.73–4.
13. Lawrence Lipking, "Night Thoughts on Literary History," in *Literary History: Theory and Practice*, ed. Herbert L. Sussman (Boston: Northeastern University Press, 1984), p. 71.
14. *Memoirs of William Wordsworth by Christopher Wordsworth, D.D.*, ed. Henry Reed, 2 vols. (Boston, 1851), II.480.
15. *Barron Field's Memoirs of Wordsworth*, ed. Geoffrey Little (Sydney University Press, 1975), p. 37, n. 43.
16. Wordsworth, *Prose Works*, II.80.
17. *The Critical Opinions of William Wordsworth*, ed. Markham L. Peacock, Jr. (Baltimore: Johns Hopkins University Press, 1950), p. 41.
18. Murray Bowen, "Toward the Differentiation of Self in One's Family of Origin," in *Family Therapy in Clinical Practice* (New York: Jacob Aronson, 1978), p. 536. I am grateful to Barbara Held of Bowdoin College for bringing Bowen to my attention.
19. The echo of Pope I don't discuss is nonetheless interesting to note. As part of

his progress piece in *To Augustus*, Pope asks, "Who now reads Cowley?" (line 75). Wordsworth begins his retrospect of literary history in the Essay by asking, "Who is there that now reads the 'Creation' of Dubartas?" (*Prose Works*, III.67).
20. Wordsworth, *Prose Works*, III.75.
21. *Ibid.*, III.77.
22. For a discussion of Pope as prophet, see Robert Griffin, "Pope, the Prophets, and *The Dunciad*," *Studies in English Literature* 23 (1983): 435–46.
23. Jonathan Wordsworth, *William Wordsworth: The Borders of Vision* (Oxford: Clarendon Press, 1982), p. 214.
24. For a discussion of the role of Milton's Satan in Tory satire, see Ronald Paulson, *The Fictions of Satire* (Baltimore: Johns Hopkins University Press, 1967), pp. 120–28.
25. Wordsworth, *Prose Works*, III.72.
26. Wordsworth to Dyce, 12 January 1829, *The Letters of William and Dorothy Wordsworth*, 2nd ed., 6 vols., ed. Ernest de Selincourt, rev. A. G. Hill (Oxford: Clarendon Press, 1979), v.3.
27. Wordsworth, *Prose Works*, III.62.
28. *Ibid.*, III.63–4.
29. My text is *The Prelude 1799, 1805, 1850*, eds. Jonathan Wordsworth, *et al.* (New York: Norton, 1979).
30. R. D. Havens, *The Mind of the Poet* (Baltimore: Johns Hopkins University Press, 1941), pp. 402, 405.
31. Richard J. Onorato, *The Character of the Poet: Wordsworth in* The Prelude (Princeton University Press, 1971), p. 83.
32. Harold Bloom, *A Map of Misreading* (New York: Oxford University Press, 1975), p. 95.
33. Peter Manning, for instance, speaks of the "double origin" of *The Prelude* "in literary history as well as in the *facta* of Wordsworth's life." "Reading Wordsworth's Revisions: Othello and the Drowned Man," *Studies in Romanticism* 22 (1983): 21. See also Mary Jacobus on the picturesque landscape of *Tintern Abbey*, in *Tradition and Experiment in Wordsworth's Lyrical Ballads, 1798* (Oxford University Press, 1976), p. 110.
34. *The Poetical Works of William Wordsworth*, eds. Ernest de Selincourt and Helen Darbishire, 2nd ed., 5 vols. (Oxford: Clarendon Press, 1940–49), IV.320, lines 412–13.
35. Hollander contrasts Milton's mode of allusion with Cowley's by noticing that in Cowley "there is no resonance of context"; *The Figure of Echo: A Mode of Allusion in Milton and After* (Berkeley and Los Angeles: University of California Press, 1981), p. 118.
36. For this relation between *Messiah* and *The Dunciad*, see Martin Battestin, *The Providence of Wit* (Oxford: Clarendon Press, 1974), pp. 58ff.
37. My language here obviously owes much to Geoffrey Hartman's formulations in *Wordsworth's Poetry, 1787–1814*, 2nd ed. (New Haven: Yale University Press, 1971), and in "Romanticism and Anti-Self-Consciousness," in *Beyond*

Formalism (New Haven and London: Yale University Press, 1970), pp. 298–310. The phrase "sovran voices" comes from Keats's *Hyperion: A Fragment* (III.115), and describes one of the things that comes pouring into the brain of Apollo. Notice that Keats is troping upon Milton's God, "the Sovran Voice" (*Paradise Lost*, VI.56), and thus turns the one god into a plurality of gods, or echoes of earlier poet-deities, that Mnemosyne evokes. I am suggesting, of course, that Pope is one of the "sovran voices" in Wordsworth's text, but that the voice is muffled or muted, "muffling" being a general condition that James Chandler has analyzed in "Romantic Allusiveness," *Critical Inquiry* 8 (1982): 461–87.

38. Jonathan Wordsworth, *The Borders of Vision*, p. 420, n. 3. I wrote to Wordsworth suggesting the source in *Aeneid* 4 that I develop in the following pages. This led to an invitation to deliver a paper on the subject at Grasmere in 1986 which I gratefully accepted. I tell this story only to prevent my being charged with lifting this material from John A. Hodgson, who independently arrived at the same source in "'Was it for this?': Wordsworth's Virgilian Questionings," *Texas Studies in Literature and Language* 33 (Summer 1991): 125–36.
39. Jonathan Wordsworth, *The Borders of Vision*, p. 37.
40. Wordsworth to Aubrey de Vere, 16 November 1842, *Letters of William and Dorothy Wordsworth*, v.1386.
41. *Ibid.*, v.471. The *Aeneid* translation has been virtually ignored. Bruce Graver's appreciation of Wordsworth's achievement is the first article since 1974; see "Wordsworth and the Language of Epic: The Translation of the *Aeneid*," *Studies in Philology* 83 (1986): 261–85. Arthur Sherbo documents very thoroughly Wordsworth's use of Dryden's and Pitt's translations, as well as Pope's Homer, in *English Poetic Diction from Chaucer to Wordsworth* (East Lansing: Michigan State University Press, 1975).
42. *Ibid.*, IV.250.
43. *Ibid.*, IV.247.
44. Field, *Memoirs of Wordsworth*, Appendix, pp. 132–33.
45. *Ibid.*, p. 37, n. 43.

4. MIRROR AND LAMP

1. *The Age of William Wordsworth: Critical Essays on the Romantic Tradition*, eds. Kenneth R. Johnston and Gene W. Ruoff (New Brunswick: Rutgers University Press, 1987), p. x.
2. Jon Klancher, "English Romanticism and Cultural Production," in *The New Historicism*, ed. H. Aram Veeser (New York and London: Routledge, 1987), p. 78.
3. Samuel Johnson, "Life of Dryden," in *Lives of the English Poets*, ed. G. B. Hill, 3 vols. (Oxford: Clarendon Press, 1905), I.411.
4. Ralph Cohen, Review of *The Mirror and the Lamp*, *Philological Quarterly* 33 (July 1954): 272.

5. Jonathan Culler, "The Mirror Stage," in *High Romantic Argument: Essays for M. H. Abrams*, ed. Lawrence Lipking (Ithaca: Cornell University Press, 1981), pp. 149–63.
6. M. H. Abrams, *The Mirror and the Lamp: Romantic Theory and the Critical Tradition* (New York: Oxford University Press, 1953), pp. 20–21.
7. *Ibid.*, p. 28.
8. *Criticism: The Major Texts*, ed. W. J. Bate (New York: Harcourt Brace Jovanovitch, 1970), p. 21.
9. *Ibid.*, p. 56.
10. Abrams, *The Mirror and the Lamp*, pp. 26–7, my emphasis.
11. *Ibid.*, p. 71.
12. *Ibid.*, p. 74.
13. Bate, ed., *Criticism*, pp. 65, 66, 63.
14. Abrams, *The Mirror and the Lamp*, pp. 29, 103ff.
15. *Ibid.*, p. 328.
16. William Levine, "The Genealogy of Romantic Literary History: Refigurations of Johnson's *Lives of the Poets* in the Criticism of Coleridge and Wordsworth," *Criticism* 34 (Summer 1992): 350. For the impact of Johnson, see also Annette Cafarelli, *Prose in the Age of Poets: Romanticism and Biographical Narrative from Johnson to De Quincey* (Philadelphia: University of Pennsylvania Press, 1990).
17. Abrams, *The Mirror and the Lamp*, p. 29.
18. *Ibid.*, p. 32.
19. *Ibid.*, p. 29.
20. *Ibid.*, pp. 57ff.
21. *Ibid.*, p. 59.
22. *Ibid.*, p. 26.
23. *Ibid.*, p. 30.
24. *Ibid.*, pp. 34, 35.
25. Plato, *Timaeus*, trans. Benjamin Jowett, in *The Collected Dialogues of Plato*, eds. Edith Hamilton and Huntington Cairns (Princeton University Press, 1961), pp. 1173, 1174. For the use of this notion in eighteenth-century poetry, see the entries under "Beam" and "Ray (visual ray)" in John Arthos, *The Language of Natural Description in Eighteenth-Century Poetry* (Ann Arbor: University of Michigan Press, 1949).
26. James Boswell, *The Journal of a Tour to the Hebrides*, ed. G. B. Hill (Oxford: Clarendon Press, 1950), pp. 34–5.
27. David E. Hahm, *The Origins of Stoic Cosmology* (Columbus: Ohio State University Press, 1977), pp. 57–90, and 91ff.
28. Stephen Gersh, *Middle Platonism and Neoplatonism: The Latin Tradition*, 2 vols. (University of Notre Dame Press, 1986), 1.9f.
29. *Ibid.*, p. 125.
30. Thomas Aquinas, *Summa Theologica*, pt. 1, q. 58, art. 4, vol. 1 (New York: Benziger Brothers, 1947), p. 290.
31. Abrams, *The Mirror and the Lamp*, p. 60.

32. John Locke, *An Essay Concerning Human Understanding*, ed. Alexander Campbell Fraser, 2 vols. (New York: Dover, 1959), I.xxxiii-xxxiv.
33. *Ibid.*, II.211–12.
34. *Ibid.*, I.xliv.
35. *Ibid.*, II.177.
36. Abrams, *The Mirror and the Lamp*, p. 63.
37. Aristotle, *De Anima*, trans. W. S. Hett (Cambridge, Mass.: Harvard University Press; London: Heinemann, 1957), sec. 430a, p. 171.
38. *The Letters of Percy Bysshe Shelley*, ed. Frederick Jones, 2 vols. (Oxford: Clarendon Press, 1964), 1.35.
39. Samuel Johnson, *Rambler* No. 4, The Yale Edition of the Works of Samuel Johnson, vol. 3, eds. W. J. Bate and Albrecht B. Strauss (New Haven: Yale University Press, 1969), p. 22.
40. Abrams, *The Mirror and the Lamp*, p. 50.
41. Joseph Addison, *Spectator* No. 416, in Bate, ed., *Criticism*, p. 185.
42. Edmund Burke, *A Philosophical Enquiry into the Origin of our Ideas of the Sublime and the Beautiful*, ed. James T. Boulton (London: Routledge & Kegan Paul, 1958), part V, section v, p. 172.
43. John Richetti, Review of W. A. Speck, *Society and Literature in England, 1700–1760*, *Eighteenth-Century Studies* 19 (Fall 1985): 135.
44. J. V. Guerinot, ed., *Pamphlet Attacks on Alexander Pope, 1711–1744: A Descriptive Bibliography* (London: Methuen, 1969), p. 267.
45. John Livingston Lowes, *The Road to Xanadu: A Study in the Ways of the Imagination* (Boston and New York: Houghton Mifflin, 1930), p. 428.
46. The most detailed treatment of the debate is Gerald Graff's *Professing Literature: An Institutional History* (University of Chicago Press, 1987). See also the useful introduction to the companion volume, *The Origins of Literary Studies in America: A Documentary Anthology*, eds. Gerald Graff and Michael Warner (New York: Routledge, 1989).
47. Graff, *Professing Literature*, p. 124.
48. René Wellek, "Prospect and Retrospect," in *The Attack on Literature and Other Essays* (Chapel Hill: University of North Carolina Press, 1982), pp. 146–158.
49. Graff, *Professing Literature*, p. 158.
50. Stanley Fish, "Demonstration vs. Persuasion: Two Models of Critical Activity," in *Is There a Text in this Class?: The Authority of Interpretative Communities* (Cambridge, Mass.: Harvard University Press, 1980), p. 368.
51. Martin Mueller, "Yellow Stripes and Dead Armadilloes," in *Profession 89* (New York: Modern Language Association, 1989), p. 27.
52. Paul Bové, *Intellectuals in Power: A Genealogy of Critical Humanism* (New York: Columbia University Press: 1986), p. 106.
53. Jonathan Arac, *Critical Genealogies: Historical Situations for Postmodern Literary Studies* (New York: Columbia University Press, 1987), p. 77.
54. Murray Krieger, *The Institution of Theory* (Baltimore and London: Johns Hopkins University Press, 1994), p. 26.
55. Abrams, *The Mirror and the Lamp*, p. 25.

56. Carol Kay, "On the Verge of Politics: Border Tactics for Eighteenth-Century Studies," *Boundary 2* 12 (1984): 197.
57. Culler, "The Mirror Stage," p. 158.
58. Abrams, *The Mirror and the Lamp*, p. 326.
59. Graff, *Professing Literature*, p. 170.
60. "I recollect Wordsworth saying to me: 'I have no need of a Redeemer'; but I believe his religion to be like [that] of the German metaphysicians, a sentimental and metaphysical mysticism in which the language of Christianity is used, which is a sort of analogy to this poetical and philosophical religion." As marked in the text, parts of this passage were transcribed from shorthand. An earlier entry shows the context in which the remark occurred and gives Robinson's sense of Wordsworth's "pride." *Henry Crabb Robinson on Books and Their Writers*, ed. Edith J. Morley, 3 vols. (London: J. M. Dent, 1938), 1.158, 87.
61. Aldous Huxley, "A Wordsworth Anthology," in *On the Margin: Notes and Essays* (London: Chatto and Windus, 1923), p. 155.
62. Douglas Bush, *Mythology and the Romantic Tradition in English Poetry* (Cambridge, Mass.: Harvard University Press, 1937), p. 3. Bush's judgment must be placed against Pat Rogers', who lists the characteristics of Pope's poetry and ends by saying: "there is myth, virtually everywhere." *Essays on Pope* (Cambridge University Press, 1993), p. 33.
63. Ernest Bernbaum, *Guide Through the Romantic Movement*, 2nd. ed. (New York: The Ronald Press, 1949), p. 3.
64. *Ibid.*, p. 4.
65. *Ibid.*, p. 5.
66. *Ibid.*, p. 304.
67. *Ibid.*, p. 338.
68. *Ibid.*, p. 334.
69. *Ibid.*, p. 8.

CONCLUSION, WITH THOUGHTS ON METHOD IN LITERARY HISTORIOGRAPHY

1. Lawrence Lipking, *Abandoned Women and Poetic Tradition* (University of Chicago Press, 1988), p. 36.
2. Barbara Packer, "Browsing Happiness," in *Profession 92* (New York: Modern Language Association of America, 1992), p. 52.
3. Thomas A. Vogler, "Romanticism and Literary Periods: The Future of the Past," *New German Critique* 38 (1986): 136.
4. Peter De Bolla, *Harold Bloom: Towards Historical Rhetorics* (London and New York: Routledge, 1988), p. 88.
5. Fredric Jameson, *The Ideologies of Theory: Essays 1971–1986*, vol. 2: *The Syntax of History* (London: Routledge, 1988), pp. vii–ix.
6. Franco Moretti, *Signs Taken for Wonders: Essays in the Sociology of Literary Forms* (London and New York: Verso, 1983), p. 19.

7. R. S. Crane, "Criticism as Inquiry; or, the Perils of the 'High Priori Road,'" in *The Idea of the Humanities and Other Essays Critical and Historical*, 2 vols. (University of Chicago Press, 1967), II.25–44.
8. Siegfried Schmidt, "On Writing Histories of Literature: Some Remarks from a Constructivist Point of View," *Poetics* 14 (1985): 279–301.
9. For a cogent critique of frame-dependent relativism, and the argument for a "partial realism," see Paisley Livingston, *Literary Knowledge: Humanistic Inquiry and the Philosophy of Science* (Ithaca: Cornell University Press, 1988).
10. Katherine Hayles, "Chaos as Orderly Disorder: Shifting Ground in Contemporary Literature and Science," *New Literary History* 20 (1989): 309–10.
11. Lacan's remark appears in an anecdote told by Richard Macksey in "'Alas, Poor Yorick': Sterne Thoughts," in *Lacan and Narration: The Psychoanalytic Difference in Narrative Theory*, ed. Robert Con Davis (Baltimore: Johns Hopkins University Press, 1983), pp. 1006–1007: "When I mentioned that another speaker had joined the group – a young philosopher named Jacques Derrida – a little cloud, like a man's hand, passed over the Master's face. As I waited for worse to come, he remarked that I was carrying a book and asked me what it was. When I replied that it was a copy of *Tristram Shandy*, his manner changed abruptly, he sighed and said, '*Tristram Shandy* est le roman le plus analytique de la littérature universelle.' (The allusion to the outrageous last sentence of Victor Shklovsky's pioneer essay on 'the parodying novel' was, I assume, deliberate.)"
12. Anthony Appiah, "Tolerable Falsehoods: Agency and the Interests of Theory," in *Consequences of Theory*, eds. Jonathan Arac and Barbara Johnson (Baltimore: Johns Hopkins University Press, 1991), pp. 63–90.
13. Lee Patterson, "Literary History," in *Critical Terms for Literary Study*, eds. Frank Lentricchia and Thomas McLaughlin (University of Chicago Press, 1990), p. 250. David Bathrick objects to the narrative that reads the history of literary theory as a succession of paradigms because it suggests a unified field where actually theory is now contextualized and de-centered. His objection does not seem to me to contradict Patterson's and others' reading of that history. Rather, the names he cites now constitute the new paradigm, "theory." See Bathrick, "Cultural Studies," in *Introduction to Scholarship in Modern Languages and Literatures*, ed. Joseph Gibaldi, 2nd ed. (New York: Modern Language Association of America, 1992), pp. 323f.
14. John Frow, *Marxism and Literary History* (Oxford: Basil Blackwell, 1986), pp. 59f.
15. W. K. Wimsatt, and Cleanth Brooks, *Literary Criticism: A Short History* (New York: Knopf, 1957), p. 546.
16. W. K. Wimsatt, "History and Criticism: A Problematic Relationship," in *The Verbal Icon: Studies in the Meaning of Poetry* (Lexington: University of Kentucky Press, 1954), pp. 254, 260.
17. *Ibid.*, p. 254.
18. Howard D. Weinbrot, "William Collins and the Mid-Century Ode: Poetry,

Patriotism, and the Influence of Context," in *Context, Influence, and Mid-Eighteenth-Century Poetry: Papers Presented at a Clark Library Seminar, 21 March 1987, by Howard Weinbrot and Martin Price* (University of California, Los Angeles: William Andrews Clark Memorial Library, 1990), p. 4.
19. Howard Weinbrot, "'An Ambition to Excell': The Aesthetics of Emulation in the Seventeenth and Eighteenth Centuries," *Huntington Library Quarterly* 48 (1985): 133.
20. Jonathan Culler, "The Mirror Stage," in *High Romantic Argument: Essays for M. H. Abrams*, ed. Lawrence Lipking (Ithaca: Cornell University Press, 1981), p. 161.
21. Mark Edmundson, "Criticism Now: The Example of Wordsworth," *Raritan* 10 (1990): 131–32.
22. Mark Edmundson, "Vital Intimations: Wordsworth, Coleridge, and the Promise of Criticism," *South Atlantic Quarterly* 91 (1992): 739–64.
23. Sigmund Freud, "Repression" (1915), in *General Psychological Theory: Papers on Metapsychology*, ed. Philip Rieff (New York: Collier, 1963), p. 111.
24. Jameson, "Marxism and Historicism," in *The Ideologies of Theory*, II.174–75.
25. Robert Folkenflik, "Patronage and the Poet-Hero," *Huntington Library Quarterly* 48 (1985): 376.
26. For a full discussion, see Shelley Burtt, *Virtue Transformed: Political Argument in Britain, 1688–1740* (Cambridge University Press, 1992).
27. Byron to Murray, 18 May 1919, *Byron's Letters and Journals*, ed. Leslie A. Marchand, 8 vols. (London: John Murray, 1973–79), VI.134.

Bibliography

Abrams, Meyer H. *The Mirror and the Lamp: Romantic Theory and the Critical Tradition*. New York: Oxford University Press, 1953.
"The Romantic Period," in *The Norton Anthology of English Literature*. 2 vols. New York: Norton 1974.
Amarasinghe, Upali. *Dryden and Pope in the Early Nineteenth Century: A Study of Changing Literary Taste, 1800–1830*. Cambridge University Press, 1962.
Anderson, Robert, ed. *A Complete Edition of the Poets of Great Britain*. 14 vols. London and Edinburgh, 1795.
Appiah, Anthony. "Tolerable Falsehoods: Agency and the Interests of Theory," in *Consequences of Theory*. Eds. Jonathan Arac and Barbara Johnson. Baltimore: Johns Hopkins University Press, 1991. 63–90.
Aquinas, Thomas. *Summa Theologica*. 3 vols. New York: Benziger Brothers, 1947.
Arac, Jonathan. *Critical Genealogies: Historical Situations for Postmodern Literary Studies*. New York: Columbia University Press, 1987.
Aristotle. *De Anima*. Trans. W. S. Hett. Cambridge, Mass.: Harvard University Press; London: Heinemann, 1957.
Arthos, John. *The Language of Natural Description in Eighteenth-Century Poetry*. Ann Arbor: University of Michigan Press, 1949.
Aylmer, G. E. "Seventeenth-Century Wykehamists," in *Winchester College: Sixth Centenary Essays*. Ed. Roger Custance. Oxford University Press, 1982. 281–311.
Bagehot, Walter. *Literary Studies*. Ed. Ernest Rhys. Everyman's Library. 2 vols. London: Dent; New York: Dutton, n.d.
Barnard, John. *Pope: The Critical Heritage*. London and Boston: Routledge & Kegan Paul, 1973.
Barrell, John. *English Literature in History, 1730–1780: An Equal, Wide Survey*. London: Hutchinson, 1983.
Barrell, John, and Harriet Guest. "On the Use of Contradiction: Economics and Morality in the Eighteenth-Century Long Poem," in *The New Eighteenth Century: Theory, Politics, English Literature*. Eds. Felicity Nussbaum and Laura Brown. New York and London: Methuen, 1987. 121–43.
Barton, Anne. "The Road from Penshurst: Wordsworth, Ben Jonson, and Coleridge in 1802." *Essays in Criticism* 37 (1987): 209–33.

Bate, Jonathan. *Shakespeare and the English Romantic Imagination.* Oxford University Press, 1986.
  Romantic Ecology: Wordsworth and the Environmental Tradition. London: Routledge, 1991.
Bate, Walter Jackson. *The Stylistic Development of Keats.* Cambridge, Mass.: Harvard University Press, 1945.
  The Burden of the Past and the English Poet. Cambridge, Mass.: Belknap Press, 1970.
  ed. *Criticism: The Major Texts.* New York: Harcourt Brace Jovanovitch, 1970.
Bathrick, David. "Cultural Studies," in *Introduction to Scholarship in Modern Languages and Literatures.* Ed. Joseph Gibaldi. 2nd edn. New York: Modern Language Association of America, 1992. 320–40.
Battestin, Martin. *The Providence of Wit.* Oxford: Clarendon Press, 1974.
Beer, Gillian. "'Our unnatural no-voice': The Heroic Epistle, Pope, and Women's Gothic," in *Modern Essays on Eighteenth-Century Literature.* Ed. Leopold Damrosch, Jr. Oxford University Press, 1988. 379–411.
Beers, Henry A. *A History of Romanticism in the Eighteenth Century.* 1898. New York: Gordian, 1966.
Bell, Ian A. "'Not Lucre's Madman': Pope, Money, and Independence," in *Alexander Pope: Essays for the Tercentenary.* Ed. Colin Nicholson. Aberdeen University Press, 1988. 53–67.
Bernbaum, Ernest. *Guide Through the Romantic Movement.* 2nd edn. New York: The Ronald Press Co., 1949.
Bliss, Isabel St. John. *Edward Young.* New York: Twayne, 1969.
Bloom, Harold. *The Ringers in the Tower: Studies in Romantic Tradition.* University of Chicago Press, 1971.
  The Anxiety of Influence: A Theory of Poetry. New York: Oxford University Press, 1973.
  A Map of Misreading. New York: Oxford University Press, 1975.
  ed. *Modern Critical Views: Alexander Pope.* New York: Chelsea House, 1986.
Bogel, Fredric V. "Dulness Unbound: Rhetoric and Pope's *Dunciad.*" *PMLA* 97 (October 1982): 844–55.
Boswell, James. *Life of Johnson.* Ed. G. B. Hill. Rev. L. F. Powell. 6 vols. Oxford: Clarendon Press, 1934.
  The Journal of a Tour to the Hebrides. Ed. G. B. Hill. Oxford: Clarendon Press, 1950.
  London Journal, 1762–1763. Ed. Frederick A. Pottle. New York: McGraw-Hill, 1950.
Bové, Paul. *Intellectuals in Power: A Genealogy of Critical Humanism.* New York: Columbia University Press, 1986.
Bowen, Murray. "Toward the Differentiation of Self in One's Family of Origin," in *Family Therapy in Clinical Practice.* New York: Jacob Aronson, 1978.
Bromwich, David. "Romantic Poetry and the *Edinburgh* Ordinances." *Yearbook of English Studies* 16 (1986): 1–16.

ed. *Romantic Critical Essays*. Cambridge University Press, 1987.
Brown, Marshall. *Preromanticism*. Stanford University Press, 1991.
Budick, Sanford. "Chiasmus and the Making of Literary Tradition: The Case of Wordsworth and 'The Days of Dryden and Pope.'" *ELH* 60 (1993): 961–88.
Burger, Peter. "The Problem of Aesthetic Value," in *Literary Theory Today*. Eds. Peter Collier and Helga Geyer-Ryan. Cambridge: Polity Press, 1990. 23–34.
Burke, Edmund. *A Philosophical Enquiry into the Origin of our Ideas of the Sublime and the Beautiful*. Ed. James T. Boulton. London: Routledge & Kegan Paul, 1958.
Burney, Charles. Review of *Lyrical Ballads*. *The Monthly Review* 29 (May-August 1799): 202–10.
Burtt, Shelley. *Virtue Transformed: Political Argument in Britain, 1688–1740*. Cambridge University Press, 1992.
Bush, Douglas. *Mythology and the Romantic Tradition in English Poetry*. Cambridge, Mass.: Harvard University Press, 1937.
Butler, Marilyn. *Romantics, Rebels and Reactionaries: English Literature and Its Backgrounds, 1760–1830*. Oxford University Press, 1981.
"Romanticism in England," in *Romanticism in National Context*. Eds. Roy Porter and Mikulas Teich. New York: Cambridge University Press, 1988.
Byron, Lord. *Works of Lord Byron: Letters and Journals*. Ed. Rowland E. Prothero. 6 vols. London: 1898–1901.
Poetical Works. Ed. Frederick Page. Corrected by John Jump. Oxford University Press, 1970.
Selected Prose. Ed. Peter Gunn. Harmondsworth: Penguin, 1972.
Byron's Letters and Journals. Ed. Leslie A. Marchand. 8 vols. London: John Murray, 1973–79.
Cafarelli, Annette. *Prose in the Age of Poets: Romanticism and Biographical Narrative from Johnson to De Quincey*. Philadelphia: University of Pennsylvania Press, 1990.
Campbell, Thomas, ed. *Specimens of the British Poets*. 7 vols. London, 1819.
Chalmers, Alexander, ed. *The Works of the English Poets from Chaucer to Cowper*. 21 vols. London, 1810.
Chandler, James K. "Romantic Allusiveness." *Critical Inquiry* 8 (1982): 461–87.
"The Pope Controversy: Romantic Poetics and the English Canon." *Critical Inquiry* 10 (1984): 481–509.
Wordsworth's Second Nature: A Study of the Poetry and Politics. University of Chicago Press, 1984.
Chibka, Robert L. "The Stranger Within Young's *Conjectures*." *ELH* 53 (1986): 541–65.
Cohen, Ralph. Review of *The Mirror and the Lamp*. *Philological Quarterly* 33 (1954): 271–73.
Coleridge, Samuel Taylor. *Marginalia: Abbt to Byfield*. Ed. George Whalley. Princeton University Press, 1980.

Biographia Literaria. Eds. W. J. Bate and James Engell. 2 vols. Princeton University Press, 1983.
Cooke, Michael. *Acts of Inclusion: Studies Bearing on an Elementary Theory of Romanticism*. New Haven: Yale University Press, 1979.
Copley, Stephen, and John Whale, eds. *Beyond Romanticism: New Approaches to Texts and Contexts, 1780–1832*. London: Routledge, 1992.
Cowper, William. *The Works of William Cowper*. Ed. Robert Southey. 15 vols. London: 1835–37.
   The Letters and Prose Writings of William Cowper. Eds. James King and Charles Ryskamp. 5 vols. Oxford: Clarendon Press, 1979–86.
Crane, R. S. *The Idea of the Humanities and Other Essays Critical and Historical*. 2 vols. University of Chicago Press, 1967.
Culler, Jonathan. "The Mirror Stage," in *High Romantic Argument: Essays for M. H. Abrams*. Ed. Lawrence Lipking. Ithaca: Cornell University Press, 1981. 149–63.
Curran, Stuart. *Poetic Form and British Romanticism*. Oxford University Press, 1986.
   "Wordsworth and the Forms of Poetry," in *The Age of William Wordsworth: Critical Essays on the Romantic Tradition*. Eds. Kenneth R. Johnston and Gene W. Ruoff. New Brunswick: Rutgers University Press, 1987. 115–32.
Damrosch, Leopold, Jr. *The Imaginative World of Alexander Pope*. Berkeley and Los Angeles: University of California Press, 1987.
   ed. *The Profession of Eighteenth-Century Literature: Reflections on an Institution*. Madison: University of Wisconsin Press, 1992.
Davie, Donald. *The Purity of Diction in English Verse*. Oxford University Press, 1953.
De Bolla, Peter. *Harold Bloom: Towards Historical Rhetorics*. London and New York: Routledge, 1988.
De Man, Paul. *The Rhetoric of Romanticism*. New York: Columbia University Press, 1984.
De Selincourt, Ernest. *Wordsworthian and Other Studies*. Oxford: Clarendon Press, 1947.
D'Israeli, Isaac. Review of Spence's *Anecdotes of Pope* and Bowles's *Invariable Principles of Poetry*. *Quarterly Review* 23 (July 1820): 400–34.
Dodsley, Robert, ed. *A Select Collection of Old Plays*. Corrected by Isaac Reed. 12 vols. London: 1780.
   ed. *A Collection of Poems, in Six Volumes, by Several Hands, with Notes*. London: Dodsley, 1782.
Dowling, William. "Ideology and the Flight from History in Eighteenth-Century Poetry," in *The Profession of Eighteenth-Century Literature: Reflections on an Institution*. Ed. Leo Damrosch. Madison: University of Wisconsin Press, 1992. 135–53.
Dryden, John, trans. *The Works of Virgil*. London, 1697.
Edmundson, Mark. "Criticism Now: The Example of Wordsworth." *Raritan* 10 (1990): 120–41.

"Vital Intimations: Wordsworth, Coleridge, and the Promise of Criticism." *South Atlantic Quarterly* 91 (1992): 739–64.
Elfenbein, Andrew. "Cowper's *Task* and the Anxiety of Femininity." *Eighteenth-Century Life* 13 (1989): 1–17.
Eliot, George. *Essays of George Eliot*. Ed. Thomas Pinney. New York: Columbia University Press, 1941.
Elwin, Whitwell. Review of *The Prelude*. *Quarterly Review* (December 1852): 182–236.
Engell, James. *Forming the Critical Mind: Dryden to Coleridge*. Cambridge, Mass.: Harvard University Press, 1989.
Erskine-Hill, Howard. *The Augustan Idea in English Literature*. London: Edward Arnold, 1983.
Fairer, David. "The Poems of Thomas Warton the Elder?" *Review of English Studies* 26 (1975): 287–300, 395–406.
"The Poems of Thomas Warton the Elder? – A Postscript." *Review of English Studies* 29 (1978): 61–6.
"Oxford and the Literary World," in *The History of the University of Oxford*, vol. V: *The Eighteenth Century*. Eds. L. S. Sutherland and L. G. Mitchell. Oxford: Clarendon Press, 1986. 779–805.
Fairington, Joseph. *The Fairington Dairy*. Ed. James Greig. 8 vols. London: Hutchinson, 1922–28.
Felperin, Howard. "Romance and Romanticism." *Critical Inquiry* 6 (1980): 691–706.
Ferguson, Frances. "On the Number of Romanticisms." *ELH* 58 (1991): 471–98.
Ferguson, Oliver. "Warton and Keats: Two Views of Melancholy." *Keats–Shelley Journal* 18 (1969): 12–15.
Field, Barron. *Memoirs of Wordsworth*. Ed. Geoffrey Little. Sydney University Press, 1975.
Fish, Stanley. *Is There a Text in this Class?: The Authority of Interpretative Communities*. Cambridge, Mass.: Harvard University Press, 1980.
Folkenflik, Robert. "The Artist as Hero in the Eighteenth Century." *Yearbook of English Studies* 12 (1982): 91–108.
"Patronage and the Poet-Hero." *Huntington Library Quarterly* 48 (1985): 363–79.
Foster, Gretchen M., ed. *Pope Versus Dryden: A Controversy in Letters to* The Gentleman's Magazine, *1789–1791*. University of Victoria Press, 1989.
Freud, Sigmund. "The Dynamics of the Transference" (1912), in *Therapy and Technique*. Ed. Philip Rieff. New York: Collier, 1963. 105–15.
"Repression" (1915), in *General Psychological Theory: Papers on Metapsychology*. Ed. Philip Rieff. New York: Collier, 1963. 104–15.
Frow, John. *Marxism and Literary History*. Oxford: Basil Blackwell, 1986.
Fry, Paul. *The Poet's Calling in the English Ode*. New Haven: Yale University Press, 1980.
Frye, Northrop, ed. *Romanticism Reconsidered*. New York: Columbia University Press, 1963.

Gardner, Brian. *The Public Schools: An Historical Survey.* London: Hamish Hamilton, 1973.
Gersh, Stephen. *Middle Platonism and Neoplatonism: The Latin Tradition.* 2 vols. University of Notre Dame Press, 1986.
Gill, Stephen. *William Wordsworth: A Life.* Oxford: Clarendon Press, 1989.
Goldsmith, Oliver. *Collected Works of Oliver Goldsmith.* Ed. Arthur Friedman. 5 vols. Oxford: Clarendon Press, 1966.
Gosse, Edmund. "Two Pioneers of Romanticism: Joseph and Thomas Warton." *Proceedings of the British Academy* 7 (1915–16): 145–163.
Graff, Gerald. *Professing Literature: An Institutional History.* University of Chicago Press, 1987.
Graff, Gerald, and Michael Warner, eds., *The Origins of Literary Studies in the America: A Documentary Anthology.* New York: Routledge, 1989.
Graver, Bruce. "Wordsworth's Georgic Beginnings." *Texas Studies in Literature and Language* 33 (1991): 137–59.
  "Wordsworth and the Language of Epic: The Translation of the *Aeneid.*" *Studies in Philology* 83 (1986): 261–85.
Greenblatt, Stephen. *Renaissance Self-Fashioning: From More to Shakespeare.* University of Chicago Press, 1980.
  Learning to Curse: Essays in Early Modern Culture. London and New York: Routledge, 1990.
Griffin, Dustin. *Alexander Pope: The Poet in the Poems.* Princeton University Press, 1978.
  Regaining Paradise: Milton and the Eighteenth Century. Cambridge University Press, 1986.
Griffin, Robert. "Pope, the Prophets, and *The Dunciad.*" *Studies in English Literature* 23 (1983): 435–46.
Guerinot, J. V., ed. *Pamphlet Attacks on Alexander Pope, 1711–1744: A Descriptive Bibliography.* London: Methuen, 1969.
Hahm, David E. *The Origins of Stoic Cosmology.* Columbus: Ohio State University Press, 1977.
Halpern, Sheldon. *Sydney Smith.* New York: Twayne, 1966.
Hartman, Geoffrey. *Beyond Formalism: Literary Essays 1958–1970.* New Haven and London: Yale University Press, 1970.
  Wordsworth's Poetry 1787–1814. 2nd edn. New Haven: Yale University Press, 1971.
  The Fate of Reading and Other Essays. University of Chicago Press, 1975.
  Criticism in the Wilderness: The Study of Literature Today. New Haven: Yale University Press, 1980.
Havens, R. D. *The Mind of the Poet.* Baltimore: Johns Hopkins University Press, 1941.
Hayles, Katherine. "Chaos as Disorderly Order: Shifting Ground in Contemporary Literature and Science." *New Literary History* 20 (1989): 305–22.
Hazlitt, William. *Conversations of James Northcote, Esq., R.A.* London, 1830.

Collected Works of William Hazlitt. Eds. A. R. Waller and Arnold Glover. 12 vols. London: Dent, 1904.

Hazlitt on English Literature. Ed. Jacob Zeitlin. New York: Oxford University Press, 1913.

ed. *Select British Poets, or New Elegant Extracts from Chaucer to the Present Time, with Critical Remarks by William Hazlitt.* London, 1824.

Hertz, Neil. *The End of the Line: Essays on Psychoanalysis and the Sublime.* New York: Columbia University Press, 1985.

Hodgson, John A. "'Was it for this?': Wordsworth's Virgilian Questionings." *Texas Studies in Literature and Language* 33 (Summer 1991): 125–36.

Hollander, John. *The Figure of Echo: A Mode of Allusion in Milton and After.* Berkeley and Los Angeles: University of California Press, 1981.

House, Humphrey. *Coleridge.* London: Rupert Hart-Davis, 1969.

Hume, David. *Of the Standard of Taste and Other Essays.* Ed. John W. Lenz. Indianapolis: Bobbs-Merrill, 1965.

Huxley, Aldous. *On the Margin: Notes and Essays.* London: Chatto & Windus, 1923.

Jack, Ian. *English Literature 1815–1832.* Oxford: Clarendon Press, 1963.

The Poet and His Audience. Cambridge University Press, 1984.

Jacobus, Mary. *Tradition and Experiment in Wordsworth's Lyrical Ballads (1798).* Oxford University Press, 1976.

Romanticism, Writing, and Sexual Difference: Essays on The Prelude. Oxford: Clarendon Press, 1989.

Jameson, Fredric. *The Political Unconscious: Narrative as a Socially Symbolic Act.* Ithaca: Cornell University Press, 1981.

The Ideologies of Theory: Essays 1971–1986. 2 vols. London: Routledge, 1988.

Jeffrey, Francis. *Contributions to the Edinburgh Review.* 4 vols. London, 1844.

Johnson, Samuel. *Lives of the English Poets.* Ed. G. B. Hill. 3 vols. Oxford: Clarendon Press, 1905.

Johnston, Kenneth R., and Gene W. Ruoff. *The Age of William Wordsworth: Critical Essays on the Romantic Tradition.* New Brunswick: Rutgers University Press, 1987.

Jones, John. *The Egotistical Sublime.* London: Chatto & Windus, 1964.

Kay, Carol. "On the Verge of Politics: Border Tactics for Eighteenth-Century Studies." *Boundary 2* 12 (1984): 197–215.

Klancher, Jon. "English Romanticism and Cultural Production," in *The New Historicism.* Ed. H. Aram Veeser. New York and London: Routledge, 1987. 77–88.

"Romantic Criticism and the Meaning of the French Revolution." *Studies in Romanticism* 28 (1988): 463–91.

Krieger, Murray. *The Institution of Theory.* Baltimore and London: Johns Hopkins University Press, 1994.

Leedy, Paul F. "Genres Criticism and the Significance of Warton's Essay on Pope." *Journal of English and Germanic Philology* 45 (1946): 140–46.

Leitch, Vincent B. *American Literary Criticism from the Thirties to the Eighties.* New York: Columbia University Press, 1988.

Le Prevost, Christina. "More Unacknowledged Verse by Joseph Warton." *Review of English Studies* 37 (1986): 314–47.
Levine, William. "The Genealogy of Romantic Literary History: Refigurations of Johnson's *Lives of the Poets* in the Criticism of Coleridge and Wordsworth." *Criticism* 34 (Summer 1992): 349–78.
Lindenberger, Herbert. *The History in Literature: On Value, Genre, Institutions*. New York: Columbia University Press, 1990.
Lipking, Lawrence. *The Ordering of the Arts in Eighteenth-Century England*. Princeton University Press, 1970.
  "The Genie in the Lamp: M. H. Abrams and the Motives of Literary History," in *High Romantic Argument: Essays for M. H. Abrams*. Ed. Lawrence Lipking. Cornell University Press, 1981. 128–48.
  "Night Thoughts on Literary History," in *Literary History: Theory and Practice*. Ed. Herbert L. Sussman. Boston: Northeastern University Press, 1984.
  Abandoned Women and Poetic Tradition. University of Chicago Press, 1988.
  "Inventing the Eighteenth Centuries: A Long View," in *The Profession of Eighteenth-Century Literature: Reflections on an Institution*. Ed. Leopold Damrosch. Madison: University of Wisconsin Press, 1992.
"The Literary Restoration, 1790–1830." *Cornhill Magazine* 46 (September 1882): 309–22.
Liu, Alan. "The Power of Formalism: The New Historicism." *ELH* 56 (1989): 721–71.
  Wordsworth: The Sense of History. Stanford University Press, 1989.
Livingston, Paisley. *Literary Knowledge: Humanistic Inquiry and the Philosophy of Science*. Ithaca: Cornell University Press, 1988.
Locke, John. *An Essay Concerning Human Understanding*. Ed. Alexander Campbell Fraser. 2 vols. New York: Dover, 1959.
Lonsdale, Roger, ed. *The Poems of Gray, Collins, and Goldsmith*. London: Longman, 1969.
Lovejoy, Arthur O. "On the Discrimination of Romanticisms." *PMLA* 39 (1924): 229–53.
Lowes, John Livingston. *The Road to Xanadu: A Study in the Ways of the Imagination*. Boston and New York: Houghton Mifflin, 1930.
MacClintock, William D. *Joseph Warton's Essay on Pope: A History of the Five Editions*. New York: Russell & Russell, 1933.
Macksey, Richard. "'Alas, Poor Yorick': Sterne Thoughts," in *Lacan and Narration: The Psychoanalytic Difference in Narrative Theory*. Ed. Robert Con Davis. Baltimore: Johns Hopkins University Press, 1983. 1006–1020.
Manning, Peter. "Reading Wordsworth's Revisions: Othello and the Drowned Man." *Studies in Romanticism* 22 (1983).
  Reading Romantics: Texts and Contexts. Oxford University Press, 1990.
Markley, Robert. "The Rise of Nothing: Revisionist Historiography and the Narrative Structure of Eighteenth-Century Studies." *Genre* 23 (1990): 77–101.

Maurer, Oscar, Jr. "Pope and the Victorians," in *Studies in English, 1944*. Austin: University of Texas Press, 1945.
McGann, Jerome J. *Don Juan in Context*. London: John Murray, 1976.
— *The Romantic Ideology: A Critical Investigation*. University of Chicago Press, 1983.
— "Rethinking Romanticism." *ELH* 59 (1992): 735–54.
Mellor, Anne K., ed. *Romanticism and Feminism*. Bloomington: Indiana University Press, 1988.
Memoirs of the Life and Writings of Alexander Pope. London, 1745.
Miller, Henry Knight. "The 'Whig Interpretation' of Literary History." *Eighteenth-Century Studies* 6 (Fall 1972): 60–84.
Milton, John. *Poems upon Several Occasions*. Ed. Thomas Warton. London, 1785.
Moretti, Franco. *Signs Taken for Wonders: Essays in the Sociology of Literary Forms*. London and New York: Verso, 1983.
Morley, Edith. "Joseph Warton: A Comparison of His *Essay on the Genius and Writings of Pope* with His Edition of Pope's *Works*," in *Essays and Studies 9*. Ed. W. P. Ker. Oxford University Press, 1924. 98–114.
Mueller, Martin. "Yellow Stripes and Dead Armadilloes." *Profession 89*. New York: Modern Language Association, 1989. 23–31.
Newlyn, Lucy. *Coleridge, Wordsworth, and the Language of Allusion*. Oxford: Clarendon Press, 1986.
— *Paradise Lost and the Romantic Reader*. Oxford: Clarendon Press, 1993.
Newman, John Henry. *The Idea of a University*. Ed. Martin J. Svaglic. New York and Toronto: Rhinehart, 1960.
Odell, Daniel W. "Young's *Night Thoughts* as Answer to Pope's *Essay on Man*." *Studies in English Literature* 12 (Summer 1972): 481–501.
Onorato, Richard J. *The Character of the Poet: Wordsworth in* The Prelude. Princeton University Press, 1971.
Packer, Barbara. "Browsing Happiness." *Profession 92*. New York: Modern Language Association of America, 1992. 49–53.
Parker, Mark. "Measure and Countermeasure: The Lovejoy–Wellek Debate and Romantic Periodization," in *Theoretical Issues in Literary History*. Ed. David Perkins. Cambridge, Mass.: Harvard University Press, 1991. 227–47.
Parrish, Stephen M. "Wordsworth as Satirist of His Age," in *The Age of William Wordsworth: Critical Essays on the Romantic Tradition*. Eds. Kenneth R. Johnston and Gene W. Ruoff. New Brunswick: Rutgers University Press, 1987. 21–38.
Patey, Douglas Lane. "The Eighteenth Century Invents the Canon." *Modern Language Studies* 18 (Winter 1988): 17–37.
— "'Aesthetics' and the Rise of the Lyric in the Eighteenth Century." *Studies in English Literature* 33 (1993): 587–609.
Patterson, Annabel. *Pastoral and Ideology: Virgil to Valéry*. Berkeley and Los Angeles: University of California Press, 1987.
Patterson, Lee. "Literary History," in *Critical Terms for Literary Study*. Eds. Frank Lentricchia and Thomas McLaughlin. University of Chicago Press, 1990. 250–62.

Paulson, Ronald. *The Fictions of Satire*. Baltimore: Johns Hopkins University Press, 1967.
  Representations of Revolution, 1789–1820. New Haven: Yale University Press, 1983.
  Breaking and Remaking: Aesthetic Practice in England, 1700–1820. New Brunswick and London: Rutgers University Press, 1989.
Perkins, David, ed. *Theoretical Issues in Literary History*. Cambridge, Mass.: Harvard University Press, 1991.
  Is Literary History Possible? Baltimore: Johns Hopkins University Press, 1992.
Pittock, Joan. "Joseph Warton and His Second Volume of the Essay on Pope." *Review of English Studies* 18 (1967): 264–73.
  The Ascendency of Taste: The Achievement of Joseph and Thomas Warton. London: Routledge & Kegan Paul, 1973.
Plato. *The Collected Dialogues of Plato*. Eds. Edith Hamilton and Huntington Cairns. Princeton University Press, 1961.
Pocock, J. G. A. *The Machiavellian Moment: Florentine Political Thought and the Atlantic Tradition*. Princeton University Press, 1975.
  "Cambridge Paradigms and Scotch Philosophers: A Study of the Relations Between the Civic Humanist and the Civil Jurisprudential Interpretation of Eighteenth-Century Social Thought," in *Wealth and Virtue: The Shaping of Political Economy in the Scottish Enlightenment*. Eds. Istvan Hont and Michael Ignatieff. Cambridge University Press, 1983.
  Virtue, Commerce, and History: Essays on Political Thought and History, Chiefly in the Eighteenth Century. Cambridge University Press, 1985.
Pope, Alexander. *The Poems of Alexander Pope*. Eds. John Butt, et al. 11 vols. London: Methuen, 1939–69.
  The Correspondence of Alexander Pope. Ed. George Sherburn. 5 vols. Oxford: Clarendon Press, 1956.
Pottle, Frederick A. "The Case of Shelley," in *English Romantic Poets: Modern Essays in Criticism*. Ed. M. H. Abrams. Oxford University Press, 1960. 289–306.
Price, Martin. *To the Palace of Wisdom: Studies in Order and Energy from Dryden to Blake*. Garden City: Doubleday, 1965.
Priestman, Martin. *Cowper's Task: Structure and Style*. Cambridge University Press, 1983.
Richardson, Joan. *Wallace Stevens: The Early Years, 1879–1923*. New York: William Morrow, 1986.
Richardson, Thomas C. "Lockhart and Elwin on Wordsworth." *Wordsworth Circle* 20 (Summer 1989): 156–9.
Richetti, John. Review of W. A. Speck, *Society and Literature in England, 1700–1760*. *Eighteenth-Century Studies* 19 (Fall 1985): 135–40.
Robinson, Henry Crabb. *The Correspondence of Henry Crabb Robinson with the Wordsworth Circle (1808–1866)*. Ed. Edith J. Morley. 2 vols. Oxford: Clarendon Press, 1927.
  Henry Crabb Robinson On Books and Their Writers. Ed. Edith J. Morley. 3 vols. London: J. M. Dent, 1938.

Rogers, Pat. "North and South." *Eighteenth-Century Life* 12 (1988): 45–75.
  Essays on Pope. Cambridge University Press, 1993.
Ross, Marlon. *The Contours of Masculine Desire: Romanticism and the Rise of Women's Poetry*. Oxford University Press, 1989.
Ruffhead, Owen. *The Life of Alexander Pope, Esq. compiled from Original Manuscripts; with a Critical Essay on his Writings and Genius*. London, 1769.
Ruoff, Gene. "Romanticism with a Difference: The Recent Criticism of Karl Kroeber." *Boundary 2* 18 (1991): 226–37.
Russo, John Paul. *Alexander Pope: Tradition and Identity*. Cambridge, Mass.: Harvard University Press, 1972.
Schmidt, Siegfried. "On Writing Histories of Literature: Some Remarks from a Constructivist Point of View." *Poetics* 14 (1985): 279–301.
Schweickart, Patrocinio. "Reading Ourselves: Toward a Feminist Theory of Reading," in *Contemporary Literary Criticism: Literary and Cultural Studies*. Eds. Robert Con Davis and Ronald Schleifer. 2nd edn. New York and London: Longman, 1989. 118–141.
Scott, Walter. *The Life of John Dryden*. Ed. Bernard Kreissman. Lincoln: University of Nebraska Press, 1963.
Scouten, Arthur. "The Warton Forgeries and the Concept of Preromanticism in English Literature." *Etudes Anglaises* 40 (1987): 434–47.
Sedgwick, Eve Kosofsky. *Between Men: English Literature and Male Homosocial Desire*. New York: Columbia University Press, 1985.
Sheats, Paul D. *The Making of Wordsworth's Poetry, 1785–1798*. Cambridge, Mass.: Harvard University Press, 1973.
Shelley, Percy Bysshe. *The Letters of Percy Bysshe Shelley*. Ed. Frederick Jones. 2 vols. Oxford: Clarendon Press, 1964.
Sherbo, Arthur. *English Poetic Diction from Chaucer to Wordsworth*. East Lansing: Michigan State University Press, 1975.
Sherburn, George. *The Early Career of Alexander Pope*. Oxford: Clarendon Press, 1934.
Simpson, David. *Wordsworth's Historical Imagination: The Poetry of Displacement*. New York: Methuen, 1987.
Siskin, Clifford. *The Historicity of Romantic Discourse*. Oxford University Press, 1988.
Sitter, John. *Literary Loneliness in Mid-Eighteenth-Century England*. Ithaca and London: Cornell University Press, 1982.
Smith, Sydney. *The Wit and Wisdom of Sydney Smith*. London, 1860.
  Selected Writings of Sydney Smith. Ed. W. H. Auden. London: Faber and Faber, 1957.
Spence, Joseph. *An Essay on Pope's Odyssey*. London, 1727.
  Observations, Anecdotes, and Characters of Books and Men, Collected from Conversation. Ed. James M. Osborn. 2 vols. Oxford: Clarendon Press, 1966.
Stallybrass, Peter, and Allon White. "The Grotesque Body and the Smithfield Muse: Authorship in the Eighteenth Century," in *The Politics and Poetics of Transgression*. Ithaca: Cornell University Press, 1986.

Staves, Susan. "Pope's Refinement." *The Eighteenth Century: Theory and Interpretation* 29 (1988): 145–63.
Stein, Edwin. *Wordsworth's Art of Allusion*. University Park: Pennsylvania State University Press, 1988.
Teich, Nathaniel. "A Comparative Approach to Periodization: Forms of Self-Consciousness in Warton's 'The Pleasures of Melancholy' and Keats's 'Ode on Melancholy,'" in *Proceedings of the Xth Congress of the International Comparative Literature Association*. Vol. 1: *General Problems of Literary History*. Ed. Douwe Fokkema. New York: Garland, 1982. 158–163.
Thomas, Claudia N. *Alexander Pope and His Eighteenth-Century Women Readers*. Carbondale and Edwardsville: Southern Illinois University Press, 1994.
Tillotson, Geoffrey, *et al.*, eds. *Eighteenth-Century English Literature*. New York: Harcourt Brace Jovanovitch, 1969.
Trapp, Joseph. *Lectures on Poetry*. London, 1742.
Trickett, Rachel. "The *Heroides* and the English Augustans," in *Ovid Renewed: Ovidian Influences on Literature and Art from the Middle Ages to the Twentieth Century*. Ed. Charles Martindale. Cambridge University Press, 1988. 191–204.
Trilling, Lionel. "Wordsworth and the Rabbis," in *The Opposing Self: Nine Essays in Criticism*. Oxford University Press, 1980. 104–32.
Vance, John A. *Joseph and Thomas Warton: An Annotated Bibliography*. New York: Garland, 1983.
Vogler, Thomas A. "Romanticism and Literary Periods: The Future of the Past." *New German Critique* 38 (1986): 131–60.
Wakefield, Gilbert. *Observations on Pope*. London, 1796.
Warton, Joseph. *Odes on Various Subjects* (1746). Ed. Joan Pittock. Delmar, N.Y.: Scholars' Facsimiles & Reprints, 1977.
  An Essay on the Writings and Genius of Pope. London, 1756.
  An Essay on the Genius and Writings of Pope. 2 vols. London, 1782.
  ed. *The Works of Virgil in English Verse*. 4 vols. London, 1753.
Warton, Thomas, the Elder. *Poems on Several Occasions* (1748). New York: The Facsimile Text Society, 1930.
Warton, Thomas. "The Pleasures of Melancholy" (1745), in *Eighteenth Century Poetry and Prose*. Eds. Louis Bredvold, *et al*. New York: The Ronald Press, 1939. 565–70.
  "The Pleasures of Melancholy" (1755), in *A Collection of Poems, in Six Volumes, by Several Hands, with Notes*. Ed. Robert Dodsley. London, 1782. IV.224–35.
  History of English Poetry from the Twelfth to the Close of the Sixteenth Century (1774–1781). Ed. W. Carew Hazlitt (1871). 4 vols. New York: Haskell House, 1970.
Wasserman, Earl R. *Elizabethan Poetry in the Eighteenth Century*. Urbana: University of Illinois Press, 1947.
Weinbrot, Howard D. "'An Ambition to Excell': The Aesthetics of Emulation in the Seventeenth and Eighteenth Centuries." *Huntington Library Quarterly* 48 (1985): 121–39.
  "William Collins and the Mid-Century Ode: Poetry, Patriotism, and the

Influence of Context," in *Context, Influence, and Mid-Eighteenth-Century Poetry: Papers Presented at a Clark Library Seminar, 21 March 1987, by Howard Weinbrot and Martin Price.* University of California, Los Angeles: William Andrews Clark Memorial Library, 1990. 1–39.

Weinsheimer, Joel. "Conjectures on Unoriginal Composition." *The Eighteenth Century: Theory and Interpretation* 22 (1981): 58–73.

Imitation. London: Routledge & Kegan Paul, 1984.

Wellek, René. *The Rise of English Literary History.* Chapel Hill: University of North Carolina Press, 1941.

A History of Modern Criticism. Vol. 2: *The Romantic Age.* New Haven: Yale University Press, 1955.

Concepts of Criticism. New Haven: Yale University Press, 1963.

Discriminations. New Haven: Yale University Press, 1970.

The Attack on Literature and Other Essays. Chapel Hill: University of North Carolina Press, 1982.

Williams, Raymond. *Culture and Society: Coleridge to Orwell.* London: Chatto & Windus, 1958.

The Long Revolution. London: Chatto & Windus, 1961.

The Country and the City. Oxford University Press, 1973.

Wilson, John, et al. *Noctes Ambrosianae.* 5 vols. New York, 1854.

Wimsatt, W. K. *The Verbal Icon: Studies in the Meaning of Poetry.* Lexington: University of Kentucky Press, 1954.

"Imitation as Freedom – 1717–1798." *New Literary History* 2 (Winter 1970): 215–36.

Wimsatt, W. K., and Cleanth Brooks. *Literary Criticism: A Short History.* New York: Knopf, 1957.

Woodmansee, Martha. "Toward a History of Modern Criticism: The Emergence of a Paradigm," in *Proceedings of the Xth Congress of the International Comparative Literature Association.* vol. 1: *General Problems of Literary History.* Ed. Douwe Fokkema. New York and London: Garland, 1985. 177–83.

Woods, George B., et al., eds. *From the Dawn of the Romantic Movement to the World War.* New York: Scott, Foresman & Co., 1941.

Wooll, John, Rev. *Biographical Memoirs of . . . Joseph Warton.* London, 1806.

Wordsworth, Christopher. *Memoirs of William Wordsworth.* Ed. Henry Reed. 2 vols. Boston, 1851.

Wordsworth, Jonathan. *William Wordsworth: The Borders of Vision.* Oxford: Clarendon Press, 1982.

Wordsworth, William. *The Poetical Works of William Wordsworth.* Eds. Ernest de Selincourt and Helen Darbishire. 2nd edn, 5 vols. Oxford: Clarendon Press, 1940–49.

The Critical Opinions of William Wordsworth. Ed. Markham L. Peacock, Jr. Baltimore: Johns Hopkins University Press, 1950.

The Letters of William and Dorothy Wordsworth. Ed. de Selincourt. Rev. Chester L. Shaver, Mary Moorman, Alan G. Hill. 2nd edn. 6 vols. Oxford: Clarendon Press, 1967–82.

Lyrical Ballads. Ed. W. J. B. Owen. Oxford University Press, 1969.

The Prelude: A Parallel Text. Ed. J. C. Maxwell. Harmondsworth: Penguin, 1971.

The Prose Works of William Wordsworth. Eds. W. J. B. Owen and Jane Worthington Smyser. 3 vols. Oxford: Clarendon Press, 1974.

The Prelude 1799, 1805, 1850. Eds. Jonathan Wordsworth, *et al*. New York: Norton, 1979.

Young, Edward. *Conjectures on Original Composition*. Ed. Edith J. Morley. London: Longmans, Green & Co.; Manchester University Press, 1918.

Conjectures on Original Composition. Leeds: The Scolar Press, 1966.

The Correspondence of Edward Young. Ed. Henry Pettit. Oxford: Clarendon Press, 1971.

Night Thoughts. Ed. Stephen Cornford. Cambridge University Press, 1989.

Index

Abrams, Meyer H. 1–4, 86, 111–28, 161, 165, 166, 167
Addison, Joseph 12, 42, 46, 47, 58, 61, 68, 72, 79, 81, 85, 93, 100, 123, 124, 166
Amarasinghe, Upali 155, 157, 158
Anderson, Robert 68, 158
Appiah, Anthony 168
Aquinas, Thomas 120, 165
Arac, Jonathan 10, 147, 166, 168
Aristotle 112–15, 119, 121, 123, 166
Arnold, Matthew 24, 25, 41, 61, 72, 128, 134, 147, 155
Arthos, John 165
Auden, W. H. 161
Auerbach, Erich 120, 126
Aylmer, G. E. 155

Babbitt, Irving 131
Bagehot, Walter 62
Baillie, Joanna 81
Bakhtin, Mikhail 86
Barnard, John 152
Barrell, John 9, 10, 86, 154, 161
Barthes, Roland 134
Bate, Jonathan 3, 4, 72, 84, 146
Bate, W. J. 65, 66, 84, 150, 155, 157, 158, 159, 160, 165, 166
Bathrick, David 168
Battestin, Martin 163
Beaumont, George 3
Beer, Gillian 35, 151
Beers, Henry A. 45
Bell, Ian A. 146
Bernbaum, Ernest 26, 130, 131, 150, 167
Blake, William 7, 14, 19, 20, 26, 29, 30, 117, 153
Bliss, Isabel St. John 153, 155
Bloom, Harold 5, 19, 27, 54, 64, 84, 99, 127, 135, 138, 140, 141, 149, 156, 157, 163, 167
Bogel, Fredric V. 148
Boswell, James 44, 45, 153, 154, 165
Boulton, James T. 166
Bové, Paul 166

Bowen, Murray 92, 107, 162
Bowles, William Lisle 25, 42, 60, 61, 70, 74, 84, 90, 156, 158
Bromwich, David 156, 158
Brooks, Cleanth 131, 159, 168
Brougham, Henry 70
Brower, Reuben 4
Brown, Laura 154
Brown, Marshall 150
Budick, Sanford 146
Burger, Peter 154
Burke, Edmund 11, 109, 124, 147, 166
Burney, Charles 12, 148
Burns, Robert 6, 7, 27, 146
Burtt, Shelley 169
Bush, Douglas 129, 167
Butler, Marilyn 2, 15, 16, 55, 70, 148, 155, 158, 161
Butt, John 151
Byron, Lord 6, 13, 16, 17, 25, 27, 42, 60, 61, 70, 84, 133, 140, 144, 145, 150, 156, 158, 169

Cafarelli, Annette 165
Cairns, Huntington 165
Campbell, Thomas 6, 43, 66, 74, 80, 152, 156, 161
Chalmers, Alexander 27, 68, 150, 153
Chandler, James K. 1, 9, 11, 61, 109, 146, 156, 164
Cohen, Ralph 112, 164
Coleridge, Samuel Taylor 3, 7, 11, 16, 19, 26, 27, 45, 60, 69, 72, 78, 79, 81, 108, 109, 113, 116, 117, 119, 127, 150, 153, 155, 157, 158, 160, 165, 169
Collier, Peter 154
Collins, William 20, 26, 57, 63, 94, 141, 156, 168
  "Ode on the Poetical Character" 63
Cooke, Michael 155
Copley, Stephen 4, 146
Cornford, Stephen 153
Courthope, William 45
Cowley, Abraham 98, 163

Index

Cowper, William 5–7, 20, 24, 25, 27, 59–63, 78–80, 90, 107, 129, 142, 146, 149, 150, 153, 155, 156, 159, 160
  The Task 59–60
Crane, R. S. 4, 136, 137, 168
Croft, Herbert 49
Culler, Jonathan 112, 127, 142, 165, 167, 169
Curran, Stuart 88, 89, 159, 162
Custance, Roger 155

Damrosch, Leopold 14, 146, 148, 151, 154
Darbishire, Helen 147, 163
Darwin, Erasmus 7, 147, 160
Davie, Donald 160
Davis, Robert Con 151
De Bolla, Peter 167
De Man, Paul 4, 146, 160
Denham, John 18, 53, 63
De Quincey, Thomas 7, 165
Derrida, Jacques 135, 168
De Selincourt, Ernest 108, 147, 160, 162, 163
De Staël, Madame 73, 133, 134
D'Israeli, Isaac 67, 79, 84, 158, 160, 161
Dodsley, Robert 74, 150, 159
Donne, John 41, 42, 47, 69, 73, 74, 79, 81
Dowling, William 54, 154
Dryden, John 6, 14, 18, 20, 26, 41, 42, 44, 47, 53, 55, 56, 58, 61–3, 90–94, 97, 101–104, 106, 109, 111, 120, 129, 140, 146, 153, 154, 155, 157, 158, 160, 161, 164
Dyce, Alexander 94

Edmundson, Mark 143, 169
Elfenbein, Andrew 156
Eliot, George 45, 67, 147, 153, 158
Elwin, Whitwell 150
Empson, William 155
Engell, James 66, 150, 157, 160
Erskine-Hill, Howard 65, 157

Fairer, David 38, 57, 58, 151, 155
Felperin, Howard 20–21, 149
Ferguson, Frances 148
Ferguson, Oliver 150
Field, Barron 91, 109–10, 164
Fielding, Henry 26, 69
Fish, Stanley 126, 141, 166
Fokkema, Douwe 150, 154
Folkenflik, Robert 58, 144, 155, 169
Ford, John 73, 150
Foster, Gretchen M. 155, 160
Foucault, Michel 135
Fraser, Alexander Campbell 166
Freud, Sigmund 28, 32, 54, 84, 92, 143, 151, 154, 169

Friedman, Arthur 159
Frow, John 138, 168
Fry, Paul 156
Frye, Northrop 20, 37, 54, 151

Gardner, Brian 155
Gay, John 48, 51, 153
Gersh, Stephen 165
Geyer-Ryan, Helga 154
Gibaldi, Joseph 168
Gill, Stephen 162
Glover, Arnold 158
Goethe, Johann Wolfgang von 59, 133
Goldsmith, Oliver 10, 14, 55, 75, 89, 153, 156, 159, 160
Gosse, Edmund 151
Graff, Gerald 128, 148, 166, 167
Graver, Bruce 89, 162, 164
Gray, Thomas 13, 26, 58, 62, 63, 65, 98, 156
  The Bard 58
  "Stanzas to Mr. Bentley" 63
Greenblatt, Stephen 10, 126, 141
Griffin, Dustin 148, 156
Guerinot, J. V. 166
Guest, Harriet 154
Gunn, Peter 150

Hahm, David E. 165
Halpern, Sheldon 71, 158, 159
Hamilton, Edith 165
Hartman, Geoffrey 102, 127, 148, 154, 161, 163
Havens, R. D. 97, 163
Hayles, Katherine 168
Hayley, William 149
Hazlitt, William 7, 69, 70, 91, 157, 158
Hertz, Neil 88, 142, 161
Hett, W. S. 166
Hill, G. B. 152, 154, 160, 163, 164, 165
Hodgson, John A, 164
Hogg, Thomas Jefferson 122
Hollander, John 102, 163
Homer 3, 44, 46, 49, 51, 53, 60, 74, 76, 90, 91, 100, 101, 104, 109, 113, 160, 164
Hont, Istvan 146
Horace 60, 72, 97, 98, 113–15, 117, 140
House, Humphrey 155
Hume, David 65, 66, 79, 160
Hunt, Leigh 61, 156
Huxley, Aldous 128, 129, 167

Ignatieff, Michael 146

Jack, Ian 72, 159
Jacobus, Mary 135, 163
Jakobson, Roman 140

186 Index

Jameson, Fredric 17, 20, 135, 136, 143, 149, 167, 169
Jauss, Hans Robert 141
Jeffrey, Francis 2, 6, 7, 24, 25, 27, 37, 65, 66, 70–77, 79, 81–4, 93, 149, 150, 157, 158, 159, 160, 161
Johnson, Barbara 168
Johnson, Samuel 6, 18, 26, 43, 44, 46, 49, 51–2, 53, 55, 56, 67, 70, 76–9, 93, 94, 109, 111, 116, 117, 119, 123, 144, 152, 153, 155, 160, 164, 165, 166
Johnston, Kenneth R. 147, 162, 164
Jones, Frederick 166
Jowett, Benjamin 165

Kant, Immanuel 88, 119
Kay, Carol 167
Keats, John 6, 7, 20, 28, 56, 61 71, 73, 150, 155, 158, 164
Ker, W. P. 150
King, James 155, 160
Klancher, Jon 164
Kreissman, Bernard 154
Krieger, Murray 127, 166
Kroeber, Karl 147

Lacan, Jacques 137, 168
Lamb, Charles 66–8, 91, 158
Leavis, F. R. 147
Leedy, Paul F. 152
Leitch, Vincent B. 148
Lentricchia, Frank 168
Lenz, John W. 160
Le Prevost, Christina 38–40, 151, 152
Levin, Harry 126
Levine, William 116, 165
Lindenberger, Herbert 64, 71, 155, 157, 159
Lipking, Lawrence 4, 19, 91, 133, 146, 149, 150, 162, 165, 167, 169
Little, Geoffrey 162
Liu, Alan 3, 4, 135, 146
Livingston, Paisley 168
Locke, John 117, 119–21, 166
Lockhart, John Gibson 150
Longinus 79, 115, 116, 142
Lonsdale, Roger 108, 148, 156
Lowes, John Livingston 125, 166
Lowth, Bishop 58
Lovejoy, Arthur O. 15–17, 19, 148
Lyttelton, Lord 90

Macaulay, Thomas 61, 68, 147
MacClintock, William D. 152
Macksey, Richard 168
Manning, Peter 11, 147, 148, 163

Marchand, Leslie A. 158, 169
Markley, Robert 151, 161
Mason, William 57, 154
Martindale, Charles 151
Maurer, Oscar, Jr. 156
McGann, Jerome J. 2, 15, 16, 23, 69, 148, 149
McLaughlin, Thomas 168
Mellor, Anne K. 149
Miller, Henry Knight 150
Milton, John 5, 18, 20, 28, 29, 34–7, 40–44, 50, 56, 57, 59–63, 64, 67–9, 81, 84, 85, 92, 103, 106, 108, 141, 151, 155, 156, 157, 163, 164
 Comus 36, 68
 "Il Penseroso" 28, 29, 34–6, 41, 57, 59
 "L'Allegro" 28, 34, 41, 57
Mitchell, L. G. 155
Moorman, Mary 162
Moretti, Franco 136, 137, 167
Morley, Edith 27, 49, 147, 150, 153, 156, 158, 162, 167
Mueller, Martin 166
Murray, John 144, 158, 169

Newlyn, Lucy 157
Newman, John Henry 67, 158
Nicholson, Colin 146
Northcote, James 65, 69, 70, 157, 158
Nussbaum, Felicity 154

Odell, Daniel W. 153
Ogilby, John 104
Onorato, Richard J. 163
Osborn, James M. 153
Ovid, 32, 69, 76, 102, 103, 106, 151
Owen, W. J. B. 151, 160, 162

Packer, Barbara 134, 167
Page, Frederick 156
Parker, Mark 16, 148
Parrish, Stephen M. 7, 147
Patey, Douglas Lane 54, 154, 157
Patterson, Annabel 22, 149
Patterson, Lee 138, 168
Paulson, Ronald 58, 147, 155, 163
Peacock, Markham L., Jr. 162
Percy, Bishop 12, 76
Perkins, David 148, 149
Pettit, Henry 153
Pinney, Thomas 153, 158
Pitt, Christopher 58, 106, 164
Pittock, Joan 151, 152
Plato 112–14, 117–19, 165
Plotinus 117
Pocock, J. G. A. 2, 8–13, 19, 54, 146, 147, 148
Pope, Alexander 1–6, 10, 11, 13, 14, 18–22, 25,

26, 28–56, 58–70, 72–4, 76–82, 84–95, 97–112, 115, 116, 122, 124, 129, 133–5, 140–45, 146, 148, 150, 151, 152, 153, 154, 155, 156, 157, 158, 160, 161, 162, 163, 164, 167
"An Epistle to Dr. Arbuthnot" 48, 70, 93, 97, 158
The Dnciad 14, 38, 43, 47, 48, 54, 55, 58, 64, 93, 94, 102, 148, 157, 158, 163
Elegy to the Memory of an Unfortunate Lady 29–31, 33, 43, 151, 156
Eloisa to Abelard 30–37, 42, 43, 84, 106, 107, 133, 134, 151, 156
Epistle to Augustus 140
"Epistle to Mr. Jervas" 70
Essay on Criticism 43, 45, 48, 78, 115, 122
Essay on Man 43, 45, 48, 122, 153
Iliad translation 68, 101
Imitations of Horace 60, 146
Messiah 46, 100, 101, 102, 163
Moral Essays 41, 68; "Epistle to Bathurst" 66; "Epistle to Cobham" 109
Pastorals 36, 43, 46
The Rape of the Lock 28, 29, 32–4, 42, 43, 46, 59, 60, 68, 104, 107
Windsor Forest 43, 46, 52, 77
Porter, Roy 155
Pottle, Frederick A. 153
Powell, L. F. 154
Price, Martin 11, 153, 169
Priestman, Martin 155

Quillinan, Edward 67, 68, 70, 158

Rhys, Ernest 156
Richardson, Joan 161
Richardson, Thomas C, 150
Richetti, John 124, 125, 166
Rieff, Philip 151, 169
Reed, Henry 162
Reed, Isaac 74
Robinson, Henry Crabb 66–8, 91–109, 129, 147, 156, 158, 160, 162, 167
Rogers, Pat 159, 167
Ross, Marlon 25, 150
Rousseau, Jean-Jacques 6, 133
Ruffhead, Owen 41, 43, 48, 152
Ruoff, Gene W. 147, 162, 164
Ruskin, John 46
Russo, John Paul 146
Ryskamp, Charles 155, 160

Saussure, Ferdinand de 137
Scott, Walter 6, 17, 53, 56, 67, 70, 75, 81, 90, 92, 98, 102, 147, 154, 162

Schleifer, Ronald 151
Schmidt, Siegfried 137, 168
Schweikart, Patrocinio 151
Scouten, Arthur 151
Seward, Anna 77, 160
Shakespeare, William 18, 20, 40, 42–4, 53, 62, 63, 65, 67–9, 75, 81, 84, 93, 116, 124, 139
Sheats, Paul D. 89, 162
Shelley, Mary 17
Shelley, Percy Bysshe 6, 7, 14, 16, 20, 118, 119, 122, 145, 150, 158, 166
Sherbo, Arthur 164
Sherburn, George 153, 155
Shklovsky, Victor 137, 168
Sidney, Philip 114
Simpson, David 9, 10, 13, 148
Siskin, Clifford 2, 3, 146
Sitter, John 53–5, 152, 154
Smith, Charlotte 17, 140
Smith, Sydney 58, 69, 70, 86, 158, 159, 161
Smyser, Jane Worthington 151, 160, 162
Southey, Robert 7, 11, 17, 18, 59, 81, 155
Speck, W. A. 166
Spence, Joseph 48, 58, 153, 158, 160
Spenser, Edmund 18, 28, 29, 32, 35, 42, 56, 61, 69, 75, 92, 143
Stallybrass, Peter 154
Staves, Susan 85, 161
Stein, Edwin 89, 162
Sterne, Laurence 60, 137, 168
Stevens, Wallace 87, 161
Strauss, Albrecht B. 166
Sussman, Herbert L. 162
Sutherland, L. S. 155
Svaglic, Martin J. 158
Swift, Jonathan 10–12, 14, 26, 41, 42, 51, 53, 54, 58, 60, 72, 79

Teich, Mikulas 155
Teich, Nathaniel 150
Tennyson, Alfred 87
Thomas, Claudia N. 151
Thomson, James 18, 69, 84, 94
Tickell, Thomas 46, 153
Tillotson, Geoffrey 153, 154
Trapp, Joseph 76, 159
Trickett, Rachel 151
Trilling, Lionel 129

Vance, John A. 150
Veeser, Aram H. 164
Virgil 22, 58, 69, 76, 100, 101, 103–10, 120, 149, 159, 164
Vogler, Thomas A. 134, 149, 167
Voltaire 41, 44

Wakefield, Gilbert 80, 161
Waller, Edmund 18, 53, 63, 65, 156
Walpole, Horace 43, 54, 154
Warner, Michael 166
Warton, Joseph 2, 6, 7, 18–20, 25–7, 35–45, 49, 53–65, 73, 74, 76, 77, 79, 82, 89–91, 107, 125, 127, 134, 142–4, 150, 151, 152, 153, 154, 156, 157, 159, 160, 161
  Essay on the Writings and Genius of Pope 18, 25, 39–45, 49, 60, 150, 152, 153, 157, 160
  "Fashion" 39
  Odes on Various Subjects 39
  "The Enthusiast" 39
Warton, Thomas the Elder 6, 18, 19, 26, 36–8, 45, 49, 53–6, 58, 59, 62, 63, 73, 82, 89, 91, 107, 125, 127, 143, 144
Warton, Thomas 2, 6, 7, 18–20, 26, 28–38, 40, 45, 49, 53–9, 61–4, 73, 82, 84, 85, 89, 91, 106, 107, 125, 127, 134, 143, 144, 149, 150, 151, 152, 157, 159
  "Ode to Taste" 37–8
  "The Pleasures of Melancholy" 28–38, 106
  "The Triumph of Isis" 57
  History of English Poetry 20
Wasserman, Earl 4
Weinbrot, Howard 141, 142, 168, 169
Weinsheimer, Joel 153
Wellek, René 1, 15–20, 71, 72, 82, 126, 128, 148, 149, 159, 166
Wendell, Barrett 87
Whale, John 4, 146
Whalley, George 153
White, Allon 154
Williams, Raymond 8–10, 13, 14, 148
Wilson, John 68, 150, 156, 158

Wimsatt, W. K. 4, 139–41, 154, 159, 168
Woodmansee, Martha 154
Woods, George 149
Wooll, John 43, 152
Wordsworth, Christopher 162
Wordsworth, Dorothy 17, 97–9, 160, 162, 163, 164
Wordsworth, Jonathan 94, 103, 163, 164
Wordsworth, William 1–7, 9, 10, 11, 13, 14, 19, 20, 24, 27, 37, 39, 46, 50, 52, 55, 59, 62, 67–9, 71, 72, 78, 79, 81, 86–113, 116, 117, 119, 128, 129, 133, 142, 146, 147, 148, 150, 151, 156, 158, 160, 162, 165, 167, 169
  "The Boy of Winander" 99–102, 107, 108
  "The Essay, Supplementary to the Preface" 7, 93–5
  Essays on Epitaphs 4, 90, 92
  The Excursion 71, 93
  Immorality Ode 101
  Lyrical Ballads 7, 10, 12, 19, 99
  Preface to *Lyrical Ballads* 24, 90, 110, 160, 163
  The Prelude 6, 55, 90, 96, 99, 100, 102–7, 119, 128, 150, 163
  Tintern Abbey 97–9, 100, 101, 102, 104, 107, 163

Young, Edward 2, 11, 25, 26, 40, 45–52, 55–9, 62, 65, 80, 127, 129, 144, 153, 154
  Conjectures on Original Composition 11, 25, 48, 49–52, 59, 80, 153
  "The Love of Fame" 47
  Night Thoughts 45, 48
  "Two Epistles to Mr. Pope, Concerning the Authors of the Age" 47–8

Zeitlin, Jacob 158

CAMBRIDGE STUDIES IN ROMANTICISM

TITLES PUBLISHED

1. Romantic Correspondence
Women, Politics and the Fiction of Letters
MARY A. FAVRET

2. British Romantic Writers and the East: Anxieties of Empire
NIGEL LEASK

3. Edmund Burke's Aesthetic Ideology
Language, Gender and Political Economy in Revolution
TOM FURNISS

4. Poetry as an Occupation and an Art in Britain, 1760–1830
PETER MURPHY

5. In the Theatre of Romanticism: Coleridge, Nationalism, Women
JULIE A. CARLSON

6. Keats, Narrative and Audience
ANDREW BENNETT

7. Romance and Revolution: Shelley and the Politics of a Genre
DAVID DUFF

8. Literature, Education, and Romanticism
Reading as a Social Practice, 1780–1832
ALAN RICHARDSON

9. Women Writing About Money
Women's Fiction in England, 1790–1820
EDWARD COPELAND

10. Shelley and the Revolution in Taste
The Body and the Natural World
TIMOTHY MORTON

11. William Cobbett: The Politics of Style
LEONORA NATTRASS

12. The Rise of Supernatural Fiction, 1762–1800
E. J. CLERY

13. Women Travel Writers and the Language of Aesthetics, 1716–1818
ELIZABETH A. BOHLS

14. Napoleon and English Romanticism
SIMON BAINBRIDGE

15. *Romantic Vagrancy*
Wordsworth and the Simulation of Freedom
CELESTE LANGAN

16. *Wordsworth and the Geologists*
JOHN WYATT

17. *Wordsworth's Pope: A Study in Literary Historiography*
ROBERT J. GRIFFIN